D0078357

MAKING ELITE LAWYERS

Visions of Law at Harvard and Beyond

Robert Granfield

Routledge

New York London

Critical Social Thought

Published in 1992 by

Routledge
An imprint of Routledge, Chapman and Hall, Inc.
29 West 35 Street
New York, NY 10001

Published in Great Britain by

Routledge
11 New Fetter Lane
London EC4P 4EE

Copyright © 1992 by Routledge, Chapman and Hall, Inc.

Printed in the United States of America on acid free paper

Interior Design by Karen Sullivan

Library of Congress Cataloging in Publication Data

Granfield, Robert, 1955-
    Making elite lawyers : visions of law at Harvard and beyond /
Robert Granfield
        p.   cm.—(Critical social thought)
    Revision of thesis (Ph. D.)—Northeastern University.
    Includes bibliographical references (p.   ) and index.
    ISBN 0-415-90408-0
    1. Harvard Law School—Students—Attitudes. 2. Law Students—
Massachusetts—Cambridge—Attitudes. I. Title. II. Series.
KF292.H328G73   1992
340'.071'17444—dc20   92-12243
                                                              CIP

British Library cataloging in publication data also available

Contents

Acknowledgments   v

1   *Power and Politics in Legal*   1
      Education

2   *American Legal Education and*   19
      the Making of the Legal
      Profession

3   *Contradictions and*   36
      Disjunctures: Motives, Values,
      and Career Preferences among
      Law Students

4   *Discovering the Law:*   51
      The Emergence of Legal
      Consciousness

5   *The Moral Transformation of*   72
      Law Students: Constructing
      Symbolic Boundaries in Law
      School

6   The Contradictions of Gender: 94
    Competing Voices among
    Women at Harvard Law School

7   Making It by Faking It: 109
    Working-class Students at
    Harvard Law

8   Learning Collective Eminence: 123
    The Social Production of Elite
    Lawyers

9   The Dilemma of Job Selection: 143
    Ideological Work among
    Harvard Law Students

10 The Public Interest Law School: 168
    An Alternative Challenge or the
    Illusion of Difference?

11 Legal Education and   198
    Professional Powers: Reflections
    on Theory and Practice

    Methodological Appendix: 209
    A Natural History

    Notes   215

    Index   244

Acknowledgments

This book represents the harvest from seeds sown more than five years ago. Along the way, I have been fortunate to have received cooperation, guidance, insight, support, and inspiration from many to whom I owe a debt of gratitude. First and foremost, I express my deepest appreciation to the law students whose voices are heard in this book. To those students who graciously allowed me into their lives, often on several occasions, and who shared with me their thoughts, beliefs, fears, and concerns, I am truly grateful. I only hope that this book does justice to their experiences.

Since this book began as a doctoral dissertation at Northeastern University, I wish to thank those faculty members who served as my principal advisors; Thomas Koenig, Elliott Krause, Craig Reinarman, and Michael Rustad. Each unselfishly offered me his knowledge, guidance and encouragement throughout this project. Tom Koenig must be especially acknowledged for his lasting influence on my thinking and his continued friendship and enthusiasm in this project. Arnold Arluke offered suggestions and valuable advice in the early stages of this research.

I would also like to thank Richard Abel who read and offered comments on this work. In addition, Gary Bellow at Harvard Law School took time to not only read and comment, but also to meet with me on several occasions to discuss the work. I also benefitted from Ron Pipkin's wisdom and experience in studying law students. Each contributed to this work and I am indebted to them. Finally, I wish to thank the Series Editor, Michael Apple for his assistance and encouragement in this project. Michael not only read early drafts of this work, but his own inquiries into social theory and education provided me the impetus to study the schooling process.

For the past two years, I have had the good fortune of supportive, caring and talented colleagues at the University of Denver who not only protected me from many of the time-consuming rigors of new faculty members, but also served as valuable role models in teaching and scholarship. I especially wish to thank Peter Adler, Paul Colomy, Nancy Reichman, and Kevin Ryan for sharing with me their insights, suggestions, and friendship.

There are also a number of dear friends that I would like to acknowledge who took the time to comment on parts of this book, especially, Augie Diana, Steven Fielding, Johanna Hadjicostandi, Daniel Lennon, Lauren Pivnick, and Robert Smith. Augie Diana must be singled out for his constant companionship throughout the various stages of this research. His consummate support, encouragement, editorial advice, and willingness to tolerate endless hours of discussion kept me going at critical times.

Dorene Miller and Tamera Trueblood provided technical assistance essential to producing the final draft. I am grateful for their efforts, tolerance, and ability to create a warm working environment.

From 1987 to 1988, I received financial support from the Spencer Foundation and the Woodrow Wilson Foundation at Princeton. Their generosity in funding my research is greatly appreciated. I would especially like to thank Barbara Heynes for her efforts in helping me receive this grant.

Portions of this manuscript have been published or are forthcoming in various social science journals. I wish to thank the editorial boards at the *Journal of Contemporary Ethnography, Critical Sociology, Sociological Quarterly, Research in Politics and Society, Social Science Perspectives, Critical Criminologist,* and *Sociological Forum* for providing me a venue to work out some of the arguments contained within this text.

I would like to thank Routledge Press for their support of my work and particularly Jayne Fargnoli for her astute guidance through the revision of this manuscript. Her editorial advice greatly enhanced & clarified the arguments contained in this book.

To my parents, Tom and Eileen, I owe a special gratitude. Their love was surpassed only by their understanding of my dreams. We all must find our own way in this life and I thank them for recognizing that. It is to my mother that I dedicate this book who sadly departed from this world before I completed this book. In her absence, she is always with me.

To my wife Marian, who still loves me after all these years despite the sacrifices she endured with my absences during several periods of this project, I owe my deepest appreciation. Her devotion sustained me, her artistic talents inspired me, her warmth and concern soothed me, and her belief encouraged me. It is because of this and so much more that I was able to complete this book.

◆ 1 ◆

Power and Politics in Legal Education

Ith the predictability of an annual migration they arrive each Fall. Beneath their prominent expressions of enthusiasm, self-assurance, and distinction there lies a sense of collective apprehension over the three-year journey upon which they are about to embark. Along the way, these wayfarers will encounter the mysteries upon which the possibility of social order is said to rest—the law. They have come for many reasons, to prosper, to pursue social justice, to fulfill childhood dreams, to be respected members of society. They profess assorted values, beliefs, and ideas about social realities culled from their own biographies. For the next three years, these students will be immersed in one of the most prestigious law schools in the world: Harvard Law School.

Throughout their stay, however, they will be in conflict with their teachers, other students, with themselves, and the law. These students will come to experience conflicts and contradictions over the nature of law and their role within the legal profession. This book is about these conflicts and contradic-

1

tions, and the identities that proceed from them. Specifically, it is about how law students at Harvard Law School construct their views of law and legal practice. It is an exploration into the making of elite lawyers.

The main thesis advanced in this book is that a law school education is deeply infused with ideological assumptions regarding the nature of everyday social life. In all societies, whether those premised upon customary arrangements or upon contractual agreements, the symbol of law represents many things. It delineates the limits and boundaries of acceptable behavior, it prescribes sanctions commensurate with the violation of those boundaries, it dictates the appropriate means to arbitrate disputes, and it is both mutually agreed upon and an arena of conflict that is negotiated and struggled over. Law is perhaps all of this but at a more rudimentary level, law is knowledge. It is a loose collection of propositions that constitute and reify ideas about such principles as rights, authority, obligations, and justice. Law then is ideological, and to study law in the halls of American law schools is to engage in a course of study in ideology.

The concept of ideology and its varigated applications has been prominent in social theories that seek to explain how domination and inequality are legitimized, sustained, and reproduced. Much of the analysis of ideology as a device for legitimating dominant forms of social organization has tendered "structuralist" interpretations that locate the cite of ideological production within epiphenomenal regions of society. Ideas and beliefs that legitimate social inequality have been seen as residing somewhere in the material conditions operating within society and reproduced within sundry institutions that indoctrinate individuals within a capitalist logic. Such a view has prevailed throughout most twentieth-century critical theory, particularly within the Frankfurt School. This view of ideology considers that various social institutions, such as education and law, advance a set of arbitrary beliefs that serve to reproduce hegemonic forms of social order.

This approach, however, mystifies ideology by not accounting for the interactional basis of its production and consumption. Although structuralist approaches to ideology like those offered by Marcuse, Althusser, Poulantzas and others illuminated the political role performed by social institutions such as education and law, they all too often took for granted tangible social processes and the shared meaning systems that emerge within the lived culture of the institution.

The assumption that a unified, dominant, and internally coherent ideology rules over individuals by subjecting them to false necessities has been severely criticized.[1] Over the past number of years, many theorists concerned with the problem of ideology have jettisoned such mechanistic conceptions concentrating instead on how world-views become meaningful, "make sense," are accommodated, struggled over, and even resisted.[2] Michael Apple argues this point when he writes that, "ideologies, properly conceived, do not dupe people. To be effective they must connect to real problems, real experiences."[3] A focus on "lived experience" replaces crude notions of reproduction with a more decentralized conception of how identity is actively (as opposed to passively) constructed within a complex process of social practice. Within recent years, attention has shifted to analyzing the ways in which collective meanings are produced through the frameworks of thought individuals use to interpret and understand the social world around them and their structural location within it.[4]

The daily experiences of students in law schools are deeply imbricated with contradictions pertaining to their future practice, knowledge of the law, and their views of justice. In law school, students develop a contradictory identity that is often experienced in ways that produce ideological orientations that are incompatible with the promotion of social justice. In the very early stages of the ethnographic work for this study, I had occasion to witness just how contradictory student identities were in law school. I interviewed a female Harvard Law student early in her second year, who at that time, expressed a fervent desire to pursue social activist legal work related to health care for the elderly. Her mother, a nurse who specialized in gerontology, had inspired her to pursue public-interest law. She considered herself far to the left and was critical of her classmates who aspired toward corporate law firm employment. The following school year, just prior to her graduation, I inquired whether she had secured a public-interest job related to health care. She told me that she was "going to Wall Street to do commercial transactions and there is nothing better I would like to do." I was stunned! The ideological distance between this student's ideals and her career decision seemed tremendous. In spite of her altered career goals, she continued to characterize herself as "public interest oriented" and someone who was greatly concerned about social justice and leftist values.

Walking away from the law school that day, I wondered how this activist-oriented student could so willingly, and even cheerfully, compromise beliefs that she was committed to uphold one year earlier. Where had these commitments gone? What was it about her lived experiences at Harvard Law School that allowed her to maintain and manage these seemingly contradictory positions?

Part of the answer to these questions, I maintain, is found in the process of schooling in which these students are immersed. Students in schools forge identities and a meaning system in relation to the societal position they occupy.[5] In school, students often construct a meaning system that explains the practices in which they engage.[6] In some cases, the identity that students

3

develop on the one hand leads them to accept social conditions that they seem to reject on the other. There are various forms of ideological contests, struggles and contradictions that take place within student experiences in schools. Schools are cultural and ideological institutions that construct social realities from which students actively attempt to derive meaningfulness. School cultures operate as regularized systems of meaning that often contain zones of indeterminacy and ambiguity to which ideologies permit various forms of situational adjustments that make meaningful the contradictions and asymmetries of social life. Culture is what is stated, ideology is what is acted through and taken for granted; it is the medium through which consciousness and meaningfulness operate.[7]

Social Inequality and the Legal Profession

In 1919, against the backdrop of a major social upheaval, prominent Boston attorney Reginald Heber Smith, cast a scathing indictment against the American legal profession.[8] In his criticism of the bench and bar, Smith charged that the legal profession displayed an ignorance of, and indifference to, the disadvantages under which the poor have struggled.[9] Echoing this view nearly sixty years later, on the occasion of the 100th anniversary of the Los Angeles Bar Association, then President Jimmy Carter leveled a similar charge. In his comments on the current state of the maldistribution of lawyers in the American society, he complained that "ninety percent of our lawyers serve ten percent of our people."[10]

Despite the continuing calls for democratic and equal legal representation, a fundamental inequality pervades the American legal profession and is, in fact, increasing. In Massachusetts alone, the number of lawyers who provide legal services to the state's poor has dropped by 24 percent in six years, while the number of clients seeking such services has risen dramatically.[11] In Denver, the local Legal Aid Society turns away as many as 650 persons in need of legal assistance each month.[12] Over one-third of the 1,500 inmates presently on Death Row are without legal representation. Few of the nation's poor are able to acquire legal advice on eviction. It has been estimated that our nation's poor receive only about 20 percent of the legal services they require.[13] Although law students are often urged to enter legal practices that provide greater access to the judicial system for those unable to afford such services, few pursue this career option. In some cases, social activist law schools have been closed and converted into condominiums.[14] In other cases, law school

4

Table 1.1   Life After Law School

Year	Private Practice	Public Interest
1978	53.0%	5.9%
1979	54.0	5.4
1980	55.1	4.3
1981	57.9	3.4
1982	59.6	3.0
1983	60.4	3.1
1984	57.4	3.1
1985	60.2	3.3
1986	61.6	3.0
1987	63.5	3.0
1988	64.3	3.0
1989	62.4	3.4

Source: National Association for Law Placement

counseling programs that encourage alternative career paths have been terminated.[15]

During the past decade, law school graduates have entered private practice in greater numbers. Table 1.1 illustrates that in 1987, roughly 64 percent entered private practice. Of those entering private practice, 14 percent took jobs with firms of one hundred attorneys or more.[16] In 1986, half of the graduates of the UCLA Law School indicated their first job as being with a firm employing more than fifty lawyers.[17] The number presently entering private practice has increased steadily since 1978, when 53 percent of that year's graduates joined law firms. In some schools, these proportions are even higher. At the University of Michigan Law School graduates entering private practice increased from 65 percent in 1971 to 89 percent in 1983.

The last decade and a half has seen a steady decline of student willingness to enter public interest law.[18] Although 21.5 percent of the 1974 graduates took government or public interest jobs, only 14.6 percent of the graduates did so in 1983. More recent figures indicate the trend is continuing. Only 3 percent of law graduates chose public interest jobs in 1989. Students graduating from top law schools choose public interest jobs in even smaller proportions. Only an average of 2 percent of the graduates from Harvard, Yale, NYU, Stanford, and the Universities of Michigan, California, Chicago, and Pennsylvania went directly into public interest practice.[19]

All this comes at a time when the starting salaries for first-year legal associates and the size of many of the largest commercial law firms are growing.[20] Many large commercial law firms offer salary increases that are as much as 25 percent above the previous year's rate. In Boston, for instance, beginning salaries at firms with more than one hundred attorneys jumped 24.8 percent from 1985 to the 1986 rate of $48,172.[21] A year later, the rate had increased to $53,200, and by 1989 new associates in top Boston law firms were commanding salaries of $68,000. In areas like New York City, starting salaries have increased significantly, reaching as high as $71,000 at some Wall Street firms.[22]

These extraordinarily high salaries have increased the compensation gap between the large law firms, on the one hand, and government and public interest jobs on the other. In 1972, starting salaries in large New York law firms were $16,000, as compared to $13,300 in the Federal government, and $12,500 in the New York Legal Aid Office. By comparison, however, large New York law firms were starting salaries at $65,000 in 1986, while the government was paying an average of $27,224 and public interest jobs were offering salaries of only $19,976.[23]

During the 1980s, the legal profession expanded dramatically. In 1980, the lawyer population in the United States was slightly above 542,000 and by 1984 it had increased to 649,000.[24] This rapid growth contributed to the transformation of employment patterns among lawyers. While the number of sole practitioners has been declining over the years, large law firms have been growing at an accelerated pace.[25] Although large firms have become increasingly diversified, they continue to disproportionately employ lawyers who graduated from elite law schools.[26]

Over the past two centuries American lawyers have plied their talents in the interests of those individuals and groups who needed and could afford their services. In most cases, this meant that lawyers, particularly elite lawyers, dealt with few of the affairs of the general population.[27] The American legal profession was born out of the intimate relationship with the free-market ethos of contemporary capitalism.[28] While legal services have been expanded in this century through state agencies, particularly during the New Deal, the role of lawyers has been one of producing and maintaining capitalism rather than significantly altering the conditions that give rise to social injustice.[29] Commenting on the role lawyers perform in the service of corporate interests, Ralph Nader has complained that

> An endemic malaise of lawyers is that 90 percent of them serve 10 percent of the people. Their development is highly skewed to available retainers—a kind of retainer astigmatism. They reject the vast majority of their potential customers. . . . This is not simply a matter of avoiding lesser remuneration, it is a choice in favor of that affluent class whose legal and illegal interests

are often directly adverse to the bottom 90 percent of the citizenry. This maldistribution of lawyers in a highly legalistic society fortifies powerful interests.[30]

Indeed, the legal resources that a single corporation can bring to bear sometimes outweigh those of the entire U.S. government, as was demonstrated in the 1979 antitrust suit against IBM.[31]

However, despite the role American lawyers play in the facilitation of dominant political and economic interests, there exist deep internal contradictions and tensions within the legal profession. For instance, lawyers are conceptive ideologists for the affluent but they also seek to remain autonomous, even if only relatively autonomous, from capitalist interests. Although the accord between the legal profession and capital has undergone change in recent years due to the growing intimacy between lawyers and business, professional autonomy continues to be valued within the legal profession.[32]

Lawyers do act as pillars of the status quo, but they also, at times, perform a "citizenship" role by extending legal services to those unable to afford them, and by supporting progressive social and legal policies.[33] Since the 1960s, lawyers have displayed increased enthusiasm over the redistribution of legal services.[34] The legal profession, for instance, unanimously endorsed the OEO Legal Services Program in 1965 and defended the Legal Services Corporation against Reagan's attacks in the 1980s. However, the legal profession has failed to make significant changes in the profession's charter that would mandate the provision of legal services to the poor. Such proposals were thought to be antithetical to the tenets of public service.

Law is considered a profession, yet variations in class, race, and gender, particularly within the twentieth century, have undermined the expression of equality and community. Indeed, a rigid system of stratification has traditionally existed within the American bar and has continued to shape the social organization of legal roles throughout the 1980s.

This book examines the contradictions prevalent within the American legal profession through an in-depth exploration of the process of identity-formation in law school. However, rather than concentrating on outcome alone, this book seeks to transcend a focus on professional socialization by examining the ways students "make sense" of the internal contradictions they experience and the implications they have for legal practice.

It has been fairly well established that law students are channeled away from public interest careers.[35] Commenting specifically on this phenomenon, Robert Stover reports that legal education produces a "mythology" of legal practice that favors commercial forms of practice over public interest ones. This mythology, Stover concludes, "discourages legal practice on behalf of the poor and the underprivileged and encourages legal practice on behalf of societal elites."[36] He maintains that students are exposed to an environment in law school that largely ignores public interest concerns. Such a view is consistent with the conclusion drawn by Shaffer and Redmount, who state that most law students "leave without any clear interest to make law an instrument for making people better,"[37] and of Foster, who writes that law students are "weaned away from previous ideas about the relationship between doing law and doing good."[38]

Law school has also been said to undermine student idealism. This was the conclusion reached by Pipkin in one of the first investigations of law school socialization. Pipkin found that the law students he studied experienced "anxiety, stress, boredom, cynicism, and psychological defenses incompatible with later ethical practices."[39] Consumers of legal education, according to Pipkin, developed high levels of cynicism and skepticism resulting in temporal and attitudinal disengagement from their legal studies.

The concern with the promotion of cynicism and the disabling of idealism in law school has been a pressing issue among law school faculty.[40] A pattern of cynical disengagement from a student's ideals seems to occur with relative frequency in law school.[41] Indeed, students internalize this cynicism at very early stages within their training and adopt it as their central intellectual orientation.[42]

While these trends are well known, little attention has been directed at understanding the ways law students make sense of and interpret their law school experiences, the legal knowledge they acquire, and their occupational choices. Over the years critical research on schooling has tended to emphasize the ways that students accept subordinate positions within society.[43] With the exception of a few studies, however, the educational experiences of students who assume positions of dominance and high status have been overlooked.[44] By focusing on students' lived experiences at Harvard Law School, this book seeks to illustrate how the process of schooling and interactions with faculty, other students, and job recruiters create a student culture that emphasizes the accommodation of corporate law firm practice, and the creation of ideological frameworks that are antithetical to the promotion of social justice.

Within most American law schools, internal contradictions and tensions are being played out in several different forms. There are few graduates of today's law schools who haven't been exposed to or confronted by the contradictions and tensions that plague the legal profession. Indeed, today's law schools have become intensely political places where the socio-political role of law and lawyers is frequently debated. Much of the tension found within American law schools has been in response to the growing politicization of law and legal practice.

During the 1980s, the ideological foundations of law in American society

8

were shaken by the winds of an increasingly politicized climate, culminating in the challenge of many progressive legal policies and rights established over the previous two decades. Few will forget the turbulent 1987 Senate confirmation hearings in which United States Court of Appeals Judge Robert Bork, the first Reagan appointee to the Supreme Court and a strict opponent of judicial activism, was repeatedly questioned on his views regarding abortion, Civil Rights, and the Constitution. The politicization of Bork's Supreme Court nomination, as well as the New Right's attempt to erode the rights of women, minorities, and labor, coupled with its efforts to enact laws that constrain governmental intervention into economic affairs and the Reagan administration's disregard for the rule of law, provided irrefutable evidence of the nexus between law and politics.

Throughout much of the 1980s, students as well as faculty within law schools were poised in bitter confrontation over the role of legal institutions (including legal education itself) in the production of class, gender, and racial domination. The voracity of these disputes at Harvard Law School lead to it being dubbed "the Beirut of legal education." There are several reasons for the emergence of the increasing tensions within American law schools. First, there has been an increased polarization of legal paradigms consisting of Critical Legal Studies advocates, a loose collection of law teachers who seek to expose the underlying ideological assumptions within law, and proponents of Law and Economics who maintain a rationalist epistemology that subjects law and legal decisions to the utility optimization principles associated with classical economic theory. Many law schools throughout the country, particularly at the nation's most elite law schools such as Harvard, have been characterized by the antagonism felt between these two jurisprudential factions. In some schools, the political discord and contentiousness has been exacerbated by the denial of tenure to some faculty members aligned with Critical Legal Studies.

A second reason for the politicization of many contemporary law schools is due to the fact that the composition of students attending law school has changed dramatically over the past two decades. While law schools in the past restricted the entrance of lower status individuals, they can no longer justify the exclusion of women, minorities, and members of the working class. Women, representing less than 10 percent of the law school population in 1970, currently occupy nearly 40 percent of the available seats. The introduction of greater numbers of women to law school has contributed to much of the growing levels of turbulence in these schools. Indeed, the elimination of the token status among women law students and the forms of overt oppression they faced in law school has facilitated the development of well-articulated feminist critiques of law and legal education.[45]

Likewise, the increasing number of minority students, although still far from being representative, presents another voice that has fanned the fires of political discord in law school by challenging not only the race-based assumptions contained within law but also by directly confronting the institution of legal education for failing to appoint minority faculty members. In 1970, minorities accounted for only 4.3 percent of the student enrollment within ABA-approved law schools. By 1986, their numbers had grown to 10.4 percent. Indeed, this increasing diversity, albeit limited, has contributed much to the growing levels of ferment felt on many law school campuses. At Harvard Law School this unrest has erupted to the point that students occupied administrative offices and brought legal charges against the law school on the grounds of racial discrimination in its hiring and promotion of faculty.

A third reason for the troubles confronting American law schools is related to the escalating debates over the public role of lawyers in society. Law students, faculty, and even law school administrators have raised the specter of concern about the long-standing service ideal associated with lawyers. Most graduates, particularly those at the prestigious law schools, have been enticed by the extraordinarily high salaries offered by the increasing number of large, high status law firms. Such giant law firms, ranging in size from one hundred to more than eight hundred attorneys, have, over the past decade, experienced tremendous growth within the legal profession. This increasing concentration of legal power in the large law firms and the growing similarity between these workplaces and the corporate clients they represent has lead many to raise critical questions concerning the direction the profession appears to be headed. This intimacy between the profession of law and corporate business interests has produced a wave of discontentment among many American law students. As a result, a number of law schools have initiated an assortment of formal and informal initiatives that seek to encourage alternative legal careers or, at least, instill in others a sense of obligation to provide legal assistance to those unable to afford these services.

This book is not intended to be a sermon excoriating law students who fail to pursue careers in social justice. In fact, it could be argued that the significance of increasing access to the legal system is limited since equal access to law in an unequal society restricts the achievement of social justice. This position has been advanced by critical legal scholars who have challenged concepts of rights and equal access commonly associated with liberal legalism.[46] Less critically informed analyses of the expansion of public interest law have argued that such efforts were primarily related to the legal profession's desire to expand its jurisdiction over more segments of social life.[47]

Over the years, legal education has been greatly criticized. Noted legal historian Jerome Auerbach, for instance, has criticized legal education for emphasizing concepts of technique and process to the exclusion of outcome.

Auerbach writes that legal education endeavors to place an "emphasis on process over substance—on internalizing certain modes of reasoning rather than on the consequences of reasoning by those modes."[48] Stronger attacks have asserted that law schools not only fail to promote a concern for social justice but unwittingly act as a barrier to its realization by training students not to care about social reform.[49] Even Harvard University's Derek Bok has criticized legal education for encouraging excessive litigation and for failing to place adequate attention on the legal needs of the poor and middle class.[50] The implication contained within such comments is that the process of becoming a lawyer in American society is seriously flawed and at variance with the actualization of a "just" society.[51]

What is it about American legal education that kindles the fears of so many in and out of the legal community? For much of the non-lawyer public, the concern over legal education is related to stereotypical portrayals of producing legal practitioners who are morally bankrupt opportunists who prey upon the problems and misfortunes of others. Others criticize legal education for producing severe alienation among law students which deadens sensitivities to social problems. More politically incisive attacks complain that legal education reproduces illegitimate forms of domination and social hierarchy.[52] Law students themselves, particularly those in their first year, often express feelings of dread with their newly honed legal understandings of the world.[53]

These sentiments underscore a basic tension; a system of law dominated by professional technocrats who sell their craft on the open market is somehow at odds with a humanistic sense of justice and public interest. While a surprising number of students enter law school with an interest in doing "meaningful" and socially beneficial, humanistic work, few take public interest forms of legal practice upon graduation.[54]

The chapters that follow explore the social processes that link the domains of student experiences in law school, their interpretation of law, and their identity-formation, to their transition into legal practice. I begin, however, by examining the socio-historical foundations of American legal education. In doing so, I investigate the ways that legal education established professional authority by cultivating various forms of social and cultural capital. Law schools not only attempted to exclude subordinate groups from their ranks, but also trained lawyers to represent the interests of social elites.

The chapters on the experiences of students attending Harvard Law School that follow are derived from an ethnographic study conducted between 1985 and 1988 during which I engaged in participant observation and conducted 103 in-depth interviews with students. In addition, I administered a survey to Harvard Law students that gathered information on 391 students.[55] Chapter 3 explores the elements of the contradictory identity Harvard Law students experience. This chapter demonstrates that while many students at Harvard Law feel as though they have become increasingly oriented towards the value of helping others and promoting social change, most make the decision to enter large corporate-style law firms upon graduation.

In chapter 4, I demonstrate the process through which students abandon their idealism about using law to promote social justice. Most of the students who, at one point in their training, expressed idealistic views about the value of law, developed an intellectual style of legal reasoning that effectively severed them from their erstwhile conceptions. Chapter 5 investigates the moral transformation accomplished by these students. This chapter demonstrates that students develop new meanings of such ideals as justice and public interest.

In chapters 6 and 7, I focus on women and working-class students in order to ascertain how individuals from subordinate positions in society experience elite legal training. Chapter 8 details how the cultural experiences in law school influence their job choice. Chapter 9 provides a close analysis of the tensions students experience in making these decisions. This chapter examines the assorted strategies they employ to resolve the tensions they experience. I follow up the observations in these chapters with a comparative analysis of a public interest law school in Boston. Finally, chapter 11 concludes with a discussion of the findings presented in the earlier chapters in relation to the future of social activist legal practice.

Theoretical Overview

Within the field of sociology there are competing and often antagonistic perspectives on the subject of professional socialization. During the 1950s and 1960s, sociological literature on professionals and their education expanded considerably. One approach to professions, and the role performed by professional education, developed from Parsonian structural-functionalism.[56] This conceptual orientation, one that dominated much of American sociology throughout the first half of the twentieth century, conceived of professional schools as an institution where the core values, skills, and controls that characterize professionals are inculcated. This model depicted individuals being inducted into a profession through a socialization process that imparts the necessary skills, knowledge, attitudes, and norms of the profession.[57] This approach maintained that learning takes place through direct teaching by representatives of the profession, as well as through informal methods in which students acquire many of the normative characteristics associated with professional life such as the quality of detached concern; the necessary balance between humanitarian values and scientific objectivity.[58] From this perspective, student identities are transformed through professionalizing and role defining activities that enable them to participate in a professional community.

The leading alternative to this approach emerged from the perspective of symbolic interactionism. This theoretical orientation differs from the above in that interactionists were skeptical about the extent to which professional values are internalized during socialization. For instance, in their attempt to grasp the subjective side of medical student life, Howard Becker and his associates portrayed medical school as an organization grounded in conflict and tension.[59] Symbolic interactionists like Becker viewed professional schooling as a dynamic process through which students collectively organize their daily activities independent from and often in opposition to the interests of the faculty.

This perspective on professional training maintains that students pursue utilitarian interests in order to survive the problems they encounter in school. Identities are transformed through the situational context of interaction occurring within schools, not through the unproblematic assimilation of core values. For instance, one consistent finding regarding professional socialization has been that the idealism of in-coming students is eventually replaced by increasing levels of cynicism as they receive the technical instruction associated with their training.[60] The result of this is a noticeable shift away from humanitarian and helping concerns to an emphasis on mastering the skills that distinguish the professional from the layperson.

While these two perspectives dominated the majority of American sociology, the power perspective of analyzing professions and their role in society gained ascendence during the 1970s. Eliot Friedson and Magali Larson, for instance, examined how professions organized themselves for the purpose of obtaining exclusive rights to practice, thereby achieving power and authority within society.[61] Such efforts not only involve obtaining power over non-professions but entail intraprofessional competition over jurisdiction.[62] More recently, Derber et al. have explored the power of the professions like medicine and law within the context of a class society.[63] While such approaches to the analysis of professional power are not without their critics, this perspective offers considerable analytic utility to the study of professions and their relation to society.

In most cases, however, advocates of the power perspective have not undertaken a systematic study of professional education. Professional schools have been seen primarily as instruments for constituting and maintaining

13

professional dominance.[64] The knowledge transmitted within medical schools or law schools has been seen as a way a profession negotiates its occupational authority, prestige, and power.[65]

While such analyses have produced great insight into the self-interested nature of professions, the micro-politics of professional schooling in relation to the larger questions of professional organization and social order have been neglected. One reason for this is that the literature on professional socialization has not kept pace with recent developments in the sociology of education. As Atkinson suggests, analyses must move beyond a socialization focus to an exploration of the processes through which professional education and the daily experiences in these schools produce and reproduce dominant world-views and practices.[66]

The theoretical perspective underlying this book is informed less by theories of professional socialization than the critical theories that have emerged in the sociology of education. This book examines how law students actively participate in their institutional surroundings to create meaning and construct elite identities. In short, it is a study of elites-in-formation.[67]

As a social practice, schooling cannot be viewed as an experience independent of power. Recognizing this point is important for illustrating how the micro-politics occurring within schools contribute to producing hegemonic forms of social life. Raymond Williams made this point when he analyzed the hegemonic characteristics of schooling. According to Williams,

> Any process of socialization includes things that all human beings have to learn, but any specific process ties this necessary learning to a selected range of meanings, values, and practices which, in the very closeness of their association with necessary learning constitute the real foundations of the hegemonic. . . . Education transmits necessary knowledge and skills, but always by a particular selection from the whole available range, and with intrinsic attitudes, both to learning and social relations, which are in practice virtually inextricable.[68]

Thus, educational institutions, professional or otherwise, involve a great deal more than providing academic instruction and socializing students. Schools represent sites where ideological struggles occur over areas of knowledge and practice, where hierarchical relations in the workplace are constituted and legitimized, where students acquire cultural codes that justify the logic of dominant assumptions, where students devise ways of accommodating conflicts and contradictions they experience in the course of schooling, where students construct new meanings about social and political life, and where students sometimes resist the ideological foundations contained within a

14

curriculum. The *social* curriculum elaborated through schooling and the processes of interpretation carried on by students constitute a critical dimension of educational practice. Indeed, the education of lawyers, particularly within the most elite law schools, provides the ideological foundation and social skills for those who are destined to become the servants of the power elite.

Since the 1970s, analyses of educational institutions have tried to illustrate the various ways that education reproduces dominant ideology, forms of knowledge that sustain this ideology, and a capitalist division of labor.[69] Since the mid-seventies, research conducted on educational institutions have focused on how forms of class, gender, and racial domination were reproduced through the process of schooling. By now, there is little doubt that education is related to social inequality. However, while there has been considerable attention given to the social processes by which this occurs in primary and secondary schools, research on professional schools has been relatively undeveloped.

Schools contribute to forms of class, gender, and racial inequality in society. Pierre Bourdieu maintains that educational institutions reproduce inequality by teaching the social and cultural dispositions of dominant groups.[70] By reinforcing cultural capital that legitimizes dominant forms of social relations and then concealing the arbitrariness of those relations, schools reproduce an unequal system of social relations based largely upon an illusion of objectively defined qualities of superiority, meritocracy and entitlement.

From the cultural reproduction perspective then, legal knowledge as taught in law school is in a sense arbitrary. There is no "ideal" law to which the curriculum corresponds. Instead, legal knowledge represents a form of cultural capital. Such knowledge represents the basis from which the legal profession derives its legitimation. Legal knowledge separates what is thinkable from what is unthinkable; what is practical from what is impractical. It identifies what is deemed important and attempts to distinguish it from the trivial.[71] As a cultural arbitrary then, professional training in law embodies a set of dispositions and outlooks that creates a practical consciousness which simultaneously directs and restricts behavior. Legal thinking, as with other forms of knowledge, represents a cultural code that is reified within the educational process. The form that this knowledge is given within law school plays a critical role in reproducing legal practice.

Legal education, like other forms of schooling, is marked by a system of "symbolic violence." Law school creates a "habitus" in which meanings, definitions, and professional behaviors are presented to students as being natural, practical, and autonomous. Through their legal education students acquire distinctive modes of perception, thinking, and practice. Such dispositions influence the way students learn to and eventually relate to the world.

·15

Such perceptions and dispositions constitute the politics of professional knowledge and the professional power of lawyers. Lawyers learn a style of thinking that represents the cultural arbitrary of the profession. The acquisition of this cultural arbitrary has important implications concerning the role lawyers play in society.

While such an approach has been of great importance in the development of the "new sociology of education," it is not without its critics. Perhaps the most stringent criticism leveled against this literature has been its tendency to take for granted the actual social dynamics within schools. By ignoring the "lived culture" within schools, this literature tends to produce a "structuralist" analysis of schools that lacks an immediate reference to human agency.[72]

Recent analyses have focused on the processes through which students construct their identities and work orientations within particular structures of existing relationships in and out of school.[73] The focus on the way students create their identities through absorbing, accommodating, and even resisting schooling practices has provided important insights into the ideological dimension of schooling.

Central to this orientation is Gramsci's concept of hegemony.[74] Hegemony refers to the varieties of lived experiences that sustain intersubjective worldviews and practices. Unlike Althusserian views that portray ideology as an unconscious and "overdetermined" reflection of ruling-class interests, the concept of hegemony offers more elasticity by being situated at the level of daily lived experience. Hegemony isn't an already accomplished social fact, but a process in which dominant groups and classes "manage" to win approval from individuals. As Williams expresses it:

> [Hegemony] is a whole body of practices and expectations, over the whole of living: our senses and assignments of energy, our shaping of ourselves and our world. It is a lived system of meanings and values—constitutive and constituting—which as they are experienced as practices appear as reciprocally confirming. . . . It is, that is to say, in the strongest sense, a culture, but a culture which has also to be seen as the lived dominance and subordination of particular classes.[75]

Schools produce a common stock of meaning structures that legitimate dominant modes of expression, beliefs, activities, and social relations. Like mass media, schools advance dominant values and dispositions.[76] However, the acceptance of these values and dispositions does not occur without the active involvement of students whereby dominant social values, practices, and images become meaningful and sensible.

One of the most important ethnographic accounts of this process in educa-

16

tion is Paul Willis' *Learning to Labor.*[77] In his elaborate study of English working-class students he articulated the social process whereby subordinate class positions are produced and made subjectively meaningful. Willis' working-class "lads" engaged in activities in school which brought them in direct confrontation with the dominant middle-class values articulated throughout their school's curriculum. These students, rejecting the middle-class ideology of delayed gratification and the value of mental over manual labor, sought various ways to avoid, resist, and delegitimize the cultural practices embedded within their school. Willis' students saw through or "penetrated" the system of class society, yet ironically, they formed identities that virtually guaranteed their subordination. These students rejected and discredited the mode of success and system of values articulated through school which would help them escape working-class status. They defined their own working-class culture, with all its brutality, prejudice, hardships, and pain, as possessing the only important social value—robust masculinity. As a result, these students eventually took jobs at the lowest level of the occupational hierarchy due to both their lack of skill—a lack of skill that resulted from, in part, their own resistance to the imposition of middle-class values in school—and their ideological preferences.

The constitution of work roles occurs through a dynamic interaction between biography and experience and contributes to the assorted life decisions made by an individual. Choice, then, becomes a critical independent variable in exploring social reproduction, but choice is always mediated by structural factors that influence the meaning systems within the everyday dispositions that individuals construct.[78] The interpretations of reality and construction of ideological dispositions always occur within a selected range of possibilities. Because of this, individuals often act in ways that unintentionally produce outcomes that are structurally reproductive.[79]

In the case of Willis' subjects, it was not necessarily the intention of the school to channel these students into less attractive jobs. Rather, it was a student's own resistance that contributed to a willingness to assume working-class occupational roles. By demonstrating the contradictory interconnection between social structure and social agency in this way, Willis draws our attention to how daily life contributes to the production of social roles. The situated context of ideological expression within schooling is best understood, therefore, as an active process that is negotiated and managed.

This literature has rescued the notion of ideology from materialist mystifications. Understanding ideology as a series of lived experiences and strategic actions in which individuals give meaning to their lives provides great insight into social reproduction. Ideologies represent belief systems that give rise to the various forms of accounts, justifications, and rationalizations law students offer in their daily lives. Conceived as such, ideology is not imposed, rather it is actively created and constituted within the situated context of one's own daily experiences. In viewing legal education as a "constructive" and "interpretive" activity, I hope to offer insight into the making of elite lawyers and the implication this has on these students' visions of law and their eventual legal practice.

◆ 2 ◆

American Legal Education and the Making of the Legal Profession

George Bernard Shaw once said that all professions are conspiracies against the public. Such a view captures the thesis articulated by Magali Sarfartti Larson who sees professional groups organizing themselves to attain market power.[1] For Larson, the French and industrial revolutions represent major transformative periods in the history of professions. Getting their start from the logic of competitive capitalism and the emergence of a bourgeoisie, professions, Larson argues, engaged in deliberate activities to establish monopoly control over various forms of services. The march toward market control involved "an attempt to translate one order of scarce resources—special knowledge and skills—into another—social and economic rewards." This great transformation was brought forth by subtle ideological devices such as the development of restricted codes of speech, the rationalization and mystification of standards, and an extended period of training through which one acquired distinctive forms of cognitive and cultural capital.

19

The movement to establish ideological hegemony and authority over the production of "goods" within the professions has been further explored by Gouldner.[2] In one of his final contributions to the study of social class, Gouldner undertakes an analysis of the role of intellectuals in the modern world. While Larson argues that the rise of modern professions represented the embourgeoisement of a professional class who were able to overcome the tyranny of an aristocratic elite, Gouldner contends that the old property class was never actually subordinated by the rising new middle class. Nonetheless, Gouldner maintains that the new class of intellectuals and technical workers did represent a serious challenge to the dominance of the old propertied class.

Before examining the ways that law student experiences contribute to the social production of career choices, values, and identities, it is necessary first to explore the historical linkages between legal education, the legal profession, and power. This chapter offers a critical social history of legal education and its importance to the rise of the legal profession, as well as provides a context for understanding the role of legal education within contemporary society.

Elite Foundations in Legal Education

There has long been a suspicion that lawyers are a group of professional "tricksters" who practice a kind of black art, the practice of which tends to undermine democratic egalitarianism.[3] Lawyers have been greatly concerned with such portrayals. One lawyer, describing what he saw as the rabid nature of this public opinion, wrote that the public views lawyers

> as species of social vampire which the greed of the dominant class has maintained to help ruin the "horny-handed son of toil"; his learning is but knavery reduced to science; his business, in a large part, when not the support of the capitalist offender, is the production of strife, that from it he may draw the enormous revenues he is popularly supposed to enjoy.[4]

Even before the rise of the modern legal profession and legal education, American lawyers were subject to negative appraisal. In Puritan Massachusetts, for instance, lawyers were banned from practicing in the Bay Colony. These Puritans possessed strong theologically based conceptions of natural law and were uneasy with a class of "pettifoggers" and sophists who passionately argued both the side of God and that of the devil. With God as the final arbiter in Puritan society, lawyers could gain little ground. Lawyers upset what might be termed the "moral economy" of justice. Disputes in Puritan society were to be decided along substantive lines as opposed to the legal-rational ones articulated by lawyers. In addition, since lawyers in Puritan society had been ensconced in the ancient traditions of English Common Law with ties to the feudal authorization of precedent, there was great fear that their aristocratic heritage would lead to the very tyranny from which the Puritans had fled.

With the beginning of the eighteenth century, however, social changes occurred that directly favored the collective position of lawyers. Various forms of commerce grew as markets for fishing, ship building, and slave trading developed. In addition, the parceling of land and ownership rights likewise emerged with the growth of an agricultural market. Burgeoning commercialization and the increasing centralization of political and economic activities fostered a mutually beneficial alliance between lawyers and the propertied classes.[5]

Public sentiment toward lawyers began to change in the eighteenth century. This was in part due to the distinctive personal qualities that had been cultivated by elite practitioners. Because there were no law schools in pre-revolutionary America, admission to practice law was generally dependent upon a period of apprenticeship. Apprenticeship could be accomplished in two ways: either through attendance at the Inns of Court in England, or through a long period of association with a practicing attorney. During this period, the organization of the profession became increasingly hierarchical with "county courts" or "inferior circuit courts" being occupied by lawyers who had apprenticed with local attorneys, while the higher "general courts" were limited to the practice of elite lawyers trained at the "Inns." Southern plantation owners, admiring the aristocratic foundations of English institutions, sent their sons to the Inns of Court to take advantage of the opportunity to learn a "gentlemanly" profession.[6]

More often than not, however, attendance at one of the Inns had little to do with learning the law. Despite its elite reputation, legal training at the Inns "had more to do with establishing one's position within the informal networks of power and influence" within the English bar than with providing "systematic instruction in the principles of English law."[7] Indeed, by 1700, the Inns had become merely a residence hall and dining club where students could meet and leisurely study law. Once described as a "university for noblemen," the Inns were accessible only to those of the highest social status.[8] Tests and exams were seen primarily as a "hollow sham" and formal requirements for admission to the bar were no more than eating a prescribed number of dinners at one of the Inns.[9] From its inception, legal education, though not yet instituted within America, reflected elite traditions.

The primary social purpose of legal training at the Inns was to cultivate and reinforce in students elite dispositions that were characteristic of the

English bar. Many of those from the colonies who attended the Inns went on to play important political roles within American society.[10] However, the opportunity to acquire such training was available only to those of colonial aristocracy. Not only did the Inns cultivate and produce a culture of legal elites, but they were also designed to exclude the "unworthy" from gaining entry.

Throughout the first half of the eighteenth century the position of lawyers in the colonies improved considerably. While the legal profession was more favored in the southern colonies of Virginia and South Carolina than in Massachusetts and New York, the "spirit of professionalism" developed rapidly after the close of the seventeenth century. Trained lawyers acquired restricted rights to establish regular practice in all colonial courts. With a drastically improved position, lawyers increased in number and assumed influential leadership roles in local governmental affairs. With the coming of the American Revolution, no less than 25 of the 52 signers of the Declaration of Independence and 31 of the 55 members of the First Continental Congress were lawyers.[11]

That lawyers were prominent in the struggle for independence must not be construed to mean that they had come to occupy the secured status of a new class. Despite the activities of lawyers during the Revolution, Colonial America never relinquished its mistrust for the legal profession. The spirit of natural law upon which the Revolution was formed placed greater emphasis on justice according to the heart instead of the head.[12] In a tone reminiscent of Shakespeare's conspirators—"The first thing we do/Let's kill all the lawyers"— hostile attention was once again foisted upon the profession immediately following the Revolution. Lawyers were thought to be undermining the very democratic process for which the Colonists had fought. Elite Tory lawyers were forced to return to England for their loyalty to the Crown. Also, Colonial lawyers were employed to collect debts that remained after the Revolution, thereby embittering many of those suffering postwar depression.[13] So acerbic was the sentiment against lawyers that occasional riots broke out in streets, courthouses were set ablaze, and resolutions were passed that sought to restrict their activities.[14] In Braintree, Massachusetts, the following resolution was affirmed in 1786:

> We humbly request that there may be such laws compiled as may crush or at least put a proper check or restraint on that order of Gentlemen denominated Lawyers the completion of whose modern conduct appears to us to tend rather to the destruction than the preservation of this commonwealth.[15]

If the American legal profession was to achieve "market control" and the legitimate status of a new class, activities which would elevate the reputation of lawyers would need to be enacted. Recognizing the problems besetting the profession, James Kent, the noted New York attorney, intoned that unless lawyers could acquire special erudite abilities "they would never make headway against the sullen resentment of the democracy."[16] Such a sentiment provided fertile ground for the development of American law schools.

Elite Practitioners and the Struggle for Control

Perhaps no other institution within society had more of an impact on the emergence of the American legal profession than that of the law school. It was within these schools that the culture of critical discourse arose and imbued aspiring attorneys with a cultural capital that challenged public resentment.[17] The effect of the law school movement is analogous to Douglas Hay's striking analysis of how the elements of ritual and dramatic spectacles provided English common law with widespread legitimacy.[18] For Hay, legitimizing oppressive criminal laws in the eighteenth century through a blend of mercy, justice, and majesty represented a critical ideological victory which helped sustain the dominance of the English ruling class. Similarly, the elements of ritual and judicial spectacle within American law schools played a formidable role in the growth and legitimation of the legal profession.

The opening of Tapping Reeve's law school at Litchfield, Connecticut in 1784, and the founding of an assortment of others which soon followed, represented early attempts to enhance the status of the legal profession. These schools, or more aptly, apprentice shops, sought to cultivate a cultural capital which would transform the legal profession from its dubious position in society to one of distinction. Gouldner's insights into the emergence of a "culture of critical discourse" offers a useful way of examining the American law school movement.[19] From his perspective, the emergence of the American legal profession represented the social accomplishment of a group struggling to achieve social status. The ideology of professionalism, including the elements of rationality, intellectual elegance, aristocratic style, and liberal, public-spirited disposition were the basic ingredients of these early law schools.

In his historical study of the development of American law schools, Stevens points out that these schools taught law as a science through which Blackstone's *Commentaries* were assiduously applied to the American scene.[20] The pursuit of an unimpassioned legal rationality represented an attempt to establish exclusionary linguistic codes. The acquisition of this code was made possible only through the study of legal reason in school. Much akin to the

Inns of Court, these early law schools allowed aspiring lawyers to "read in law" as well as helped them cultivate personal distinction and oratory skills. By elevating the study of law to an exalted position requiring superior habits of mind, lawyers sought to gain the special status of a learned profession.

The success of Litchfield's law school has been characterized as legendary.[21] Of the 903 graduates between 1774 and 1833, 2 became vice-presidents, 28 were elected to the U.S. Senate, 101 became Representatives, 16 were assigned to the post of chief justice, 14 became state governors, and 10 became lieutenant governors. There was a distinct elite tradition associated with this school. Litchfield lawyers assumed upper-class prerogatives and considered themselves above the multitude.[22] Indeed, they were a collectively eminent group. A girls academy was founded in 1792 in Litchfield that served to introduce ladies of refinement to Litchfield students. Many of these women went on to marry men at Litchfield.[23]

The momentum of the private law school movement, however, was slowed by the development of university-based law schools. Several university law schools emerged to compete in the production of qualified attorneys.[24] While there had already been law professors at various colleges, no established, university-based law school existed before 1817, the year that saw the founding of Harvard Law School. Harvard Law School was "essentially a school of the Litchfield type; it afforded an improved method of study under a preceptor in a law office."[25] With the appointment of Joseph Story as Dane professor, academic lectures that communicated the traditions of English Common Law replaced the "rule of thumb" methods of the lawyer's office. Within time, this "taylorization" of law teaching in the university became viewed as a more appropriate form of instruction than "crasser" vocational methods employed at the private schools. The development of the university law schools amounted to the death knell of the early private schools. By 1826 enrollment at Litchfield began to decline and in 1833, with only six students enrolling, the school was forced to close.[26] Other private schools also closed or were absorbed by universities as was the case at Yale, Tulane, and the University of North Carolina.[27]

These initial developments within American legal education, however, must not be viewed as a complete success. Many university law schools opened shortly after Harvard only to be abandoned a few short years later.[28] These unsuccessful efforts would seem somewhat incongruous with Tocqueville's assessment regarding the aristocratic foundations of the American legal profession. If, as Tocqueville claimed, lawyers constituted a dominant social class within society, what explains the collapse of university law schools?

It has frequently been argued that the populist spirit of Jacksonian democracy arose to challenge the authority of all elites, most typically symbolized by wealthy land owners, emerging industrialists, and by professional lawyers who did their bidding.[29] Entrepreneurial groups since the revolutionary period had sought an alliance with the legal profession to advance their own economic interests. The populist mood within Jacksonian America represented a public challenge to this new economy—an economy increasingly dictated by market practices that eroded the moral economy of fair and just prices. The transformation of American laws of property and contract signified the accomplishment of lawyers and legislators in facilitating the interests of "commerce and industry at the expense of farmers, workers, consumers, and other less powerful groups within the society. Not only had the law come to establish legal doctrines that maintained the new distribution of economic and political power, but, wherever it could, it actively promoted a legal redistribution of wealth against the weakest groups in the society."[30] It was this affiliation with the commercial class that ignited public hostility towards the legal profession.

Jacksonian democracy, with its ideological support for free trade existing along side its opposition to large corporations, greatly limited the opportunities of lawyers to organize as a profession. The legal profession, and with it legal education, underwent significant transformation. Massachusetts and New Hampshire abolished apprenticeship requirements entirely. As early as 1829, students not qualified for admission to Harvard College could enroll in the law school—indicating an erosion of requirements. The school's program was scaled down from three years to just eighteen months.[31] By 1840, apprenticeship was required in only eleven of the thirty jurisdictions, and only "9 university-affiliated law schools with a total of 345 students" were to be found.[32] In several other states, the practice of law was open to any voter of "good moral character."[33] Such an atmosphere certainly did not bode well for lawyers as a profession.

Although elites in the profession were concerned with the leveling of requirements for admission to the bar, there is some question regarding the adverse effects such "democratizing" trends had upon trained lawyers.[34] The commitment of Jacksonian democracy to classical liberalism and the promotion of capitalism may have proven beneficial to elite lawyers who had already cultivated an alliance with the commercial class. As Stevens suggests, despite claims of demoralization within the profession, "there seems little doubt that in the major cities like Boston the leading members of the bar played a role, led a life, and enjoyed a status in 1830 little different from their counterparts in 1800 or 1900."[35]

The changes enacted in the law which directly extended the economic power of the commercial class coupled with the birth of law firms such as Cravath, Swaine, and Moore, and Cadwalader, Wickersham, and Taft created unprecedented opportunities for elite lawyers to enhance their own position while contributing to social changes which they perceived as positive. While the ideology of Jacksonian democracy restricted the opportunity of lawyers to organize as a group, the leveling of requirements for legal practice represented more the activities of progressives to "liberalize" law in order to provide greater access to the middle class than a direct assault on professional powers.[36] Lay practitioners at this time sought to provide legal services for those who could not afford to pay elite lawyers.[37] Elite lawyers during this period, however, continued to be vital in the industrial revolution. The owners of slaves, steamboat monopolies, and banks found they needed the services these elite lawyers could provide.

The relaxation of entrance requirements for the practice of law, therefore, did not pose a direct threat to the economic position of elite lawyers, since their position had been secured through informal networks of family and close associates. What elite lawyers did fear, however, was that the relaxation of standards would further tarnish the public reputation of lawyers, thereby lowering its prestige and influence. Perry Miller, in his brilliant study of the legal mind in America, identified how elite lawyers sought to maintain a degree of legitimacy through a glorification of legal rationality, praising the intellectual acumen of academically trained lawyers, and underscoring the moral earnestness and Christian character of the "competent" attorney.[38] While the period of Jacksonian democracy did not seriously impair the economic position of elite lawyers, it did represent a period of contested struggle over the character and culture of the profession. As Lefcourt points out,

> the established lawyers of the colonial and post-revolutionary periods, allied as they were to the economic and other interests of the ruling classes . . . sought to control its (legal training's) direction and reform through an ideology that distrusted a more democratic participation in legal study and practice.[39]

This period within the history of the American legal profession was a time when conflicting ideologies of legal practice competed for dominance. It would be simplistic and misleading, however, to portray elite lawyers of this period as merely a self-interested group whose sole intention was to exploit the opportunities of a growing commercial market.[40] Such instrumental descriptions are limited because they fail to consider the ideological assumptions upon which elite lawyers premised their activities.

Lawyers are producers of ideology and possessors of a legal consciousness.[41] That elite lawyers felt threatened by the democratic challenge posed by the entrance into the bar of the great "unwashed" masses should not obscure the dangers that such developments seemed to pose. Elite lawyers sought to prevent the installation of new standards that could potentially disparage the cultural capital they had succeeded in cultivating over the years. Not only did elite attorneys fear that these democratic legal reforms would assault professional dominance, but they could produce a trend that could, in the end, upset the natural virtues upon which law and social order were based.

What was at stake throughout this period was no less than the fundamental elements of culture and ideology—ideas, values, habits of mind, and dispositions—which were to be considered appropriate for professional lawyers. For elite lawyers, it was the academic study of law in law schools where the appropriation of professional "capital" was to be acquired. Opening the doors of legal practice to those not steeped in these professional traditions was seen by elite lawyers to threaten the very existence of social order. Law school, therefore, had become more than simply an educational institution where students would learn the law; it provided a way through which elite lawyers could produce, control, and disseminate an ideology consistent with their own world-views. In short, these early law schools, although few in number, instilled an ideology and culture that propagated a justification for elite views of law and legal practice.

For the elite lawyer, law schools were to function as the appropriate transmitter of established legal culture. The creation of an established discipline, however, preserves the dominance of those who establish it. As Foucault points out,

> Disciplines constitute a system of control in the production of discourse, fixing its limits through the action of an identity taking the form of a permanent reactivation of the rules. . . . This amounts to a rarefaction among speaking subjects: none may enter into the discourse on a specific subject unless he has satisfied certain conditions. . . . Education may be the instrument whereby every individual can gain access to any kind of discourse. But we well know that in its distribution, in what it permits and in what it prevents, it follows the well-trodden battle-lines of social conflict. Every educational system is a political means of maintaining or of modifying the appropriation of discourse.[42]

It is apparent from the brief survey of the early history of the American legal profession outlined above that law school training symbolized a great deal more than simply acquiring the skills needed to practice law. More than just an institution of training, professional law schools during this period sought to ritualize language, elite traditions, legal consciousness, social characteristics, and political thought. While the law school movement in the first half of the nineteenth century failed to establish dominance over the production of lawyers, it provides a useful illustration of the importance elite lawyers placed on legal education as a primary cultural and ideological device in the making and shaping of the American legal profession.

The Rise of the Modern Law School

If the initial phase of the American law school movement was viewed as an important conduit for instilling the values and ideologies associated with nineteenth-century elite lawyers and the prestigious clients they represented, the emergence of the modern law school movement was related to the rise and consolidation of advanced corporate capitalism. With the growth of large corporations and the concentration of power in state structures, lawyers strategically positioned themselves to exploit the opportunities offered them by a changing society. Legal services became essential to big business for the management of their investment interests,[43] tort liability,[44] the enforcement of contracts,[45] and the control of labor.[46] Lawyers had increasingly become the "intellectuals" who would translate the wishes of the bourgeoisie into appropriate legal channels.[47] Imitating the entrepreneurial spirit of the time, lawyers increasingly organized themselves into corporate and contingent-fee styles of practices whose main activities were in the interests of business.[48]

The historical account of the rise of modern legal education is substantially well-documented.[49] The modern law school movement may be said to have begun in 1870 at Harvard—the "high citadel" of legal education—and radiated outward over time.[50] While there are various accounts providing informative chronologies of modern legal education in America, they are absent of a theoretical analysis. What these comprehensive works produce are interpretations that depict modern law schools as evolving naturally out of "the transformation from a rural-agricultural to an urban-industrial civilization."[51] For instance, according to Pound, modern legal education arose because

> there was a need of legal provision for many things which were not dealt with by English legislation and which English judges had had no occasion to consider. It was needful to develop a system of law adapted to a new and growing country to work out certain detailed precepts to the requirements of American life. Apprentice trained lawyers knowing chiefly the mechanisms of procedures and thinking locally, could not meet this demand; only law schools and law teachers could.

Such portrayals, by reducing the development of modern law schools to functionalist imperatives, inadequately address the self-generating ideological formulations that legal education provided in the shaping of legal conscious-ness, professional values, and the subsequent practice of lawyers.[52]

It has been observed that modern legal education paralleled the rise of corporate-style law firms.[53] Some have argued that modern law school was directly related to the efforts of elites to structure social life and commercial enterprise in the post-bellum period.[54] From this perspective, the modern law school can be best conceived as a defense of elite authority whose sturdiest foundations lay within the professions. For instance, Harvard University President, Charles W. Eliot, and first law school dean, Christopher Columbus Langdell (the latter considered by most as the founder of modern legal education), were instrumental in creating the elite culture and ideology associated with legal education. Both men were members of the American Social Science Association, an organization that emerged "in response to a nine-teenth-century crisis of authority experienced most acutely by members of the traditional, college-educated, professional and gentry classes."[55]

The collective project by which professionals obtained monopoly control over the provision of professional services, however, was related not only to the social and economic transformations within corporate capitalism, but also to the various social problems that such changes seemed to produce. Dramatic social changes of the time brought new paradigms of thought that sought not only to provide the intellectual impetus for industrial growth, but also to help ameliorate problems associated with its expansion.[56] Out of this period there rose an expert class whose social position supported the economic transforma-tions occurring within corporate capitalism, but whose professional ideology permitted the appearance of autonomy from elites. The development and application of expert knowledge premised upon an ideology of scientific neutrality and disinterestedness, as well as a dedication to public service, provided a justificatory rationale through which professionals pursued their own legitimation. Through the various forms of ideological work they carried out, professionals adopted a view of themselves as a "classless" class.

1. Sources of legitimation in the modern legal profession

The primary sources of legitimation within the legal profession during the late nineteenth and early twentieth centuries included the application of the scientific method and a dedication to public service. The appeal to science in which "objective" standards of law were to be discovered in law school is best seen in the installation of "Langdellian formalism" and the creation of the "case method" of legal education. According to Langdell,

Law, considered as a science, consists of certain principles or doctrines. To have a mastery of these as to be able to apply them with constant facility and certainty to the ever-tangled skein of human affairs is what constitutes a true lawyer; and hence to acquire that mastery should be the business of every earnest student of law. Each of these doctrines has arrived at its present state by slow degrees; in other words, it is a growth, extending in many cases through the centuries.[57]

The cultivation of the spirit of legal positivism provided a source of authority for the legal profession which transcended the favoritism of politics, the corruption of personality, and the exclusiveness of partisanship characteristic of elite antebellum lawyers.[58] The separation of law from politics and the assignment of law and the legal profession to the position of a neutral and universal mediator of conflicts in civil society represented a significant ideological accomplishment in the rise of the American legal profession. The movement to establish a science of law, an elaboration on what Charles Eliot viewed as "progressive education," transferred the problems of social order from traditional sources of legitimation to formal-rational ones. Much like the professions of medicine and social work, lawyers employed a scientific paradigm as a way of accomplishing eminence within society. The crusade of elites to establish rational social order parallels the rise of moral crusades whose purpose was the reconstitution of elite authority.[59]

The legal profession's appropriation of science, however, cannot be completely viewed as a professional conspiracy. While lawyers and others no doubt realized the market potential for establishing professional standards, strict reliance on instrumentality obscures an understanding of the ideological role performed by "legal science." Indeed, the translations of various behaviors into legitimate diseases, disorders, and pathologies represent forms of scientific ideology that provided professionals with a conceptual framework through which they were able to derive a sense of indispensability, eminence, and social status. Like medical and social work professionals, legal professionals adopted the norm of scientific neutrality with the belief that such neutrality would lead to the betterment of society. As the following passage from the 1879 American Bar Association meetings suggests, the science of law was seen by elite lawyers as critical to the evolution of modern society:

[T]he best growth of liberty is law. The product of order, it is a constant science. It vindicates the right and condemns the wrong; it upholds just authority, and forbids and punishes tyranny. It is the dispenser of justice; the exponent of public and private morality; the shield of innocence; the guardian of the defenseless; the comfort and consolation of the good, and the confusion of the wicked. By its regular course and operation, the fruits of peace are secured, and the evils of war are diminished and assuaged by it. Without it a republic is impossible.

This new scientific authority, however, continued to serve the interests of social elites. A symbiotic relationship existed between legal science and the attempt to defend the authority of a gentry class.[60] The changes in the character and nature of capitalism required law schools to train elites to facilitate capital accumulation and provide the decentralized capitalist class with a national administrative framework for rationalizing competition. However, this point must not be overstated. While the substantive content of modern legal education included courses in property, contracts and corporations, the Harvard Law School faculty were opposed to teaching business, insurance, corporate finance, or taxation.[61] Students were often advised not to become too wedded to the interests of business.[62]

The legal profession also pursued its legitimacy through an ideology of public spiritedness that was to be acquired in law school.[63] The assumption of disinterested public service, in fact, is related to the scientific endeavor whose project it is to advance the good of humanity.[64] This dedication to public service explains why institutions such as Harvard Law School could appear to reject the corporate interests its graduates represented. Concerned about their reputation within society, professional lawyers sought to demonstrate their public spirited intentions. While the American legal profession has historically failed to provide adequate legal services to the public, its rhetoric has promulgated a commitment to public service.[65] In an address delivered to the Minnesota State Bar Association in 1921, Herbert Hadley defined this public role of the profession in the following way:

> The character of the general and of the professional education to be required of those admitted to the practice of law must be considered in full realization of the fact that it is upon the lawyers that the world must largely rely, both for guidance and execution in the working out of those great problems which will determine not only the future welfare but the continued existence of that complicated system of relations, adjustments, and reactions which we call modern civilization.[66]

This statement reflects the nature of the long-standing service ideal promulgated by the legal profession. Elites in the American legal profession, however, never considered the provision of advocacy services to the poor and common citizenry as the exclusive definition of public service. The bar's commitment to the public, at this time, represented more an abstract paternalistic benevolence in the shaping and ordering of society than any collective attempt to

31

remedy the inequities and injustices fostered by the growth of corporate capitalism. Because of their eminence, lawyers viewed themselves as contributing to the public good even though they were not directly serving the public. In this way, the legal profession sowed the seeds of its own legitimacy. It is not that lawyers had not cultivated a close bond with the capitalist class. Tocqueville's assessment of the legal profession as belonging to the aristocracy by habit and taste remained true for early twentieth century lawyers. However, modern legal education provided an ideological set of values, justifications, and rationales which served to mask the gross recognition of that relationship for themselves and the public. And where that relationship was apparent the service to capitalism was seen no less than the service of the public who would be its beneficiary.

2. Sources of crisis in legal education

The legitimation crisis that modern education resolved for elite practitioners was by no means unchallenged. Ideological disputes over the form and content of legal education were frequent during this time and continued through the Progressive Era and beyond. The primary foci of these running contests occurred in three distinct areas: (1) the appropriate means of legal instruction, (2) the growing incursion of private part-time schools, and (3) the role of the lawyer in society. These tensions produced considerable turmoil between partisans of opposing positions. Indeed, the third phase of the law school movement represented a period of contested struggle over law school training in which new elites, challenged from below, attempted to gain exclusive control over legal education. The eventual institutionalization of Langdell's scientific method, for instance, was not easily won. Indeed, this period represented cultural wars over the appropriate character and substance of modern legal education. As Johnson points out,

> The dispute over case study reveals a larger problem. By 1900 the sources of agreed upon principles of justice and fairness had become objects of disagreement. . . . The older generation of lawyers, trained in the nineteenth century but completing their careers as eminent practitioners in the twentieth century, would continue to rely upon broad moral principles as the basis for justice. Case lawyers, especially those who were taught in the major universities, would, in contrast, rely upon a narrow scientific historicism for their source of justice. . . . Against this background, the battle over the form and purpose of the university law school would continue in the twentieth century.[67]

In addition, many non-elite practitioners believed that the new form of legal instruction failed to provide necessary clinical training that could assist lawyers in the delivery of legal services to the poor and middle class. In fact, some of the first legal aid clinics that made their appearance in the late nineteenth century were affiliated with law schools which rejected Langdell's method.[68] Many schools which had affiliated legal aid programs emphasized clinical training in law school as opposed to instruction in pure law.[69] In the minds of elite academic law teachers, however, clinical training smacked of the crass vocationalism reminiscent of the earlier apprentice forms of legal training.

A second major contest over the structure of legal education grew out the increasing number of part-time law schools that appeared at the turn of the century. Indeed, the greatest number of law schools in the early twentieth century were part-time programs. There were approximately 40 full-time law schools in 1890 and 20 part-time ones, as compared to 83 full-time schools and 107 part-time schools by 1938.[70] The introduction of the part-time law school movement led to considerable tension between elite law teachers and part-time law school advocates.[71] The antipathy which developed between elite lawyers trained in prestigious law schools and non-elite lawyers who had attended proprietary part-time schools was great. Elite lawyers perceived these interlopers, who were mostly working-class minorities, as ill-mannered, incompetent, and above all, immoral. Part-time law schools were seen as a "rank weed" to be "dried out." Their students were said to be "shrewd young men, crammed so that they could pass the bar examination, all deeply impressed with the philosophy of getting on, but viewing the Code of Ethics with uncomprehending eyes."[72]

Early legal periodicals often derided these attorneys for preying upon the public as an easier method of earning a living than by manual labor or engaging in small business enterprises. Hostility directed at graduates of part-time law schools even took the form of degrading poems published in lawyer magazines. One such poem, entitled "The Evolution of the Ambulance Chaser," was particularly acerbic.

In the Year 2.

A way back in primeval time, when Mother Earth was new,
There wandered aimlessly through space, its mysteries to view.
Two spirits from another world, some shining, distant star,
To note the change resulting from the last creative jar.

"Aha," cried one, methinks I see another world,
Which from creation's workshop hath recently been hurled.
Lets' hie us to this new-born globe. I'd dearly love to see
What kind of living creatures its inhabitants may be.

They rested on our Mother Earth, and paced its barren strand,
It was void of population, a rocky, sterile land.
No green thing grew upon its face, nor flower, nor vine, nor tree.
While far beyond them as they stood, there stretched the shifting sea.

Upon its glassy surface those spirits gazed with awe,
Struck dumb with consternation at the carnage they saw;
For its waves were thickly peopled with creatures hard of shell,
With eyes protruding from their heads, whose presence was a knell.
Of death, to any living thing within those waters black,
If once those awful scavengers should get upon their track.
One spirit spoke, "What were those fiends, who feed on luckless mites?"
The other answered, "From their nerve, I'm sure they trilobites."

In the Year 1902 A.C.

When many eons rolled along, these spirits did return
To visit Mother Earth again, its present state to learn
How vast the change! The desert spot had blossomed into flower
Where once was dearth and barrenness, now countless cities tower.

A myriad peoples crowded where once no foot had pressed;
They ruled the land, they tilled the soil, they rode the billow's crest.
Man's mind had chained the elements to do man mighty will;
Man's work had left its imprint on harbor, vale and hill.

The spirits gazed in wonder upon the surging throng;
The haughty and the humble, the feeble and the strong;
Each in a feverish scramble to reach a common goal;
The great almighty dollar, regardless of his soul.

And fiercest, midst this monster host, were by the spirits seen
A swarming blood of creatures of a most rapacious mien,
Who pushed and crushed and struggled to lead in the array,
While, like vultures over carrion, they gloried in foul play.

"Who are these greedy objects who swarm the city street?"
The spirits asked of an old friend, whom they had chance to meet
"Oh those, sirs, are the lawyers who in accidents delight,
The chasers of the ambulance,—the modern trolleybite."[73]

Although part-time law schools eventually acquiesced to the demands of elite institutions, the struggles that occurred are indicative of the disharmony that existed concerning the culture and ideology of legal education.

Finally, the contest over the dissemination of an appropriate culture and ideology in law school was witnessed with the rise of Legal Realism. Reacting against the dogma of Langdellian formalism, legal realists reconceptualized the role of the law and the lawyer in society. Challenging the authority of precedential reasoning, legal realism sought to wed law with social science in order to promote desirable social and legal reforms. The realists combined an analysis of law and legal decisions with establishing progressive social policy.[74] Realists considered that such an approach was best suited to elucidate and maximize the public interest. While legal realism failed to establish itself as the dominant method of legal analysis, it did arouse great antipathy among more traditional legal practitioners and law school faculty. Indeed, this hostility towards unorthodox methods of legal analysis continues today in the critique of Critical Legal Studies.

This chapter has sought to provide a social history of law school culture and ideology. My brief account of the rise of the American legal profession has suggested that while legal education has been a critical component in its ascent, the character and composition of legal education was a subject of bitterly contested struggle. The appropriate culture and ideology required for the practice of law in American society has been an ongoing concern within the legal profession. As illustrated in this historical overview, law schools, particularly elite law schools, served an important cultural and ideological purpose in the rise of the American lawyer. More than simply providing training in law, these schools sought to inculcate social characteristics, ideological dispositions, and hierarchical organization that not only provided public legitimacy for a growing legal profession, but also imparted a self-legitimating ideology that justified the activities in which they engaged as lawyers. How these ideologies and cultural dispositions are developed in law school, and whose interests they ultimately serve, is the subject of the present investigation.

◆ 3 ◆

Contradictions and Disjunctures

Motives, Values, and Career Preferences among Law Students

Despite the ongoing calls for redistribution of legal services, despite the politically liberal orientation of those who choose law as a career, and despite what appears to be a genuine interest in justice by many students who attend law school, a serious and pervasive maldistribution of legal talent continues to serve the interests of wealth, power, and status. The conflicts that this contradiction generates, the direction in which these conflicts are resolved, and the cultural processes through which this resolution is legitimized, are all components of a law school experience in which students accommodate contradictory tendencies that pervade their daily lives. The culture students create and experience within law school transmits messages to law students which effectively encourage them to accommodate the values and interests of the corporate marketplace.

The experience of attending law school produces in law students a disjunction between substantive views of justice and the profession's emphasis on technical rationality; between an individual's search for democracy and the

36

profession's ethic of eminence; between the recognized need to provide egalitarian forms of legal service and the desire to accommodate those with a generous supply of economic and cultural capital. Harvard Law professor Duncan Kennedy has conceptualized this disjuncture as a tension between individualism and altruism.[1] This disjuncture and the conflict it creates constitutes a central element of student experience in law school.

Nowhere is this disjuncture more apparent than in the occupational choices made by students during law school. In this chapter, I demonstrate that law students who enter law school for altruistic reasons experience a "disjuncture" between their personal interests in justice and the ones articulated in law school. In the chapters that follow I illustrate that such disjunctures, while at times disturbing, are resolved in ways that allow students to make occupational choices that favor corporate practice.

Student Motives for Attending Law School

The decision to enter law school is often complex. Students study law for a variety of reasons. In his comparative study of six law schools, Stevens found that students entered law school for career, intellectual, and social justice reasons.[2] Stevens found that the desire to restructure society and to serve the underprivileged ranked significantly higher than the desire to go to Wall Street or to enter politics. More recently, Hedegard examined the reasons why students attend law school.[3] In his study of Brigham Young University law students, he found that 18 percent ranked the desire to help the underprivileged as being of great importance in their decisions to enter law school. A desire to restructure society was ranked as a reason of great importance by 31 percent of these students. Also, Zemans and Rosenblum report that about 18 percent of the Chicago lawyers they studied ranked an opportunity to be helpful to others and/or useful to society as the most important reason for entering law school.[4] Similarly, Katz and Denbeaux found that the opportunity to be of "great service to the community" ranked third among a list of factors affecting students' decisions to become a lawyer.[5]

A considerable amount of time has passed since these studies were conducted. Most were conducted in the 1960s and 1970s during the height of student activism. Indeed, the late 1960s and early 1970s generated the activist energies of many law students, who took a significant role in the newly created O.E.O. Legal Services programs and other public interest programs that began at the time. However, law students of the 1980s, it has often been said,

Table 3.1   Student Motivations for Attending Harvard Law School

| | RANK ORDER OF IMPORTANCE | | |
| | *First* | *Second* | *Third* |
	N (%)	N (%)	N (%)
CAREER			
Social Status	12 (3.8)	28 (11.6)	13 (11)
Monetary Reward	20 (6.3)	34 (14)	31 (26.3)
Job Security	6 (1.9)	6 (2.5)	9 (7.6)
Career Advancement	85 (26.6)	36 (15)	12 (10.2)
Job Change	4 (1.3)	5 (2.1)	1 (.8)
ACADEMIC			
Education	20 (6.3)	8 (3.3)	3 (2.5)
Academic Interest	56 (16.9)	54 (22.3)	13 (11)
ALTRUISTIC			
Help People	39 (12.5)	21 (8.7)	13 (11)
Social Justice	25 (7.8)	15 (6.2)	8 (6.8)
Social Change	17 (5.6)	6 (2.5)	1 (.8)
OTHER			
Politics	8 (2.5)	10 (5.0)	2 (1.7)
Default	24 (7.5)	16 (6.7)	10 (8.5)
Personal Autonomy	4 (1.3)	3 (1.2)	2 (1.7)
	320 (100)	242 (100)	118 (100)

like contemporary college students, have been swept up in the wave of political conservatism associated with the Reagan years. It has been argued that "yuppie culture," with its fast-paced life, sensual vanities, and great affluence, has produced a generation of young people who are devoid of any social interest outside their own immediate experience.[6] Certainly this has been the case for many students in the 1980s whose desire to achieve a high standard of living supersedes all other interests. However, there is evidence that student activism and interest in social issues continues to rank high among a significant proportion of students in law school. For instance, in a 1984 portrait of four hundred American law students conducted by the student division of the American Bar Association, a concern for social justice and service to humanity ranked above a student's interest in financial considerations and job security.[7]

Both the statistical data and in-depth interview data summarized below provide strong evidence that large numbers of students at Harvard Law School attended for altruistic reasons. The following table provides a rank ordered breakdown of student motivations for attending Harvard Law School.

While career reasons were the most frequently cited by students at Harvard Law School, many entered expressing altruistic concerns. Nearly 26 percent of the Harvard law student sample indicated a desire to restructure society, help others, or seek social justice. The desire to help others, for instance, was expressed by a son of a Black minister:

> The main reason I chose to come to law school was because of my family. My father was a minister and this is important in the Black community. I thought that the many activities my father's church engaged in could have benefitted by having legal counsel. I came to law school greatly influenced by this and with a commitment to public interest law.

Another student who worked as a community organizer prior to law school verbalized a similar concern:

> I was interested in helping people and using the law for rights and the idealistic stuff that most people don't do.

In addition to wanting to help people, many law students saw an opportunity to reform what they saw as unjust social practices. Three law students described their reasons for attending in the following way:

> I had a good sense of what I wanted to do which was work in the labor movement and organizing. I was initially interested in using law as a vehicle of social change, and more broader public interest goals. (Third-year male)

> I decided to go to law school when I was thirteen because it was then that I became aware of the civil rights movement. I came because I was interested in these issues. (Second-year male)

> I had idealistic notions of doing good. I wanted to do something in the public interest sector. I came in really interested in Native American rights. (Third-year female)

Still others arrived with intentions of using their legal and advocacy skills to help foster social change initiatives:

> I was heavily involved in radical politics at college. I decided that things were too fucked up to go study in a library so I decided to come to law school. I came with the feeling that law school would empower me. I'm a believer in power, mobilization, and change. I came to law school because I was interested in transformative politics. (Second-year male)

39

I really feel strongly about social change and I thought that the law is a fair instrument for that. I think that everyone has a responsibility to help society. I believe it's a moral obligation. (First-year male)

I was interested in political things and social progress and I thought law school would be helpful. I don't necessarily want to work at a corporate firm. I would like to use it to get involved in the legal system and effect change. (Third-year female)

Many students choose law school for the opportunities it would provide in realizing their substantive interests in social change. Thus, a significant number of law students at Harvard had interests in law and legal practice that extended beyond the abundance of material rewards and professional prestige that an Ivy League law degree could bring.

The Special Sadness of the Law School Student

Over the years, writers on the subject of law school have expressed misgivings with the purported cruelties of contemporary legal education. The popularized version of this uneasiness is contained within *The Paper Chase,* where the central character, Hart, explains how he is being reshaped and manipulated by the facile intellect of his professors. Speaking of his contracts teacher, Professor Kingsfield, Hart complains that he is "like the air or the wind, he's everywhere. You can say you don't care, but he's there anywhere, pounding his mind into mine. He screws around with my life." A similar trepidation is contained in Scott Turow's chronicle of his first year at Harvard Law School: "They're making me different. . . . They're turning me into someone else, someone I don't want to be. I have the feeling all the time that I'm being indoctrinated."[8]

The apprehension expressed in these voices reflects a concern with the deadening effects of the law school experience; a fear that students who attend lose their sense of personal competence and humanism, only to emerge three years later as disaffected technocrats whose search for justice has been subsumed by the tough-minded and calculating rationality of rules, limiting principles, balancing tests, and line-drawing. Indeed, the phrase exhorted by the mythical Kingsfield that he would turn "minds of mush" into thinking lawyers expresses the reputation of contemporary law school education.

Research on the experiences of law students has consistently noted that they become increasingly alienated, progressively isolated and chronically distressed.[9] This has been said to be particularly evident among women.[10] In one Harvard Law student publication, law students even complained of suffering a form of mental illness.

> The richer we are, the more opportunities we have for success, the harder it is to accept failure. And failure is defined, not by ourselves but by those we don't even like or respect. The world is designed, financed, packaged and marketed by people we would never want to be like, never want to talk to, never want to sleep with. We are aliens in our own culture. It's no wonder so many law students are suffering mild forms of mental disease.[11]

These students feel alien in the very world that is being offered to them.

Most often, the students who experience these disabilities had not brought this condition with them into law school. By all accounts, such behaviors are the products of the process of law school socialization, a process not unlike boot camp, that attempts to dissolve a student's previous conceptualizations of the world and replace them with a set of values consistent with the ideology of professional culture. "The student is stripped naked, so to speak, so that he may be remade a lawyer."[12] While not all those who attend law school complain of these experiences, most altruistic-oriented students are confronted with a perspective that seriously upsets their view of justice. A third-year law student described how dreadful her first-year experience was; an experience that left her completely uncertain about her own values.

> Everything in my life was challenged which seriously doubted my foundations. You come in with a system of beliefs that you base your life on and I think it's valuable to question presumptions, but to have the whole base blown away without any substitution of something I could believe in was very disturbing. I talk to people now and I listen to them and say, "well I guess you're right," knowing full well that if someone else was giving me the opposite side, I would say, "I guess you're right." I can walk away from discussions now with no strong feelings of my own. I guess this is what it means to be a lawyer, you're taught to see that there are two equal sides of any issue.

The discomfort reported by this student is closely related to the individualist/altruist disjuncture noted earlier. These students had brought a sense of justice into law school that did not resonate with what they found in law. The "professionalization" process conflicted with their entering values and ideals.

Despite the traumatic and unsettling experiences reported by many of these law students, the overwhelming majority expressed the feeling that law school had been positive and enriching. In spite of the reported alienation and personal discomfort, law students generally believed that they were better able to assume eminent roles in society after having attended law school. Rarely, however, did these roles include public interest forms of practice. Indeed, while many students arrived at law school with altruistic orientations to legal practice and developed attitudes in law school that would seemingly be consistent with public interest practice, few students actually pursued this option. Given that so many students report possessing altruistic interests, what effect do they perceive law school as having on their personal and professional interests?

To investigate this, I examined student perceptions of the effect of law school. The next section suggests that despite instances of alienation and isolation among many students, most see their law school training as personally and professionally empowering. In addition, some students even report having developed attitudes about law and legal practice that seem to correspond to public interest roles. Not only did many of these students begin their law school career motivated by social interests, but many developed a self-image that would make the practice of public interest law seem more likely.

The Political Education of Elite Law Students

It is important to understand how law students see their development in relation to their training. Despite the many claims made by those who criticize law school education for having a conservatizing effect, most law students at Harvard Law School perceived themselves as having become far less conservative in their political ideology.

Walking through the labyrinth of underground tunnels that connect the various buildings on the Harvard Law School campus, one is immediately struck by the politically liberal and left-liberal atmosphere that prevails. Organizations and law reviews such as the *Harvard Civil Rights/Civil Liberties Law Review,* the *Environmental Law Review,* the Civil Rights Action Committee, the Committee on Gay and Lesbian Legal Issues, the Harvard Labor Law Project, and, the Prisons Legal Assistance Project reflect politically liberal and sometimes radical concerns. Located in other buildings are the office of the Students for Public Interest Law, which represents Cambridge tenants in hearings before the rent control board, as well as provides legal assistance to low and moderate income tenants; and the Harvard Legal Aid Bureau, which provides legal services to approximately 1,000 indigent clients each year in landlord-tenant disputes, welfare issues, consumer law, and family law. The Harvard Legal Services Center operates a clinical program for students who provide legal aid to Boston residents in the areas of government benefits, immigration, and housing, while the Harvard Fellowship in Public Interest Law raises money through student and alumni contributions to fund students dedicated to working in public interest law. In 1984, this last organization raised approximately $50,000 to provide funding for students to work with the Mississippi ACLU, the El Paso Legal Assistance Society, and the Massachusetts Advocacy Center.[13]

Recently constituted organizations include Harvard Law School's Children's Rights Project, in which students research legal programs available for youngsters throughout the country and write model legislation;[14] the Project of Law and Social Thought, which received $80,000 from the law school to start up an interdisciplinary speaker's program that would bring faculty in anthropology, literary studies, and social theory to the law school to lecture;[15] and a small, but highly active collection of semi-militant students calling themselves "The Counter-hegemonic Front" who, among other things, are opposed to "illegitimate hierarchies," reification, mystification, private property, minority rule in South Africa, and all Boston sports teams.[16]

In addition to this, the law school contains perhaps the largest contingent of Critical Legal Scholars in the country and has one of the only public interest placement centers in the country, a program that was terminated in 1989 by incoming law school dean, Robert Clark, a militant proponent of Law and Economics.[17] This program was reinstituted shortly thereafter, however, due to overwhelming student opposition. In many ways, the atmosphere within Harvard Law School suggests an orientation that would be consistent with the promotion of social justice careers and values.

All of this is very confusing particularly when so many students from Harvard accept legal positions in large corporate law firms. The environment is liberal and to the left while the occupational decisions that students make are corporate-oriented. Although few enter public interest legal practice, more than one third, 38 percent, of law students at Harvard believed themselves to have become more radical while in law school. When asked, students generally perceived themselves as having political ideologies that they characterized as on the left. Cross-sectional data between each class indicates that third-year students were more likely to perceive themselves as becoming more radical than their first- and second-year counterparts.

In addition to this, more than half (53 percent) of the Harvard sample indicated that they had become more interested in pro bono legal services

Table 3.2 Self-reported Shift in Political Attitudes of Harvard Law
Students by Year

	More Radical	Same	More Conservative
First	30.2%	40.3%	29.5%
Second	38.1	26.5	36.4
Third	45.8	20.8	33.3
	(N=143)	(N=115)	(N=124)

Chi Square = 14.09; P<.007

during law school. As table 3.3 demonstrates, there is a statistically significant pattern between students. Third-year students report having become more interested in pro bono than first-year students.

Similarly, nearly half (49 percent), perceived themselves as having become more interested in public service. Furthermore, over one half (55 percent) believed themselves to be more involved in politics since entering. These students did not consider themselves politically conservative. In fact, 51 percent of the Harvard sample reported having become more interested in restructuring society while in law school, and 49 percent felt that they had become more concerned with resolving the various social problems presently confronting society.

Many students believed they had become more interested in politics and had developed greater concern with the myriad of social problems confronting society. This is partially due to the fact that many students were relatively apolitical before law school. As one twenty-four-year-old female student who came to law school to advance her career but also with a strong interest in "helping people" explained,

> I don't think law school has depoliticized me. I came here not having much of a sense of politics at all. I have a much greater sense of it now. I never realized law was so political. I rarely had a political thought before I came

Table 3.3 Self-reported Student Interest in Pro Bono Legal
Services by Year

	More Interested	Same	Less Interested
First	48.3%	38.3%	13.4%
Second	46.5	33.3	20.2
Third	64.0	16.0	20.0
	(N=201)	(N=114)	(N=67)

Chi Square = 18.23; P<.001

here and suddenly I'm thinking about what they are trying to get across in the decision, who are they trying to oppress. I think now that I'd really like to have some sort of effect on integration or the redistribution of wealth. I believe these are important issues, but as a lawyer I don't know how I can do that.

At the time she expressed these thoughts about her political consciousness she was in the first year of her legal studies. She had come to law school directly out of a prestigious college in the south where she had majored in English literature. During her first year she had been exposed to classes that were taught by faculty who were active in the Critical Legal Studies movement, and came away from that experience feeling that she had been radicalized. Her level of altruistic concern, she felt, rose dramatically during her first year so much so that she expressed concern over being on the "right side" in her moot court competition. On the evening of her moot court she expressed this concern:

My partner and I are representing a Black guy who was convicted of inciting a riot. I was really afraid that I was going to have to take the state's side of the case. I think that this is a racially motivated case that probably would have been settled out of court if he were white. I convinced the other students that we should flip a coin to determine who should argue the state's side. Fortunately, my team won the coin toss so I feel comfortable about what I'm about to argue.

Indeed, this student *had* become more sensitive to the legal and social issues involved in the case, but she was unwilling to let her "sensitivities" get in the way of being a lawyer. In her mind, the case was an example of racial oppression, but as a lawyer it simply represented a toss of a coin. For this student, being a lawyer ultimately meant not standing on principles that were outside legalistic conceptions of justice.

In keeping with what she defined as her new-found radicalism, she participated in a trial advocacy workshop during her second year that contained a clinical legal services component. She described this as "particularly rewarding" because she was providing legal services to poor people. While she described this experience as the most favorable one she had while in law school, and considered herself more radical because of it, she chose to work at a large firm after graduation. Becoming radical in law school and engaging in activities that are "public interest" does not necessarily foster a commitment to practice public interest law. Her experiences in law school confirmed to her that she was properly concerned about these issues but need not put that into practice when she graduated.

45

Research has demonstrated that as law students begin their legal studies they tend to exhibit more sensitivity to their clients than do students who are approaching the end of their legal education.[18] This, however, is not the view Harvard law students have of themselves. In contrast to the "case-hardened" and insensitive image, these law students believed themselves to have become more sensitive to client needs. Nearly 40 percent said they had become more empathetic towards client problems while being in law school. In addition, they claimed to have become more issue-oriented as opposed to mere technocrats. Forty-five percent of the sample believed they had become more concerned with substantive interests, while only 21 percent believed they had become more technically-oriented. Indeed, they did not believe they had lost their sensitivity.

The contradiction that prevails within the lives of Harvard law students is seen further in their evaluations of substantive areas in law. They generally favored legal specialties that were associated with public interest forms of practice over those that were associated with corporate and commercial practice. More than half, 59 percent, 64 percent and 54 percent, felt that corporate law, tax law, and real estate law, respectively, were unchallenging and personally unrewarding areas of legal practice, while 75 percent and 73 percent considered public interest law and civil rights work, respectively, both challenging and personally rewarding.[19] In addition, more than half, 51 percent, indicated that they found poverty law fulfilling and rewarding.

Legal Education as a "Radicalizing" Effect

From the data reported above, it would appear that many law students at Harvard believed they had become "radicalized" in law school. Most reported becoming more interested in social change, most felt that courses in public interest law were more challenging and rewarding than corporate-oriented classes, most had become more interested in public service, and more than a third characterized themselves as having become more radical. Even conservative students believed there to be a "radicalizing" trend at Harvard Law School.

When students' reasons for entering law school were controlled, this pattern of radicalization became even stronger among certain groups. Students who came to law school with altruistic motivations tended to believe themselves to have become far more radical than their career-oriented counterparts. Of the students entering law school for altruistic reasons, 63 percent considered that law school had further radicalized them, while 33 percent of the career-oriented students believed themselves to have become more radical.

What is interesting about the comparisons between the career-oriented students and those who chose to attend law school for altruistic reasons is the fact that, other than feeling that they had become more radical and more opposed to business interests, altruistic students were often indistinguishable from their careerist counterparts. Both groups had become more concerned with pro bono legal services, 61 percent and 54 percent, respectively. In addition, 50 percent of the career-oriented students expressed increased interest in public service, compared to 62 percent of the altruistic-oriented students. While there is a difference, it was not statistically significant. Each group had developed more interests in helping to resolve social problems. Fifty-two percent of the career students and 59 percent of the altruistic students felt that they had become more concerned about various social problems during their law school socialization. Each group felt they had become increasingly interested in social change, 65 percent and 50 percent, respectively. Also, each group tended to see public interest law as challenging and rewarding; 88 percent of the altruistic group and 70 percent of the career group, respectively.

Diminishing Expectations

Observers of professional socialization have shown that students experience dramatic shifts in their occupational orientation as they move through their schooling. Divergence from a student's original goals has been a common finding in medical school, professional schools for nursing, and even police academies.[20] Alterations in occupation goals seem to be a natural outcome of any professional socialization process. As students acquire new norms, they are often exposed to a wide variety of different specialties and career options, and frequently develop a sense of efficacy in areas that might not coincide with in-coming orientations. Students who enter professional schools possess interests that are based on their non-professional image of professional work. As they become socialized into the profession, however, many undergo significant change.

A common complaint among observers of legal education has been that students enter law school with a public interest orientation, yet their interests in pursuing this form of practice erodes significantly over time. The career intentions of Harvard law students seem to confirm this pattern. First-year students at Harvard were more likely to begin their law school careers expressing interest in forms of practice other than large private firms. While there

47

were certainly large numbers of students expressing interest in these law firms, the proportion was significantly less during the first year than in subsequent years. In the Harvard sample, 55 percent of all first-year students surveyed indicated that their most likely future practice after graduation would be in settings other than large law firms. These students more often saw themselves as interested in social or public interest types of work, government service, or in some cases, as sole practitioners or practitioners in small law firms. In a separate poll of first-year Harvard Law students conducted in 1986, 70 percent expressed a desire to practice public-interest law.

As one third-year student commented, however: "The conventional wisdom is that everyone comes in saying they don't want to do corporate law, but when they leave everyone does just that." The assessment of this student appears correct. There is a statistically significant increase in the number of second- and third-year students considering careers in larger law firms. On the whole, few third-year students perceived their initial legal position as being in settings other than a large private law firm. Of those third-year students reporting this, only 2 percent indicated a preference for legal aid jobs and only 5 percent were still considering public interest jobs. As one third-year Harvard student explained,

> I came to law school with the idea of doing social policy and public interest. I have instead decided to go into a large private firm. I really didn't know what kinds of opportunities were available to me. I just didn't know what kind of ticket this was.

The fact that a significantly greater proportion of third-year students report having become more radical and antibusiness in law school as compared to first-year students makes this finding particularly ironic.[21]

This is a common tendency even among the most committed students. While no first-year student entering for altruistic reasons had desires to work in large law firms, almost all of these most public-interest committed students were intending to join corporate law firms. One third-year student, who initially expressed a deep commitment to public interest practice, described his future career track:

> I'm clerking for a very prestigious court in the D.C. circuit. After that I plan to go work for [a large New York firm]. This is a change for me. I can't go into some public interest job straight out of here. It's not really because of my loan debt though. If I really wanted to take a public interest job I could get the school to forgive my loan. The question is do I really want to live on $30,000 a year. I think I want to buy a house and be comfortable for awhile.

Maybe I'll move into public interest work after a few years in a big firm. This all leads to a mainstream corporate job for me. I guess I want to keep my options open. I've gotten into the habit of going for the brass ring and so I don't want to slip. The problem with the brass rings are that they don't conform to a non-mainstream career route. In public interest jobs it's not clear where you go to be on top. I'm caught on a success treadmill and it remains clear to me where the successful firms are. If you get on a partner track at a large New York law firm then it's clear that you're still on track. I'm keeping my options open.

With this student, at least, it seems that the desire to succeed overwhelmed his desire to do good. This student sums up all-to-well the pattern of most students at Harvard Law School. Despite their humanistic concerns and their growing desire to contribute to society, most of these students accepted jobs working for America's power elite.

The data presented in this chapter illustrate that significant proportions of students enter law school with some degree of interest in public interest law. Many of these students expressed specific interests in working with disadvantaged groups, working for community groups on environmental or housing problems, or working for labor unions. Others were less specific but generally wished to be involved in providing legal assistance for progressive causes. More often than not, first-year students saw themselves as planning a career in non-corporate forms of legal practice so that their altruistic goals might be realized.

Many of these students, as well as their less social-justice-oriented counterparts believed they had developed a greater "public interest" orientation while in law school. Most believed themselves to have become more interested in social change, resolving social problems, and public service. Despite the numbers of students expressing these interests, however, most end up planning legal careers in large corporate law firms upon graduation. This represents a basic anomaly.

Many legal professionals and legal scholars have registered deep dissatisfaction with the seeming unwillingness of graduating law students to accept public interest jobs. Former deans of the Harvard Law School have criticized the numbing effects of legal education and its failure to produce more public interest lawyers.[22] Journalists, as well, have launched sharp attacks against legal education for seemingly facilitating the corporate path taken by so many law students.[23] Renowned legal activists like Ralph Nader have sternly criticized the failure of law schools to promote and support alternative career choices among law students. The President of the American Bar Association has recently raised the specter of concern about the needs of the poor and their lack of legal representation.[24] Many law schools, including Harvard, have begun to take measures to redress the maldistribution of lawyers by forgiving student loans if they take lower paying jobs upon graduation.[25] At the present time, however, there is no indication that loan forgiveness programs will be able to alter occupational trends of law students.

The chapters in this book examine the experiences of students as they undergo their legal education, and pay close attention to the ideological transformations that occur. These chapters will demonstrate how the experiences of students, both in and out of their classes, and the values they adopt, produce visions of law and legal practice that direct them into America's elite law firms.

♦ 4 ♦

Discovering the Law

The Emergence of Legal Consciousness

I t has been alleged that educational institutions reproduce forms of consciousness required for the perpetuation and legitimation of the social relations prevalent in a class society. Much in keeping with Marx's dictum that the ideas of the ruling class are in every epoch the ruling ideas, some social scientists have argued that consciousness is formed and structured in various institutions according to the dictates of a capitalist logic. Within the educational literature, the most vivid articulation of this correspondence view has been advanced by Bolwes and Gintis in their study of American education.[1]

While schools frame consciousness in ways that give meaning to the social and political world, meaning itself always involves an interpretive activity in which students struggle to "make sense" of the new world-views, norms, values, and dispositions to which they are exposed.[2] The question of *how* knowledge, consciousness and subjective identity are activated by students, a question that correspondence approaches fail to address, is essential to any analysis of the role educational institutions play in mediating the relationship between dominant and subordinate interests within society.

In this chapter, I first examine the pedagogical foundations associated with the production of legal consciousness. Legal consciousness is typically referred to as the ability to "think like a lawyer." While the process of linguistic conversion is central to a law school experience, learning a particular mode of cognitive analysis lies at its core.[3] Although the practice of thinking, as a physiological activity, requires little socio-cultural information, the concepts and methods used to articulate thought are socially constructed. As Mannhiem's sociology of knowledge instructs, "It is not men in general who think, or even isolated individuals who do the thinking, but men in certain groups who have developed a particular 'style of thought' in an endless series of responses to certain typical situations characterizing their common position."[4] Legal consciousness is a social artifact derived from a particular social context where ideas, concepts, propositions, intellectual styles, and principles become meaningful.

Law students are not simply empty vessels into which knowledge and consciousness is poured. Rather, they react to, struggle with, and interpret law. For most, this sense-making activity produces a consciousness about the nature and role of law that severs students from their nascent idealistic views of social justice. The formation of this type of consciousness often promotes the adoption of moral and ethical orientations that are incongruous with a student's personal views of ethics and justice. During their law schooling, most students replace a justice-oriented consciousness with a game-oriented consciousness.

The Elementary Form of Legal Consciousness in Law School

A law school education in American society is typically a challenging intellectual experience. Legal education, particularly in elite law schools, has the reputation of cultivating the sharpest minds in American society and preparing students for positions of leadership. From the legal profession's standpoint, law school hones the minds of bright students to enable them to expertly handle the assorted policy-related problems confronting society. In the words of Edwin Griswold, former dean of Harvard Law School, "the functions of law school should be primarily to teach a capacity to face new problems successfully, to find solutions to questions never before dreamed of."[5] The laurels of the legal profession, thus, hang on the finely-tuned intellectual talents of its members.

The process of learning law is a demanding intellectual endeavor. This is particularly true for first-year students who must navigate through the difficult process of learning a new and often complex language. Learning law involves assimilating a unique form of speech which is at once highly specialized and conceptually ambiguous. Embedded within legal discourse is a collection of competing and contradictory assumptions, world-views, and values from which students endeavor to discern meaningfulness and, at least initially, certainty. The development of linguistic competence in law demands a significant investment of time and energy, particularly for first-year students. Fifty-five percent of first-year law students at Harvard, for instance, reported spending between thirty and sixty hours per week preparing for their classes.

In the course of their training students become conversant in extremely technical concepts in law. During their first year, these law students are faced with difficult legal concepts such as promissory estoppal, contractual consideration, res ipsa loquitur, res judicata, and fee-tail. Even mundane terms such as mortgage, conveyance, property, and negligence take on new meanings for neophyte law students. Lengthy esoteric discussions involving the use of these concepts and their subtle interplay frequently engulf students during their first year, very often superseding other personal interests. One third-year Harvard Law student recalled how other non-legal interests became less important during his first year:

> I was walking back from Civil Procedure with several other first-year law students from my class. We were embroiled in a discussion of rule 23-B1 of the procedural code. As we approached the Hark (student center) I overheard several other students nearby talking about the Grenada invasion that had just been reported in the news. I barely stopped to listen and instead continued discussing the procedural rule. This was strange for me because I consider myself a political person who is concerned about foreign policy and American Imperialism.

The law is often so complete and engulfing that outside events become increasingly irrelevant. This process undermines radical thought by teaching a logic and vocabulary that isolates law students from social contexts. This ability to disregard social contexts is part of the self-alienating ideology associated with legal consciousness.

The consciousness that students develop about the role and nature of law has significant implications for the practice of law in society. What are, as Goodrich has recently queried, the implications of having a powerful group of individuals who are trained to think in ways that are quite different from the public run the government, head or advise multinational corporations, determine standards of morality or immorality, and advise leaders throughout the world?[6]

The legal consciousness these students developed consisted of three fundamental attributes. These included: (1) the ability to conceive of legal analysis as justification, (2) the ability to draw connections, and (3) the ability to pose arguments and counterarguments on a variety of legal and social policy issues. In the following sections, I explore the ways in which these skills are developed.

1. Law as justification

During their initial year in law school, students often struggled to identify the conceptual logic beneath the legal rulings they read. Despite the existence of what Duncan Kennedy refers to as multiple gaps, conflicts, and ambiguities in the law, students typically endeavored to discern the line of reasoning a judge used in writing a judicial opinion.[7] Students carefully searched through judicial opinions in order to locate their logical foundations. Many first-year students even participated in study groups to help them facilitate this skill.[8] As students continued to read and discuss the various cases, however, they frequently discovered that each case contained competing and often contradictory interpretations. This occurred primarily because the cases explored in law school involve the juxtaposition of complex social issues. In these cases, students were presented with concurring and dissenting court opinions registered by different justices, each offering reasonable justification for their respective position. For instance, public liability for personal harm was juxtaposed with individual responsibility, civil freedoms with the power of the state to restrict those freedoms, or the economic needs of individuals versus the economic needs of corporate institutions. These are difficult issues, and, rarely, if ever, were they resolved in class. In fact, answers, while sometimes offered, became less immediately realizable to students. A second-year male law student described how he experienced the curriculum as a newcomer.

> I got frustrated the first year because I was looking for answers but there really aren't any answers. I think this is how law has to be. There aren't any simple answers.

Students began to view the justificatory process itself as the paramount lesson to be learned within their law classes. One second-year student, for instance, described how she grew to recognize the importance of justification.

> We don't find answers. I took an exam where there was a hypothetical that was like the one in our study guide. I was really upset because I didn't come

out the same way the manual did, but I still did well on the exam. What I realized from that exam was that thinking like a lawyer is how you can take a case and make it say what you want to say. I got the impression that there is no right or wrong. You can justify almost any position it seems.

This process of legal justification is central to legal consciousness. As the noted scholar, Karl Llewellyn once remarked: "the opinion is an explanation, a justification of the decision, and one at least acceptable to the court which decided."[9] In short, judicial opinions represent social constructions that are frequently arbitrary.

During law school, students were taught the ability to justify their opinions on legal grounds as opposed to ideological or substantive ones. This is fundamental to the development of legal consciousness for lawyers. Developing legal consciousness, however, is often difficult and occurs only after one's complete immersion in law. The identification and construction of justification seems to be what Llewellyn meant when he proposed that: "If law makes you blind, more law will make you see."[10] Law students come to "see" the law only after they have struggled with it. Students, however, are frequently frustrated with this constructive process; a process many believed was at variance with their personal views of justice.

However, the more students participated in this justificatory process the more they perceived such abilities as necessary. A second-year student explained his reaction to this process.

It [legal consciousness] bothered me a lot more before than it does now. You find out that law is really justification; you can always find a case to support your argument. To me it called into question the legitimacy of the whole process. What's supposed to happen is that two people go to court with a dispute and the rule is supposed to govern the dispute and someone comes out a winner. However, I've learned that I can bring a case that I want to use to win and the opposing lawyer uses the same case to argue what he wants. The more cases I read and courses I took the more I realized that I wasn't going to find right answers. I've grown to accept that.

Throughout the first year, students often expressed fears of losing sight of their values. The development of legal consciousness was disturbing to many of these law students. A first-year student, discussing what he considered the shortcomings of his legal education, complained that

The law is not guided by fundamental principles of right or wrong, but rather the ability to twist the law as much as possible to make a coherent argument. What we are taught here is how to construct "good" but not necessarily moral arguments.

Law school may be viewed as cousin to Erving Goffman's concept of "total institution." According to Goffman, a key organizational prerequisite of the total institution is to detach entering "inmates" from their previous or "presenting culture."[11] This presenting culture is defined by Goffman as "a record of experience that confirmed a tolerable conception of self and allowed a set of defense maneuvers, exercised at his own discretion, for coping with conflicts, discreditings and failures." It is the design of such institutions to strip away past individual loyalties, and in their place, construct a set of legitimate and homogenous values, identities, and practices that are consistent with the institutional image. In the words of Bonsignore, law students are "caught in a paradigmatic squeeze" that significantly effects the way they look at the world.[12]

2. *Drawing connections*

In addition to learning that judicial decisions are mere justifications, students were taught the ability to distinguish similar cases and draw parallels between distinct ones. In their classes, students were encouraged to engage in techniques of argumentative manipulation and synthesis as a way of developing these skills. Students learned that the practice of law involved a process of creative argumentation in which they must be able to create the appearance of logical consistency and coherence. They soon realized that they would be evaluated on their ability to make creative arguments.

The recognition of this tended to exaggerate the level of anxiety experienced by many first-year law students who felt unable to make such arguments. These students experienced considerable uncertainty about their ability to learn the law due to their failure to see the connections made by their professors. It was not that these law students had failed to see these connections; they simply had not seen the ones made by their professors or other students. Not recognizing at first that law and the facts surrounding a case can be manipulated in multiple ways, many first-year law students felt inadequate for failing to anticipate an argument. The collective anxiety that students experienced actually served to intensify the learning process by encouraging students to engage in efforts to ascertain deeper understandings of material they read. Although most students didn't seem to recognize it in the early stages of their training, legal reasoning is a bit like mixing two or more puzzles together and using the assorted pieces to construct an entirely different image. For example, in a first-year contracts class the following interaction occurred in which the professor masterfully discussed how two seemingly disparate cases could be synthesized.

T: Miss ———, what is the promise in the American case?

S: Timely delivery of produce.

T: What is related to this reliance?

S: Expenses and costs.

T: What are the expected damages?

S: I don't know if you can calculate any.

T: (To another student) What are the expenses?

S: Exposure to the weather that ruined the produce that was in the freightcar.

T: What would be the money value for this? How could you go about making your point for compensation?

S: Publicity, you could use the media to show how the railroad contributed to the damages of the crop.

T: Is that fair for the plaintiff?

S: You would have to bargain for payment of X amount of money with the railroad company.

T: To me, the expected reliance is the fairest. These are the expectations the plaintiff was to receive. To recover lost profit, you have to show some certainty. The courts are skeptical about expected lost profit. Does this argument tell us anything about the Hawkins case? Miss ———, how would the argument go?

S: (Apparently not listening) In what? (She doesn't respond further.)

T: Mr. ———, make the argument.

S: Yes, in Hawkins there is a risk in the operation like profits. The loss of the perfect hand, which was promised by the doctor, could be seen as similar to lost profits in the previous case.

T: (To student that did not respond) You see Miss ———, there are various ways to go. (To other student) Go on now.

S: In Hawkins the doctor knew what the possible pre- and post-operative problems might be.

57

T: Yes, there is a reliance in this case that corresponds to the American case? Let's move on. Miss ———, what is the promise in the Grove's case?

This interaction demonstrates that the process of drawing connections, as spurious as they sometimes may be, represents a central pedagogical lesson in law school. In the above case, damaged fruit in a freightcar became equivalent to a hand damaged by a physician. This ritual practice of drawing similarities between differing cases and distinguishing like cases constitutes a paradigmatic component of legal consciousness.

3. Learning to argue

After learning that judicial opinions represent arbitrary social constructions and that dissimilar cases may be synthesized to form apparently coherent arguments, students were taught to make legal arguments from mutually opposing positions. This intellectual activity commenced at the earliest stage of students' law school training. One first-year male explained that

> teachers ask us to discuss the holding of a case and then ask us to distinguish it from other cases and then force us to argue the other side. We are taught how to flip arguments and how to maneuver around principles.

This pedagogical activity was designed to foster an ability to construct winning strategies. In fact, students soon learned that winning superseded the search for truth. A second-year student described this process.

> Since coming here I've learned to attack every argument and to be able to see both sides of everything. We're taught to win, not necessarily find right answers.

Students were formally introduced to this intellectual orientation through class interactions with their teachers and with other students. During their first year, for instance, these students were routinely exposed to exercises that often lead them to question their own sense of justice. A common pedagogical device used to challenge a student's conception of justice was the "slippery slope." This technique involved a faculty member who engaged a student in a debate over a legal issue and challenged the student to argue positions with which he/she may feel uncomfortable. For many, this intellectual cat and mouse game was very disconcerting, particularly since it was being acted out in front of a group of 150 law students. One third-year student who was particularly disturbed by these classroom dynamics recalled her experiences of having to perform.

> They [teachers] lock you into an argument and push you along until you die. If you say something at one point, the professor shows how it can be used to support something you disagree with. Somehow you're wrong because you can't support both things. You can't support the position you started with and the one you ended with. This is really intimidating because the class is so big.

In addition, first-year students participated in small research seminars that promoted this skill. These seminars, conducted by second- and third-year student advisors, consisted of three two-hour sessions in which first-year students were given instructions in legal research. In one such session a student instructor was teaching neophytes how to utilize the law library to conduct legal research. In the course of his explanation, a first-year student queried whether two mutually opposing positions could be supported in the same jurisdiction. This student was obviously concerned about an intellectual exercise that bore no relation to the discovery of what she saw as the truth. Her question was responded to in the affirmative by her student advisor. The student then inquired as follows:

S: If this is the case, how then does one ever derive the truth, or know what is right or wrong?

A: You don't. This is what it means to be an advocate. You are not there to uncover the "truth" but to advocate your client's case. It is your client that defines what is right. You select those cases which support his case and disregard the rest.

S: (Looking a bit concerned) I don't know if I like this.

A: You'll get used to it.

Such skills were also taught to students through examinations where students were expected to develop both sides of a legal issue in order to receive good grades.

Students soon realized that excellence in law was not related to the simple acquisition of knowledge, but rather, to the ability to "think like lawyers." A second-year female explained the importance of learning these new skills.

> I have learned to think and approach issues better since coming to law school. I've been reassured in a sense that I now know how to do it. Coming in I

59

was uncertain and very nervous. The first couple of weeks I tried to write everything down. I soon realized that this wasn't like college. The main thing is getting the mode of argument down. I realized that that was all I needed to do with any case. In terms of acquiring knowledge, that's not important in law school. Seeing how the process of legal thinking and legal argumentation operates in different legal contexts is what's really important.

Although students became competent in these skills, many continued to express fears of losing their personal values. A second-year female student complained:

We learn here how to construct arguments. I have begun to look at things in completely different ways. What we learn is to be able to defeat or at least meet the argument posed to you. I have become flip about how easy it is to construct legal arguments. What bothers me though is that you tend less to take a position because you think it's right than because it will work, or maybe [laugh] you're client wants that.

While many expressed initial reservations about being able to argue any position, these students most often began to redefine this as a necessary skill. A second-year student, while somewhat skeptical, believed there was a purpose in mastering this skill:

I often wonder whether there is any inherent worth to this work. I feel that I'm constructing a clever loophole in an argument and the other law firm will think of another clever argument, but are you adding anything worthwhile to society. I'm certain there is value in this somewhere.

The process of professional schooling is an interpretive one in which students reconceptualize their consciousness in ways that are compatible with professional culture.[13] Students achieve new insights only by making sense out of the professional framework within which they are immersed. The importance of frameworks cannot be overstated, for as Goffman instructs they render "what would otherwise be a meaningless aspect of the scene into something that is meaningful."[14] Goffman's concept of frames, like Bourdieu's notion of "habitus," offers heuristic insight into the ways individuals live through and interpret experiences in school.[15] For many students, making sense of the new realities to which they were exposed during law school involved a dramatic process of adjustment and redefinition in which they came to see the logic behind law. The process of acquiring a professional framework, however, often poses considerable conflict that is resolved only after students transcend their "naive" world-views and accommodate the collective rationales of the profession.[16] In the following section, I explore the interpretive process through which law students adjusted to legal consciousness. For most of these students, adjustment to legal consciousness produced a "fate of idealism" that was associated with the development of a gamesmanship orientation to law.

Adjusting to Law: From Idealism to Gamesmanship

The adjustment to legal consciousness entails an interpretive activity whereby students develop new ways of defining reality. Upon entering law school, many of these students frequently reported having certain presumptions about law and legal practice. Within a short period of time, however, most of these preconceptions underwent significant modification.

The effect of this process was often dramatic. Many law students believed they had become increasingly more cynical and disillusioned as a result of their legal education. Sixty-three percent of the Harvard students, for instance, reported that they had become more cynical as a result of their law schooling. This belief did not vary by a student's motivation for attending law school. Of those expressing monetary interests as their primary reason for attending law school, 69 percent believed they had become more cynical. Similarly, of those who entered law school for altruistic reasons, i.e., helping people and promoting social change, 66 percent reported increasing levels of cynicism, while 55 percent of those entering law school for other reasons, such as intellectual interests and political aspiration, perceived themselves as having become more cynical.

The development of cynicism is by no means unique to the law school experience. Indeed, Becker and his associates investigated the various ways that medical training contributed to the development of cynical attitudes among medical students.[17] In that study, students became frustrated with their inability to "learn it all." Realizing this, medical students began to exercise ways to minimize their work load. Eventually, these students became less idealistic about the practice of medicine and about the school's ability to produce competent physicians. In addition, student desires to "serve humanity" became less intrinsically apparent as they progressed in their training. The inability to keep up with their work coupled with their failure to realize their original goals produced widespread cynicism that replaced a student's erstwhile idealism.

Many of these law students, like the medical students studied by Becker and others, reported experiencing increased levels of cynicism during their training. Law students are taught to question convention, to reject the irrational, and to celebrate logical inquiry. Indeed, the ritual of classroom interactions in which cases are dissected and scrupulously analyzed fosters these skills. These are important skills, even for those outside the legal profession. However, like law, cynicism is a double-edged sword. There are forms of cynicism that are transformative and empowering. In such cases the cynic calls into question the "false necessities" and naturalistic assumptions about social life.[18] Such forms of thought may be conceived of as transformative cynicism. Most law students studied here, however, developed a debilitating form of cynicism, one that engendered a sense of detached relativism.

This had significant consequences for those students who entered law school with idealistic views of law and legal practice. Such students were most often surprised to find that the legal system did not operate according to their expectations. One third-year student who came to law school with the intention of working as a sexual violence prosecutor commented that

> I originally had a very idealistic view of the law. I think now that it was a limited view. I knew that there was civil law like divorce, not corporations though. I had a very idealistic notion of how perfect the system must be. I thought that there were some problems but that you could use political arguments to make changes, like in criminal law or civil rights. If you made a just or moral argument you would win. That's not the case though.

This conception of law and legal practice was typical among students who entered law school with the altruistic concerns of helping people and promoting social justice. Like other students who held these views, however, this student had what she had come to define as a "limited" conception of the activities of lawyers and the varied uses of law. Her attention was focused almost exclusively upon criminal law and civil rights as it applied specifically to issues of sexual violence against women. Her pre–law school image of law and its value in society led her to believe that law school would be a place where issues of justice would be explored and where she could acquire the skills necessary to work toward empowering women.

The emphasis on law as providing a useful service to oppressed groups was commonly expressed by these students. A third-year male law student whose father was a plaintiffs' attorney described his preconception of law in the following way:

> I thought the nature of the work was representing the little guy against the big interests. That was my understanding of what a good person and lawyer did. You could do good things and help people.

This student subscribed to the view that law could be used to help people resolve the assorted legal problems they experienced. For this student, legal work meant providing assistance to individuals who had been victimized by others, not simply for the sake of his own profit, but for communitarian values.

While these students each possessed altruistic views, they shared an additional characteristic. Despite the fact that each had elected to go to law school to help people and contribute to social change, they had completely abandoned their initial career intentions and were instead planning to join large private law firms where their ability to work toward their original goals would be minimized. In addition, they had each come to the realization, after two or three years of law school, that law was not what they had originally thought. In each case, these students came to interpret law not as a collection of principles that would lead to just decisions, but rather as nothing more than a game performed by practitioners for the sake of being victorious.

In describing their present conceptions of law and legal practice, law students frequently used the metaphor of a game. While this initially posed a concern for these students, most quickly became adept at playing the game. As one second-year Black woman commented:

> The fact that it's all just a game bothered me more before than it does now. The first two weeks of criminal law blew my theory of justice away. The first week we learned that if a person did something wrong you could get them off in different ways. Then you learn that attorneys can manipulate the law in any way. By the third week I was thinking that the defendants are not right, the lawyers aren't right, so at least there's a judge but then we find out the judge manipulates the law. After this I thought, well even if all these people manipulate things, at least the criminal process works; but then we find out that nearly all the cases involve plea bargaining.

Another student, a second-year male, reported a similar interpretation of legal knowledge.

> The whole thing is just a game. The teacher asks you to discuss the holding of a case, then he asks how would you distinguish it, and how would you argue the other side. We are taught to flip arguments and how to weasel around principles.

During law school, students internalized a perspective of detached cynicism. For many students, the growth of cynicism was particularly disturbing. However, most adjusted to this legal consciousness by assigning value to it.

A second-year female commented on her own emerging legal consciousness in the following way:

> Since I have been here I've realized that law doesn't achieve much and since I have realized what it does achieve, that it can't achieve a whole lot more. You do your best with what you've got but the possibilities are less grandiose. You realize that the system is set up and you can't change it. I've become really cynical. It's all a game. I'm not sure what's right or wrong anymore. I guess that I'm just understanding things more than I did before. Things are more complex now.

This student's comment offers deep insight into the way in which law school was experienced by many of these law students. Ironically, she had equated legal thinking with not being able to tell right from wrong, or justice from injustice. Instead, she had come to associate cynicism with intellectual development and sophistication. That law school training had triumphed is evident in the words she used to bemoan her current state. She felt powerless about making any significant contribution as an attorney and had begun to view her pre–law school beliefs as naive. Eventually, many of these students found solace in their ability to play the game well. A second-year Black male commented on how he had come to redefine the nature of legal consciousness.

> It's interesting though. At first, I didn't see it as a game. I was trying to figure out the rules and what the words meant. After a while, though, I realized it was all just a game. We learn to hide the ball. Sometimes students would try to make some ridiculous arguments because of this. It became fun, although at first I was really disturbed by it.

These students, while initially uncomfortable with legal consciousness, eventually accommodated themselves to its necessity. The ability to define problems in this way constitutes a primary form of cultural capital which these aspiring lawyers acquired while in law school. Such skills and abilities are typically defined as being the trademark of a "professional" attorney. From such a perspective, then, in law school

> [t]here begins a process of developing skills in the dialectical method of law. Ultimately, students learn to depend on these skills to provide solutions to many real and different problems in life about which they must make decisions. An orderly process of weighing and interpreting many life events results. The analytic experience is made easier by the fact that the entire process and result is impersonalized and viewed largely from an intellectual context. So far as the experiencing of problems, particularly other persons'

problems, is made completely impersonal, the development of legal skills is reassuring.[19]

The ability to "depersonalize" legal issues becomes a central part of these student's consciousness.[20]

The development of cynicism, however, carries with it significant consequences for a student's life in the law. While removing personal biases from students is an important component of professional training, the adjustment to the "necessity" and "naturalness" of gamesmanship disables idealist students from their previous aspirations of "doing good." Indeed, cynical relativism regarding the nature of one's actions is a type of consciousness that is contrary to the pursuit of social justice. The maintenance of social justice ideals demand that a particular ideological and normative view of legal activity be cultivated. The culture of cynicism promoted within law school produces an intellectual orientation that undermines a student's interest in social justice.

Eventually, many students even become removed from law altogether after having become bored with legal consciousness. Although many found the classroom interactions stimulating and engaging, students grew tired of this intellectual exercise, often by the middle of their second semester. After discovering the mystery of law, i.e., legal consciousness, many found little substance left in it. One third-year student complained:

> It's been very boring since my first year. The topics are dull. They act like there's going to be all this interesting academic stuff, but in reality, it's all the same. Once you have the legal thinking stuff down, there isn't much else to learn. I don't think much about the law anymore.

For most students, this completed their removal of any involvement in the law as a search for justice.

Resisting Cynicism

Although a culture of cynicism pervaded the law school experience, there were students whose interpretation of law and legal consciousness was contrary to the game orientation. While most of the literature on professional schooling demonstrates a pattern by which a transformation of idealism is reproduced, little attention has been devoted to the phenomenon of resistance and the efforts made by students to maintain their idealistic commitments. Most of the literature on professional schooling assumes that all students experience their training in similar ways. The process of schooling, however, is filled with various forms of resistance.[21] Resistance in school, when it does occur, is often carried out by subgroups who rebel against the schools' attempts to reframe beliefs, values, and consciousness. Students who resist have been said to engage in collective strategies that seek to directly challenge the representatives of authority within school.

Although few in number, the law students who resisted the gamesmanship orientation to legal consciousness ranked social change as their principal reason for attending law school. In most cases, these students adhered to strong ideological and political positions that corresponded to radical social thought and practice. Often guided by strong desires to promote social change, these students decided to attend law school in order to facilitate their political interests. Many of these students had pursued previous careers as labor and community organizers, human service workers, and, in some cases, academics.

Unlike students who became cynical, however, these students did not come to law school expecting to "discover" the values of truth and social justice. Because of their ideological leanings and social activist backgrounds they recognized that social justice was a constant struggle between conflicting interests. For these students, justice was not embodied in legal doctrine simply awaiting application. Unlike their cynical counterparts, these students were much less disturbed by the contradictory nature of law and legal practice. This difference constituted the central intellectual characteristic that distinguished the cynical students from those who resisted becoming cynical. Cynical students expected to find answers to the problems that confront individuals on an everyday basis and became disillusioned when they were presented with the "janus-faced" nature of legal discourse. These students retreated from their idealism (and often from any plans for pursuing careers in social justice) by redefining the "real" nature of law and legal practice as a game. Those who resisted this orientation, however, had no illusions about finding any abstract sense of justice in the law. Consequently, they were less cynical about law when presented with its inherently contradictory tendencies. Moreover, the contradictory attributes contained within the legal process were viewed by these students as empowering, since they allowed for greater flexibility in "constructing" legal arguments.

Like those students who became cynical, students who resisted this form of legal consciousness reacted negatively to the values contained within their education. Indeed, much of the alienation and conflict that these students experienced during their first year centered on their opposition to dominant forms of legal consciousness. One third-year student who continued to be adamant in her rejection of legal consciousness commented:

I came to be able to argue both sides of the law and what I have found is that I have totally resisted it. I don't want to learn it. I don't talk in class. I refuse to take a position where I have to argue things I don't believe in.

Such students often resisted the technocratic orientation of their schooling. For instance, the emphasis placed upon technical approaches to social problems was particularly disturbing for these students. As one second-year student complained:

I think law school is basically conservative. There's a lot of people like me who are just pissed off all the time because they see the segregation case and the professor is talking about procedure or exclusionary zoning. It's hard to deal with the emotional, the feeling that it's unfair because you're supposed to be methodical and system-oriented. Precedent is suppose to be a big deal. I think it's bullshit. I don't think law really has that much legitimacy.

Such a technocratically-oriented, procedural approach to human problems was often seen by these students as emphasizing values that were incompatible with their own personal notions of justice. For these students the initial introduction to the law was very disconcerting. One second-year student interested in representing working-class laborers explained:

I don't want to negatively affect someone's life for the sake of profit. That's what the law tells you to do and should do, protect profits. I wonder at times whether I can be a lawyer because there's so much about it that I disagree with. I'm more interested in issues of social justice, you know, people who get screwed but can't do anything about it. I consider myself a principled person and there are no real principles in law.

Although the criticisms of law made by these students resemble those enunciated by their cynical counterparts, those who resisted the game orientation possessed greater ideological intensity. Many, for instance, felt that law maintains a system of structural injustice and inequality prevalent in capitalist society. A first-year student, a twenty-four-year-old male, who held particularly critical views commented that

I think that law perpetuates an unjust system that I think should be destroyed. There's no way that I would work for a corporate law firm. I'd wait on tables before I'd do that. I'd like to do something in the general public interest, like legal services. I want to feel as though I'm doing something useful with my life and I don't feel that working for corporations is useful. I don't have the illusion that I can change the world, but I want to help people in some way. That's not emphasized here though and that's a real problem for me.

Given the ambience of cynicism, these students struggled to maintain their normative position on law and legal practice. In a sense, these students attempted to maintain what Mannheim referred to as "evaluative thought." In the middle of a long footnote in Mannheim's *Ideology and Utopia,* he offers, I believe, an insight that helps us understand the experience of those law students who resisted the dominant consciousness. He states that "the exposure of ideological and utopian elements in thought is effective in destroying only those ideas with which we ourselves are not too intimately identified."[22] Those who resisted the dominant form of legal consciousness identified themselves intimately with critical and social-justice-oriented conceptions of law and legal practice and tended to be vehement in their criticism of the law. A third-year student at Harvard who devoted a great deal of energy to radical activities on campus and had accepted a post-graduate job as a community organizer in Chicago held strong views regarding law. In discussing the matter of equal representation, an ideology that is prominent in the legal profession, he angrily stated that

It [law] doesn't really do that. Poor people don't get representation. It's not about both sides of the fence, it's still the same side. I hate when people say that stuff because it's a lie. The one with the cash always wins.

In addition to drawing upon political ideologies such as Marxism, these students sometimes relied on theological orientations to buttress maintenance of their personal values as opposed to the professional ones they were being encouraged to adopt. For some, religious ideology provided a defense against the moral relativism that was encouraged through thinking like a lawyer. One student who professed strong religious beliefs felt compelled to take a job that provided legal assistance to the poor.

The idea around here is that being a public interest lawyer is nice, something to do for humanity, and that makes us feel good. But there's no sense that people who make that decision have got to make it on principle. There's no sense that it's a principled decision. I'm making a principled moral decision by doing public interest law. Basically I believe in liberation theology, so my actions are not preferential. If you're a Christian you have to work for the poor.

Contrary to idealist students who were disturbed by the indeterminacy in law, these students often found the indeterminacy in law a form of political and social empowerment. While cynical students began to view law as a game, resisters conceived of law as a "tool." This metaphor of law as a tool or an instrument to be used, as one student stated, "against the law's normal inclinations," protected these students from the disabling effects of cynicism. The ability of normative values to "protect" individuals from contrary norms and behaviors has been noted in the sociological literature. In the case of these law students, legal consciousness was seen not as a game, but as a means of achieving the normative values they held. One second-year Harvard law student from a working-class area in New York, who was committed to the advancement of the labor movement, stated that

> A lot of people are cynical about learning to argue both sides of a case. I think that's silly. I definitely want to know how to argue both sides, then pick my side and stick to it. I'm very interested in working in the labor movement as a legal representative. Being skillful is important.

Many of these students engaged in oppositional strategies that were collectively based. In most cases, students who resisted accommodating the dominant mode of legal consciousness tended to associate with each other. Many were members of the same law school organizations, such as the Labor Law Project, Students for Public Interest Law, Prisoner's Legal Assistance Project, and the Legal Services Center. Some of these students even formed unofficial organizations such as "The Counter-Hegemonic Front," which sponsored a lecture series on alternative approaches to law and legal practice, actively challenged the appointments of faculty to the law school in order to achieve greater diversity, circulated flyers that, among other things, defied the meritocratic ideology contained within the law school culture with statements that mocked the grading system, organized grade burning rallies, and submitted proposals that sought to change law school grading practices. As one of the organizers of the postering campaign described, their activities caused considerable anger among other law students.

> We organized a campaign around grading. We started propagandizing around Christmas when exams were coming up and people got irritated. People got very angry. We put up one poster that read, "fuck studying, grades are random" and that blew people away. The posters were up for about a half-hour before students began ripping them down.

In addition, a number of these students chose alternative summer legal internships working for such groups as political prisoners in South Africa, Amnesty International, and Native American Indians.

Ironically, there were students that possessed conservative political ideologies who also failed to become cynical. While such students were few in number and complained of the "liberal tyranny" at the law school, they frequently reacted against the moral relativism that dominated the law school environment. One third-year female, who characterized herself as a political conservative, explained her view of law.

> A lot of people become cynical after a while of reading cases in a technical way. They think it's a game. In the real world the way that law works is not a game. In the real world one lesson that you learn is that judges base their findings on facts. If equity is not in your favor you're not going to win. I feel the world runs like we think it runs. I just don't buy anyone who is disillusioned about law school in that way. Anyone who thinks law is a game doesn't know what they're talking about.

Such a reaction from the right, unlike that from students on the left, represents opposition towards the moral relativism encouraged by legal consciousness, but not a rejection of the normative foundations of law itself.

The promotion of cynicism in law school is a central aspect of training students to be professional lawyers. The development of this intellectual disposition, however, is one that restricts the possibility for producing lawyers that are interested in the promotion of social justice. Indeed, "thinking like a lawyer," as experienced by most students, is incompatible with encouraging careers that provide legal assistance to subordinate groups in American society. In learning to think like a lawyer many students became cynical. The result of this cynicism was to produce in most students a game-like orientation of law and legal practice.

Cultural symbols always involve interpretation. Because of this, cultural symbols often become a matter of ideological struggle. For those students at Harvard Law School who sought to maintain their normative ideals about justice, consciousness was a cultural artifact that was struggled over on a daily basis. Unlike the cynical student who conceptualized law as a game, resisters perceived it as a tool. Conceived as such, these students experienced their education in dramatically different ways than their cynical counterparts. Differing modes of interpretation constitute the everyday micro-politics contained within the daily lives of these students.

Those few students who chose legal jobs working for the poor, the working class, or other social causes remained committed to their beliefs. Many of these students found various strategies of preserving their beliefs. Associating with other students who possessed these ideals was perhaps the most useful strategy for these students. Without a community of opposition, cooptation becomes increasingly more probable.[23]

Among the students who remained committed to their social-justice-oriented goals, the experience of law differed significantly from those who became cynical. Those who remained committed to a social justice orientation engaged in different types of resistance strategies that sought to undermine the mystique of the law school. The fact that these groups experienced the educational process differently and resisted the dominant interpretation of legal consciousness suggests that interpretation and definition are major components of life within educational institutions. This fact directs our attention to the ways that meanings are produced and consumed within educational discourse.

This chapter has demonstrated that a conflict exists in law school regarding the values associated with law and those of the individual student. While some retained their ideological views on the role of law, the vast majority of students developed a type of cynicism that drew them away from altruistic interests of pursuing justice. Ironically, most students come to accept the status quo even in the face of extreme disillusionment.

The process by which this occurs is explored in the next chapter. As I shall demonstrate, hegemonic notions regarding the role and nature of law and legal practice are rooted in the symbolic boundaries erected within law, and are shared by faculty and students. These symbolic boundaries lead students to redefine the concepts of justice and social activism in ways that are consistent with liberal legalism. The establishment of these boundaries represents a movement away from a student's personal morality to a professional one. For most students, these newly established boundaries come to represent a higher form of morality; a morality that comes to command greater authority.[24] These boundaries, consequently, represent a critical dimension of law school training by contributing to the normalization of prevailing forms of legal discourse, values, and practice.

◆ 5 ◆

The Moral Transformation of Law Students

Constructing Symbolic Boundaries in Law School

A s a social institution, law wields great power and authority in American society. The power of law comes not necessarily from its direct reflection of instrumental interests or systemic needs, as many have argued, but rather from its ability to define truth and construct social reality. Property law, for instance, does not simply reflect the economic imperatives of capitalist society. Rather, it constructs a notion of right as it relates to the ownership of property.[1] Rape law does not merely exist as a reflex of patriarchy. It also produces images about the social context and social relations within which rape occurs.[2] In a similar way, discrimination law and the drama of the court actively constructs accounts of racism that obscure its structural foundations.[3] Thus, the power of law lies in its ability to "normalize" everything that enters its field of vision.[4]

However, the power of law lies not only in its ability to construct reality but also in its capacity to limit alternative visions of social life.[5] Legal norms monopolize discourse in ways that exclude alternative views of justice. As

Gary Peller points out, "the violence of legal thought consists in the arbitrary exclusion of other ways of understanding the world."[6] There is, as Burton argues, "no purchase" within law for alternative paradigms of thought and expression.[7] Law's internal rules bracket moral issues in such a way that they are stripped of any fixed convictions or principles. Law, consequently, possesses symbolic power that constructs a moral order through the categories, classifications, and traditions it creates.[8]

Students learn law through collective identity work occurring within the interactional dynamics of schooling.[9] The professional identities that emerge lead students to construct new symbolic boundaries that are established through the "sense-making" activities they carry out in law school. It is through this process that students adopt not only a professional identity but a moral one as well. Law schooling, thus, represents a moral transformation through which students dissociate themselves from previously held notions about justice and replace them with new views consistent with the status quo.

This chapter examines how these new symbolic boundaries are constructed by Harvard law students. Specifically, I explore how new meanings about justice, social activism, and public interest are constructed within the context of law school education. This chapter first examines the subtle ways that classroom experiences and the informal student culture in law school establish boundaries upon conceptions of justice and public interest. Next, I explore the ways that law students construct a higher sense of morality through legalism and professionalism. While in law school, students struggle over the symbolic boundaries created by law and legal discourse. For most, this process culminates not in a loss of values, but rather in a redefinition of students' nascent views about justice and social activism. Students undergoing professional training do not simply abandon their previously held morals and ideals.[10] Instead, they redefine their understanding of these issues in ways that are consistent with their professional status. Students are, therefore, not passively subjugated by legal rational knowledge, but rather actively create views of social reality that are consistent with it.

Professional Identity as Symbolic Boundary

Contemporary research in cultural sociology has demonstrated how the generation of moral, social, and cultural boundaries create collective identities that legitimize social inequality. Lamont, for instance, has found that morality and social status are frequently used to assess superiority and inferiority in

73

American society.[11] In a similar way, Bourdieu has argued that class divisions in French society are maintained through the establishment of cultural boundaries associated with taste and distinction.[12] These boundaries define reality in ways that normalize dominance and inequality in society.

In a similar way, the professional community establishes a type of symbolic boundary that contributes to professional power and dominance.[13] The ideology of professionalism secures its dominance from the application of expert knowledge accumulated through many hours of study in a professional school. In these schools, aspiring professionals acquire methods, skills, expert knowledge, and responsibilities that separate them from "ordinary" occupations. Indeed, these traits helped produce the monopoly professionals have achieved over the past century.[14]

More than just knowledge accumulation and skill development, however, professional training represents moral instruction. These morals emerge from the collective values of the specific professional community and are often seen as necessary components of a complex social order.[15] Among most professional groups, this emerging morality is considered to be superior to the mundane morality of the private citizen. Professionals, once accepting this new morality, are often unwilling to renounce it. Professional morality, consequently, represents a higher moral order for those within a profession, and it is this belief in the virtues of this morality that insulates professionals from public condemnation and control.

If legal education teaches anything it teaches aspiring lawyers that there are no simple answers, only simplistic solutions. The boundary construction process inherent within legal education illustrates to students that "naive" views of justice and social activism are characteristic of the non-professional mind, one untrained in the skills of legal rational analysis. From the outset of their legal training, students are taught to approach issues pragmatically and to suspend personal views of justice. Law school training transforms students from outsiders, who are seen as possessing elementary perceptions of justice, to professionals who recognize the true complexity of social relations and social policy questions that await them in the future. This tempering of simplistic views represents a central aspect in the constitution of a moral identity among professionals.

Establishing Symbolic Boundaries in Law School

During the early phase of my fieldwork, I attended classes with some first-year Harvard law students. All of these classes utilized the case method of instruction which generally involves the careful dissection of legal cases. In several classes the cases discussed involved situations that were extremely unusual and unlikely to occur again. Arcane cases are, in fact, legendary among first-year law students at most law schools.

On one particular day that I attended class with a student, a case was discussed that involved a proprietor of a hotel who rented a room to a newlywed couple. Sometime during the course of their wedding night the couple discovered that the proprietor, one Mr. Perry, had rented them a room with a two-way mirror installed for his own viewing pleasure. The class then proceeded to discuss the legal issues that could apply to the case. After class I asked the law student whether cases like these were common. The student responded in the affirmative and proceeded to tell me about another unusual case he studied in his criminal law class:

> There was this case in my criminal class where this guy kicked his former girlfriend in the stomach. She was pregnant at the time and the kick resulted in a spontaneous abortion. The problem was that the laws pertaining to criminal procedure did not allow the defendant to be charged with homicide since the fetus was not "legally" considered a human being in the state in which the case was tried.

This was a particularly gruesome case, one that greatly angered this student: "I think this guy should be strung up by his balls! I know I shouldn't feel that way because the law doesn't allow it and everyone is entitled to representation. I suppose I'm not being professional enough." For this student, law had no room for emotion. The discovery of a new morality, a morality that is based upon a redefinition of law, is a central component of law school training. These boundaries are generally demonstrated to students in the classroom as well as through interaction with other students.

1. *Symbolic boundaries and the faculty*

How is this moral identity generated and what effects does its adoption have on the views of law students? The constitution of moral identity is accomplished through both formal and informal mechanisms. For instance, the occasional comments by case-hardened law professors who try to quell a student's outrage over the legal treatment of rape cases with comments such as "Calm down, let's approach this like lawyers" or "Is that what you're going to tell the judge?" or even, as one student was told when she expressed concern over pornography and violence against women, "We're not here to study politics, but law" are ways of signifying to students the boundaries present within legal discourse. Politically charged comments are often dismissed by professors. In some cases students are chastened for raising moral or ideologi-cally-charged issues. One third-year student, a twenty-six year-old white male on the Law Review, recalled an event during his first year.

> I had this professor who only wanted to talk about civil procedure and precedents that amounted to taking things from poor people without a hearing. When I tried to bring up that this wasn't fair because of differing levels of power, he said that I was getting some ideological buzz out of the case. After that he wouldn't leave me alone and he kept asking questions to try to embarrass me. People in my section saw what was going on and they flipped out. It was intimidating.

Another student, a third-year white male, reported a similar experience.

> The way this one professor deals with things is that if you start talking about an emotional side he will tell you that that's all well and good but it has no relationship to what we're talking about. He'll just stare at you or he'll go to someone else. He also punishes people. I got called on five days in a row because he said something about all labor law being a way that drunks can keep their jobs. I raised my hand and told him that was ridiculous. I got called on for the next five days.

The experience of having political and ethical comments attacked by law professors occurred with some frequency. While only 26 percent of the total Harvard sample agreed with the statement that "faculty members downgrade students for political opinions expressed in class," 40 percent of those entering law school with social activist interests concurred with it. This difference is no doubt explained by the fact that activist-oriented students at Harvard are more politically vocal in class and therefore subject to more criticism. Students often complained of being "mocked" by faculty members when they offered political, ethical, or moral arguments. Some reported feeling intimidated by professors and were, as a result, rarely if ever willing to take sides or offer a passionate argument for fear of reprisal. Such experiences erect symbolic boundaries that students are expected to adopt. Their purpose, in both their direct and subtle forms, is to construct a professional identity. Such practices constitute a degradation process by which law professors attempt to strip students of "non-professional" conceptions of the social world. Alternative paradigms are challenged since they violate the ideology of professionalism.[16]

Very often, cases are presented to students in which the real life elements of the case are suspended. Students learn, for instance, that a case like *Bowers v. Hardwick*, a case involving the police persecution of a gay man in Georgia, is not *really* about gay rights, but about legal strategy.[17] Students often begin to focus on the technical aspects of winning a case as opposed to its merits. One third-year student described this process in the following way:

> *Bowers v. Hardwick* is a case that ruled that homosexuals have no right to engage in sodomy. It was a horrible and awful case. It was a right of privacy case in the courts though. I remember that I was in class and went crazy when the professor presented it as if it was independent from gay rights. That's what a lawyer does though; makes arguments. Very little about law now shocks me. I look at the jury and I think, OK, how can I best manipulate them?

In many instances, students found themselves initially reacting to the human dimensions of a case only to realize later that they had missed an important legal point. One woman, discussing a case in Texas, described how she became disturbed upon finding the legal issues superseded human concerns.

> I remember I was in contracts and we had this terrible case. The case involved a man's responsibility to his illegitimate children. Under Texas law, a man's responsibility is zero. I thought this was outrageous and wrong. The woman was suing to make it his responsibility. This case really has to do with the fact that this will mean poverty for the woman and her child. It's not like they were similarly situated and they're trying to put this burden on each other. He had the money and she didn't. However, the legal issue in the case isn't about this issue. It's not about sex discrimination, it's about contracts. It's about a technical argument that has nothing to do with the people involved. I was so wrapped up with the people in the case that I totally missed what the legal issue was.

Such a pedegogy represents to students moral boundaries within the law. The real life drama of human events in law school as well as its social context is considered superfluous to the the legal issues at hand. More than simply ways to illustrate the law, legal cases contribute to the production of a professional identity by desensitizing students from the ethical implications of a case. Not unlike the use of cadavers in medical school to train doctors to approach patients as "objects," law school teaches students to disassociate themselves with the cases they handle. As one second-year woman explains,

> When the professor starts talking about the doctrine you start to forget who the people in the case are. It's a widow, who is poor with two children and has mouths to feed and this man is trying to enforce a contract. When you study law though, and practice it, all human interactions are translated into abstract events. You go to the statute books and *U.S. Supreme Court Reporter*

77

to find some more cases to support your position on either side. Everything seems to become less emotional.

The legitimacy of this professional morality is premised upon an ideology of neutrality. Professionals are expected to suspend any personal bias they may have regarding the situations they confront. Professionalism demands the separation of personal values from professional ones. The ability to accomplish this separation, to live with a sort of sanctioned schizophrenia, is a trait that divides "laymen from lawmen."[18] In law school, students often replace what they see as their own biased views with professional values that are perceived as neutral. They learn to see the law as distinct from other issues and even come to see the superiority of these views over alternative perspectives.

2. *Symbolic boundaries and students*

Much of the censuring of pedestrian positions, however, takes place informally, at the level of student culture. Severe sanctions often come from fellow students in the form of hissing, laughter, and general disdain directed at anyone who fails to accept a narrowed perspective. When boundaries of liberal legalism are breached, students often impose discrediting sanctions. One student, a vocal social activist who was known throughout the campus for his involvement in radical causes, explained some of the problems he encountered with his classmates.

> I had a bad experience in my labor law class. The professor was talking about what the law should be in secondary boycotts. Management has a right to carry on its business and how do we weigh that right against the right of workers to have an effective strike? Most of the students in the class said that there needs to be a balance. This is a typical legal argument. I said that I didn't think management counts for very much. I think that workers should be able to do what they want. It's a legal position. I just wanted to scrap part of the National Labor Relations Act. People were taken aback. Mostly everyone in the class laughed. I was going outside the legal framework. This often happened in my corporations class. I would say that the obvious answer to various problems would be to socialize the means of production. The students all laughed at this. If you make these types of arguments you're made to feel immature and silly. I know that that's how I'm seen by most students here.

Students who violate the legalistic norms of objectivity and neutrality are often held in contempt by their classmates. Many are criticized for being irrelevant, or worse. One student characterized such students as "crackpots."

Even professors who teach from the perspective of Critical Legal Studies are denounced by students. One student described a well-known faculty member as a "crackpot" who had ideas that "no one who was sane would have anything to do with." Other students held even more astringent views about these professors.

In many cases, students were criticized by their classmates for being naive and immature. Students who make moral arguments on the basis of equity or social justice are considered intellectually soft and often ridiculed by other students. One woman in her second year at the law school complained about an incident that occurred during her first year.

> When you get upset over the outcome of a case it's harder to talk about it legally, particularly in your first year because you don't really know much law. There's no room for saying, well I feel this is morally right. You just can't say that here. I made a comment in class during my first year about violence against women. It wasn't a legal point but I felt it was important to say. After class this guy came up and said that what I had said was totally inappropriate and how could I bring this up. He said it was completely out of context and ridiculous since we had been talking about the law which had nothing to do with what I said. It was terrible. I felt awful and so alone.

Such negative reactions from fellow students not only signify the violation of moral boundaries, but also curtail the articulation of an alternative voice. One particularly vocal student described how this informal pressure effected him.

> During my first year I made some fairly radical comments in class. Pretty soon I came under suspicion. I started receiving these anonymous notes from students about how much of a jerk I was. After that I decided not to talk at all or express my opinion.

Such a reaction from other students often contributes to silencing many of those who challenge the hegemony of liberal legal thought.

Students who approached issues from an emotional, ideological, or social science orientation were often subjected to disparaging assessments by other law students.[19] Despite the fact that most law students at Harvard have liberal arts backgrounds, such knowledge became viewed as irrelevant. Possessing "ideals" and basing argument upon those ideals was considered a sign of intellectual mediocrity. Students felt compelled to stick with the legal issue, not to stray, and to avoid fairness arguments. In short, law students learned to narrow their perspective. Such is the case even with those students who consider themselves strong public interest advocates. One third-year student who possessed social activist ideals commented that

> I think that it's important to become hardheaded. I made certain *naive* emotional and political arguments before law school that I no longer buy into. Part of me feels, well, there are certain things that are just right and wrong and then there's another part of me that says, well, wait a minute, things aren't that simple in the real world and you really can't go around making silly emotional arguments about what's right or wrong.

Harvard Law students believed that they had a tremendous responsibility to be leaders in society. Such responsibilities are assumed to require sharp analytical resolve undistracted by the simple arguments that are characteristic of the non-lawyer public. In the early phase of their training, these students learned that there was never a right or correct answer. Arguments, when posed, were always met with counterarguments. Every belief, value, ideal, and commitment was challenged and called into question. Students became less passionate in their beliefs primarily because they say that all such beliefs can be torn asunder. As one second-year student on Law Review commented:

> What happened to me my first year was that I began to realize that in law there are no principles. You can always construct an argument for anything. As I began to realize this, I became less invested in the ideas and beliefs I once had. I often wonder what I believe now. I could represent anyone you asked me to, but ask what I believe, I don't think I could really say.

Such experiences often posed considerable conflict for those students with activist ideals. As one third-year student reported:

> It's the thing that I don't like about being taught here. I was trained as an organizer before law school. The way you make things happen is to knock on doors and bring people together. You can't organize if you're trying to see all sides. You have to be emotionally involved. I came here and within three days I could feel that something was wrong. What felt particularly wrong to me was that we would read the cases and I would think about who was getting screwed. I would come to class ready to talk about that but that wasn't what we would do. All along the way I felt like this annoying fly—don't raise these issues, this has nothing to do with the law. I felt that we were being asked to drop our ideological baggage at the door.

Students who persisted in "non-legal" forms of argumentation were often subject to public ridicule and isolation. Public denigration imposes pressures on students to accept legal boundaries. In almost conspiratorial fashion, a game called "turkey bingo" is played in which students try to guess which of their classmates will speak out most often. This classroom game was played by designing a bingo card using students instead of numbers. When a student talks his or her square is checked off. When bingo is scored the winner answers a professor's question using a preagreed code word thus informing the other players that bingo was reached. One student explained how deeply effected she was by this practice.

> It's hard to be a talker here. I found out that I was on a turkey bingo list and I was appalled. The resentment of me, I discovered, was strong. I passed people in the corridors and they would snub me. In a way that kept me silent. After that I just went to class and kept my mouth shut.

The practice of "turkey bingo," aside from serving as a release from the day to day law school grind, sends an obvious message to students. Implicit in this game is the notion that students should not become overtly serious about "the law." Students who continued to be outspoken about their ideological positions were often the "turkeys." While this collective criticism did not deter those firmly committed to ideological positions, it was particularly destructive to those whose ideologies were not firmly established. One student explained that

> You have to watch what you say here. If you talk a lot in class and keep making the same point you'll lose your reputation. Having a good reputation is important here because if you get labeled as a talker people stop associating with you. I try not to say things that are inflammatory.

Constructing the Self through Symbolic Boundaries

Throughout their schooling, an ideology of pragmatism is systematically conveyed to these students in a variety of formal and informal ways. In the words of Domhoff, lawyers "are the supreme 'pragmatists' in a nation where pragmatism is a central element in the self-deceiving ideology that the country has no ideology."[20] Learning a pragmatic discourse instills in students an intolerance for forms of speech that are viewed as unrealistic, and thus outside the parameters of legal analysis. Formal instruction in the classroom as well as informal interactions between students serve a boundary-maintaining function that imposes collective limits upon forms of communicative discourse within law.[21]

While students generally didn't believe that law school changed them dramatically, most felt their pre–law school ideas concerning such things as social change, justice, and social activism underwent significant reorientation. These students underwent a process whereby they surrendered their "simple" and "naive" views about the world. Many reported becoming more "realistic." As one student commented, "I don't think I've changed in law school. I've picked up skills, but as a person I haven't changed." Another student, a third-year male, claimed: "I am as idealistic as I was when I was a high school and college student." However, the power of professional training lies in its ability to teach neophytes to accept and accommodate new realities and definitions about the social world. One twenty-five-year-old woman commented:

> My opinions have become more tempered, I think. It's hard to have a radical left or right position. I think I've remained radical but it's a pragmatic sort of radicalism.

Continuing, this student described what she now saw as the opportunity for radical practice. Asked what she thought of some of the more vocal radical students at the law school, she expressed a need to become more realistic.

> I don't want to sound like a right-winger but what the hell good do rallies really do? I think it's important for lawyers to develop a sense of empowerment, that they can change the firms, that they can go out and ask their firm to set up a corporation to do this or that. There's no stopping what you can do. You can be a corporate lawyer and go out and help people doing income tax types of problems in what you would think of in a left kind of way. Tax is a way of saving money. I like it, it's not dirty like I used to think. I don't think any longer that tax or corporate law is, by definition, bad, and that family law, by definition, is good. You can't say that. I don't think that I have lost any of my commitment. People go out and they are doing projects and different kinds of things, and they are thinking about themselves as lawyers in a certain kind of way. I think that, as a lawyer, I have to be *more realistic* about things.

What once appeared to these students as black and white soon became seen as complex. This process has the effect of narrowing a law student's perspective. As Worden writes:

> A very complex and subtle array of messages that are embedded in the daily interactions of law school life operate to channel [law students] into a

particular mode of behavior when participating in law school and the legal profession. . . . Directly or indirectly, these messages obviate alternative approaches to law and enforce a kind of legal/cultural uniformity. It is through these messages that law schools propagate intense pressure to "conform" without seemingly having any identifiable source intentionally initiating it.[22]

In law school, students learn to define their initial perspectives concerning law and society as markedly inferior to their newly honed legal views. While many students initially complained of experiencing a sense of personal loss at the beginning of their legal studies, most, after a short time, began to reconceptualize this "loss." For law students, what was defined as confusion became redefined as a higher form of intellectual competence. A comment by a third-year student who had been very active in public interest groups during law school but had accepted a position in a large firm in Washington captures this point.

> I have begun to question some of the things I thought were right and good. I have begun to see more gray areas. Things are much more confusing than they once were. I don't see this as indoctrination, but a learning and developing process.

Such experiences were common among these law students. The culture of legal discourse tends to render a student's previous conception of law and justice untenable and inferior. In some cases, students even learned to define their uninformed conceptions of law and justice as symbolic of their own relative immaturity. One second-year Harvard law student, a twenty-five year-old white female who characterized herself as politically radical and initially interested in public interest health care law, stated that she thought that she had become more realistic in her views about justice. When asked to explain, she commented, "I guess I'm just understanding things better now than I did before." Another student, a third-year student who likewise entered law school to pursue a career in social activist law commented, "I think I used to be more to the left but it's not really feasible if you really want to do something that's socially good."

This process of redefining reality in particular ways is fundamental to the production of professional identity in law school. Identity production is less a matter of measurable changes than an ongoing process of redefining social situations. As Goffman astutely pointed out in his analysis of the "moral career" of mental patients, the process of redefinition is an ongoing activity within all institutions that impose a degree of control over a person's daily life.[23] In law school, much like prisons, boarding schools, and army training camps, students undergo an identity transformation process in which they develop new understandings of themselves and the world around them.

This new perception, while at times unappreciated by the general public, offers what law students believe to be more pragmatic solutions to the problems that confront society. In fact, professional schools encourage this pragmatism.[24] Medical students, for instance, become less idealistic only to emerge a few years later with a renewed sense of idealism about helping patients. Through their participation in the student culture of medical school, students construct a more "realistic" attitude that replaces "earlier grandiose feelings about medicine."[25] This transformed idealism, however, differs from earlier visions of medical service, being premised instead upon "realistic" attitudes of practice. Becker and his collaborators view this reclamation of ideals as a victory for medical students who are able to integrate their technical abilities with their erstwhile idealism. These authors maintain that the graduating student's idealism

> is more informed and knowledgeable, for he has learned a lot about what to expect and fear in medical practice. He has picked up some ideas about how one can overcome some of the problems to be faced. His idealism is more specific and more professional than it was when he entered. The layman, not seeing things the way the student does, or indeed the way the doctor does, may miss the idealistic content of much of these student concerns. From a medical point of view, however, this idealism is evident.[26]

Indeed, successful identity production in professional schools involves the redirection and channeling of nascent idealistic concerns into a professional ideology of pragmatism.

However, pragmatism is an ideologically loaded term which, when adopted, has significant political implications. Law students redefine the nature of their own idealism and that of others as being unethical, irresponsible, and self-interested. For instance, Harvard law students learned that they were ethically bound to represent interests that may be at variance with their own values. While the public often does not understand this professional attribute, law students learned to manage this problem by appealing to professional ethics rather than personal ones.

Relying on the ethics of the profession relieved students from any discomfort they experienced over advocating a position they might not agree with. In some cases, the ability to convincingly argue positions they disagreed with became seen as a form of "toughness." As one Harvard student who planned to be a litigator in a large firm commented:

To be a litigator it takes lots of guts. You have to be able to convince people that you're right when you know the case is really against your client. I see that as the sign of a really good litigator that when things are against you you still win. That takes balls.

Even a student's conception of social change underwent transformation. While many Harvard students continued to see themselves as radical and deeply interested in progressive social change, they often developed an ideology of social change which was fixed to the boundaries of legal discourse. Much like Becker's medical students who constructed new definitions of idealism, many Harvard law students redefined their own idealism as being sophomoric and quixotic. The ability to draw upon a collectively redefined sense of idealism insulated law students from the criticism that they had renounced their idealism. One student, who characterized herself as radical and primarily interested in social change, illustrates this point.

I still believe that law can be used as a tool for social change, but it's different than when I came in here. I don't anymore think law is a tool of social change where you go out and change laws and society. I think this view is a bit naive. I think that you need legal structures to help set up organization which will promote social change. People off the streets just can't go in and change property codes, you have to be an expert in property tax. You need lawyers to deal with the huge legal apparatus that relates to all of this. That's a lawyer doing social change. It doesn't look like social change on the outside but it is. I'm much more positive about what I think my classmates will do in the future.

In most cases, students began to see and accept the boundaries within law and legal discourse. This often meant accepting ideas that students would have rejected only months earlier. As one first year student commented:

I've come to accept things now that in college I would have been appalled by, like how much corporations control and how few people control. I've learned that the system is set up and can't be changed. I have begun to work inside the system to make a perverse system work the best it can. I don't think about things as moral problems anymore. *I accept a lot of things now but the acceptance comes from greater understanding.*

Contrary to the criticisms regarding the "conservatizing" effects of legal education, many students at Harvard Law School experienced their world from what they perceive to be a liberal-left political perspective. The numbers of ideologically committed conservatives actually tended to be small among the student body. Those who identified themselves as political conservatives characterized the tenor of the law school as "tyrannically liberal" and considered themselves a minority. Very often students who failed to demonstrate sufficient liberal sentiment or made blatantly conservative comments were disparaged by being hissed at in class. The professional ideology constituted by students was, thus, a liberal legal view which combines compassion and a desire to help effectuate social change with rationality and pragmatism.

Several years ago, Duncan Kennedy criticized the handicapping results of legal education, writing that law school makes students sharp by making them narrow.[27] In this early polemic against legal education, Kennedy argued that law school strips away the already diminished political sensibilities of law students. However, while professional schooling involves an identity stripping process it also includes a process whereby identities are constructed. Consequently, the ideology of legal education may operate not through the wrenching-out of the critical perspectives of law students, but rather, through a subtle process by which law students discover and "make sense" of the law. Many Harvard law students constructed an identity whereby they learned that they should be concerned with progressive reform and that they should have a direct role in these reforms. However, while students learned to be reform-minded they additionally developed a collective ethos that such concerns are separate from one's professional work as an attorney. This dynamic of separating the private, subjective realm from the public, professional one is a central component of identity construction in law school. A third-year Harvard law student who entered law school with a public interest orientation illuminates this point.

> I used to think that you could either do good things for people or not. I don't think that anymore. I don't think you can really do all that much for people with law. I'm no longer troubled by the idea of being a corporate lawyer as opposed to being a public interest one because I don't think that's the end all of being a good, or even effective person. I'm still concerned about social problems like poverty or poor housing but I'm not sure that being a public interest attorney is the way to work to resolve these things. I just don't believe it's that easy. There is value in doing corporate law. You need lawyers to get the business things done in society that help little people too. If most of the wealth goes into the pockets of the rich, well, I don't think that's an unmitigated bad for society. I'm not looking for my career as my way of contributing. There are two worlds, the public world and the private world. I consider myself to be far more on the left than I was when I came here and I think you have to do something to contribute to society. I intend to get myself involved in community things. It's funny, the more

accepting I have become of corporate law the more committed I believe I am to doing other things in my life that will help people.

The law school experience of this student and the identity she had constructed taught her that it was not necessary to "live" her politics in her professional work as an attorney. Much like law itself, this student had learned to balance opposing interests that were presented to her. During her first year at Harvard, she participated in several public interest workshops that were conducted by the placement office to promote careers in public interest practice. At the same time, however, she was also confronted with a culture within the law school that communicated a pervasive message: she could practice commercially-oriented law within a capitalist framework while preserving her idealism through activities in her private life.

The difficulty in this student's life over serving corporate interests produced tension throughout her law school career. Entering law school with a combination of career and socially motivated interests, she frequently found herself juxtaposing two polarities which she had initially seen as mutually exclusive. Through this student's contact with other students and with law firm recruiters who were more than willing to appease her social interest by offering her pro bono opportunities, she was able to resolve the apparent contradiction in favor of doing corporate legal work.[28] In fact, she was so able to resolve the conflict that her definition of those who engaged in public interest work was drastically altered. This student had internalized the symbolic boundaries of professionalism that demanded the adoption of pragmatism.

> I used to worry about selling-out. I was uncomfortable for a long while because I thought that since I was thinking of doing commercial work that I would be branded by my public interest friends. I don't think anymore that I've sold-out. I know that I can still do good things for society, maybe even better things, as a corporate lawyer. Plus, I just don't like the attitude of public interest people. *They're so single-minded at times and I think a little naive.* They've really pushed me away from wanting to do public interest work as a full-time occupation.

> I: When did you begin to realize that you could do corporate work?

> It was sometime during my second year. I met a lot of people who were like me, you know, people with good politics but who were interested in a career. I realized that they weren't hating what they were doing [working in large firms]. It's not as bad as my public interest friends told me. The people at

the firms are nice people, they're not all money hungry, and they have a real social conscience too.

Ironically, this student believed that she had become more radical in law school as well as increasingly interested in contributing to social change. Her experiences in law school, however, confirmed in her mind that it is possible to remain committed to these idealistic values while engaging in commercial types of legal practice. In fact, her identity work, supported by her law school friends, convinced her that this type of practice would be a more effective form of social activism. For this student, pro bono legal service came to be defined as public interest and social activism. Consequently, corporate law firms became the reasonable center for "radical" legal practice. As she explained:

> I don't know how much good I can do representing an individual client. The needs of the people that public interest lawyers serve are just beyond what I can do as one attorney. I think I can do more good for people if I commit myself to working with community groups or activities in the bar during my spare time.

In law school, this student had learned to be concerned about social problems, to sympathize with the underdog, to believe in one's responsibility to help those who were less privileged. However, the professional identity she had constructed taught her that the way to make one's contribution felt did not necessitate a strict diet of public interest practice.

The ideological transformation of this student represents the central feature of identity production with the law school. This student had not simply been depoliticized by law school in the way that critics have described.[29] Such analyses rely on reproductive metaphors and typically maintain the view that law school dupes students into believing law is just. Rather, through her "lived" experiences in law school, this student constructed a professional identity whose orientation may be described as conservative radicalism. She described herself as "fairly radical but not as *extreme* as her public interest friends." She had learned to define the radical activities of her social activist friends as *extreme* and more naive than her own well-reasoned, pragmatic radicalism. Through this redefinition of radicalism she was able to assume the role of a corporate attorney in a firm that had what she called "progressive attitudes" and confine her interests in social reform and justice to her private life. With her self-identity as radical intact, she could feel secure about her politics while practicing law for America's elite.

These subtle processes through which students redefined concepts such as justice, social activism, and public interest contributes to the constitution of a professional identity in law school. For many students, it was not that their ideology has changed. Rather, their conception of what constitutes justice, social activism, and public interest had changed. A student's nascent moralistic definition of justice, social activism, and public interest was washed aside by a definition that was based exclusively on professionalism. This resulted in taming these concepts while at the same time encouraging a definition of those who exceed this "tamed" image as extremists, immature, and ideologues.

Many first-year students expressed great concern over the pragmatic focus of their education. Very often, these students were unwilling to accept the value of professional idealism, even when such idealism was supported by other students. During an interview, a twenty-three-year-old male in his first year of law school expressed his interest in justice and social activism as well as his condemnation of those who accept the ideology of professional idealism in the following way:

> I came to law school because I didn't want to be involved in business or corporations. That's why I'm interested in public interest law. It seems to me that working at a large firm is the same thing as business. I think we need a redistribution of wealth in this country so I don't want to work for business interests. I think that there is a real split here. A lot of third-year students call themselves radical but go into the power structure to make change. I don't think they're radical at all. Radicals like myself have real problems with that. I'm really interested in doing public interest work.

At this early point in his law schooling, three-quarters of the way through his first year, he had developed a noticeable hostility toward the "professional" approach to social problems that was being articulated in his classes. He was disturbed by what he referred to as the law/morality separation in classes and how easily other people start, as he put it, "buying into this false dichotomy." He was especially critical of people who emphasized procedure at the expense of justice. He considered that most perceived him as immature for being too radical. As he referred to it, he was not buying into "the system." He also was disturbed by self-proclaimed radicals who chose to enter commercial law firms instead of remaining committed to social activism. During his first year, he was an active participant in a program that provided legal assistance to prisoners and maintained the view advanced recently by critical legal scholars that "law is politics."

The degree to which this student had constructed a new identity with its related redefinitions became evident in a follow-up interview conducted just five months before graduation. To my surprise, he informed me that he was no longer going to be "strictly" a social activist lawyer. Despite his altered career track, however, he still considered himself "very much on the left." He did not feel that law school had affected him in any way aside from making him more competent, more "realistic," and more "pragmatic."

> I have decided to take a position with a medium sized law firm, around sixty lawyers. I have a real bias against large firms. I worked in a medium firm over the summer and I realized that there's some good that smaller types of firms can offer. I still consider myself a public interest lawyer because I won't be making anywhere near the amount of money I could make if I worked at a large firm. Plus, the firm I'm working at does a lot of pro bono as well as title 7 and sex discrimination cases. They take cases that are really public interest that other firms turn down.

While he continued to see himself on the "far left," he had successfully redefined the nature of social activism in legal practice.

> Law is a business; it's a group of people who decide something for money. You've got to understand if there is no money in it, you're taking a loser and that means you'll spend a lot of money and time in deposition costs and things. When I came into law school I thought I wanted to work for legal services. I worked there for a three-month clinical and I just realized that you can only do so much because they have so few resources. I decided that the "private" public interest jobs were the best of all possible worlds. The firms have given me a good idea of what public interest could be. I talk to people in their first year now and they say how can I work for a commercial firm and still consider myself public interest. I almost have to laugh when I hear this because I know that most of them will probably work a summer job in a commercial firm and they won't be asking these questions in the future.

While this student experienced his world from a leftist perspective, his emerging professional identity had allowed him to successfully redefine the conceptual categories of public interest and social activism. Consistent with the findings reported by Stover, this student had become far more pragmatic in his approach to social activism and had come to believe that commercial practice could successfully address the problems which he felt only public interest lawyers could or would resolve.[30]

One other transition had occurred as well. During his first year, he spoke in terms of social class interests. His emphasis on redistribution of wealth and poverty during his first year had given way to a concern for individual clients in his latter years. As he put it, "I'm going to go to work and try to do a good job for my clients." Despite his leftist political persona, this student had begun to focus upon the individualist orientation associated with the legal profession. In some cases, students themselves recognized that they had surrendered their focus on structural inequality. Many came to realize that such issues would have little to do with their own professional practice. Similar to Stover's finding that law students become more concerned about their future work life, many law students at Harvard began to focus on their future practice.[31] One student reported having become less concerned with social class issues and more concerned with issues of gender.

> In my professional work, I realize that I probably will not come into contact with poor people. Class issues will not be important on a daily basis. However, to be a politically correct professional it's important for me to be sensitive to gender issues.

From the perspective of these students, they had not tempered their political fervor. In short, they had not, to appropriate a phrase from law student culture, "sold-out." What they had done instead was to define the situation differently. These students had successfully redefined the context of their activities to allow them to engage in commercial forms of legal practice. They had not simply been depoliticized, they had additionally become "professionalized."

The essence of identity work in professional schools, very often, involves dramatic change. Medical school, for instance, teaches physicians that they must lower their expectations of what they can accomplish as professionals. Professional schools separate what is thinkable from the unthinkable, what is practical from the unpractical.[32] In this sense, professional schools and the lived experiences in them construct symbolic boundaries that limit and restrict the possibilities, practices, and types of interventions available to professionals.

Like medical students, Harvard law students learned that they needed to temper their unrealistic idealism in order to function as competent professionals. Violators are often degraded both in and out of class for failing to be sufficiently practical. This pragmatism represents the paradigmatic model of identity construction within law school. Students interpreted this pragmatism not as a fundamental change in themselves but rather as a positive attribute, one that is necessary for professional attorneys. For them, pragmatism was apolitical; it simply related to becoming more mature and intellectually competent. As one twenty-eight-year-old white male on Law Review commented:

> I don't think I've really changed at all. I come from a very radical family, way, way, way to the left. I remember growing up and my parents would have reading groups where they would discuss Marxism and things. Since

91

being here I've become steadily pragmatic. I think that I just used to believe in things that I didn't have much understanding of. I'm more to the center because I've matured. I still share an aversion to law firms but I'm realizing that I can go into a law firm and have some impact. By virtue of my credential I can aspire to have jobs that are fairly powerful. Given that that's the case I've become more pragmatic. It's a question of looking more realistically at a system which I'll be a part of.

Another student, one who was proud of the fact that he retained his social activist commitments during his first year by working for a public interest energy group, commented:

I used to hate it when people would tell me that when I turned twenty-five I'd be different. It has happened. I think it is that I've just grown up. I've become more realistic. The visceral reaction I had against corporations before [during the student's first year] was based on limited insight. I've had more exposure to the world which makes suspect a lot of what I believed. God forbid we do away with corporations tomorrow. We'd be at a loss. They're good given 1988. When I came in here I would never have said that. Last year [second year] I saw them as neutral. This year I see them as necessary.

For these students, becoming professional meant becoming pragmatic. However, the adoption of this ideology led to a significant transformation of student identity, one that ultimately disconnected students from an orientation toward social justice.

The constitution of identity involves a labor process in which individuals actively engage in identity work. The labor of producing identities typically involves struggles by students to "make sense" of the new symbolic boundaries that have been constructed in school. For these Harvard law students, the production of a professional identity meant becoming pragmatic and defining non-legal views of justice and social activism as naive and immature. For most, this new identity also entailed the formation of new definitions of public interest. Providing pro bono services, subsequently, became seen as promoting effective social justice. This professionalization of justice, however, individualized conflict in ways that obscured various forms of class, gender, and racial inequality within society.

The politics of legal education are carried on at a cultural level. The notion of culture consisting of symbols which give meaning to social practice is a useful way of examining the politics of legal education. The legal culture in which students live during law school is an all-embracing one. Students participating in this culture learned to adopt new orientations, new definitions of their social world. This redefinition process consisted mainly of separating one's personal values from legal issues, and becoming, above-all, pragmatic. Such a culture, however, has real-world ramifications. The professional consciousness most students experienced in law school severed students from their previous views of social justice. Such experiences make it extremely unlikely that students will choose legal careers in public interest law. Because public interest law is a lower paying form of legal employment and one that has less prestige, the attraction to it comes from the very values, principles, and ideologies that were usually disparaged and often assaulted in law school.

Contemporary students with activist inclinations face greater problems than did their 1960s counterparts. For activist students in the 1960s who became lawyers, there were at least some options for radical practice. The late 1960s and 1970s saw the development and expansion of neighborhood legal service clinics for the poor and assorted state-sponsored and community based public interest programs. While limited in scope, they provided activist students with opportunities to pursue activist careers in law.

Today's potential activist lawyer faces an entirely different political climate. Legal service programs for the poor have been effectively dismantled with the rise of the New Right. Many community based public interest programs have lost their funding necessary to continue. Occurring alongside this trend has been the recent reemergence of a Progressive movement resembling that of the first two decades of the twentieth century in which professionals, lawyers, engineers, and scientists decide on the nature of the perfect society. Contemporary progressivism, however, calls for strategies such as private-public partnerships as a way of resolving the problems that confront today's society.[33] Rather than challenging the free market ethos associated with capitalist economy, contemporary progressives place their faith in the economy as a way of eradicating social problems. Among many of these progressives as well as those who identify with the New Right, corporations are seen as being well-suited to contribute to social reform. Influenced by such a climate, it is not surprising to find that many students attending Harvard Law School come to associate social activism and justice with pro bono practice in large commercial law firms.

Recently, Barbara Ehrenreich has called for a critique of the discourse associated with the ethos of professionalism and its support for the status quo.[34] Such a critique, according to Ehrenreich, holds the promise of promoting an equalitarian and activist spirit among professionals. She maintains that alternative practices will emerge from non-traditional students, women, members of the working class, and minorities, who gain access to the status of professions. The next two chapters examine this possibility and the limitations of such arguments.

◆ 6 ◆

The Contradictions of Gender

Competing Voices among Women at Harvard Law School

There is a large feminist literature arguing for the existence of distinct social differences between males and females. Using these gender classifications as unidimensional categories, feminist theorists have identified a distinct male/female dualism in regard to differences in knowing and thinking, morality and "voice," and personality orientation.[1] Much of this literature advances the theme associated with psychoanalytic and radical feminism that women, because they occupy a separate sphere of social life that is distinct from men, tend more toward social integration, community, relationality, cooperation, and an ethic of caring.[2]

Women attending law school have been characterized as having unique gendered experiences because of their distinct qualities. Studies on women in law school have reported that they are more alienated from the process of learning the law,[3] as well as experience greater stress and difficulty, reduced classroom participation,[4] and marginality.[5] In surveys, women have been found to possess different motives for attending law school,[6] different career goals,[7] lower levels of satisfaction[8] and academic performance,[9] and have tended to feel incompetent and oppressed.[10] The experiences of women in law school have been summarized by Worden, who writes that women feel "judged and excluded by a standard which one may not hold or understand."[11] Women are "unable to follow the professor's reasoning because their mind just does not work that way."[12] Such findings would seem to support the views advanced by the feminist scholars mentioned above.

Within the past few years many feminist scholars have begun to examine the contradictions and differences that exist between women. Cynthia Fuchs Epstein addresses this point in her recent critique of gender research where she states that social categories like gender

> may be based on only one or a few of the attributes of the discrete items being grouped. Thus, a person may be part of a category by virtue of one attribute, such as age, but not on the basis of another, such as ethnicity. All men are brothers by one logic, but by another they are all competitors for rank and resources. Particulars are denied or overlooked in each categorization. To believe that all men are brothers, one must overlook their differences; to believe they are competitors, one must ignore their similarities and common interests. The extent to which people attribute qualities and capacities to the sexes is an example of how the concepts "male" and "female" cause the sorting and skewing of perception of reality by a focus on differences rather than similarities. Often these distinctions are based on very slim evidence.[13]

The identification of both similarities *and* differences among women has become of great theoretical and political concern within contemporary feminist thought, thereby challenging the dominant feminist assumption that women speak in a unified voice.[14]

In this chapter, I demonstrate that women react in sharply different ways to their legal education depending on the values with which they entered. This chapter specifically explores the "politics of difference" that exists among women undergoing legal education at Harvard Law School. By examining the interactions between gender, student experiences, and motivations for attending law school, I seek to identify areas in which women participate in an intersubjective world in common with other women in law school. However, this analysis also demonstrates that significant differences between women exist that subsequently produce differing interpretations of their law school experiences.

95

Feminism and the Critique of Legal Education

The experiences reported by women at Harvard Law School offer some support for the thesis of gender difference. The initial comparisons between males and females appear consistent with the findings reported in earlier research. Female Harvard law students, for instance, were significantly more likely to perceive themselves as becoming more radical since attending law school. Forty-three percent of the women reported that they had become more radical during law school.

Table 6.1   Self-reported Change in Political
Views During Law School by Gender

	Male	Female
More Radical	34%	43%
About the Same	28	32
More Conservative	37	24
	(N=236)	(N=146)

Chi Square = 6.8; P < .03

The belief in this growing radicalism was also consistent with their views on social change. A significantly greater proportion of women claimed to have become more interested in social change then their male counterparts. Two-thirds of these women believed they had become more concerned about social change while in law school, compared to less than half of their male counterparts.

Table 6.2   Self-reported Change in Attitudes towards
Social Change During Law School by Gender

	Male	Female
More Interested	42%	66%
About the Same	37	26
Less Interested	21	8
	(N=228)	(N=139)

Chi Square = 22.11; P < .000

Also, a higher percentage of women at Harvard Law School reported experiencing differential treatment in their classrooms. Similar to data reported in previous studies, a majority of women, 53 percent, felt oppressed by faculty members.

Despite the existence of apparent divisions between women in this sample,

Table 6.3 Self-reported Belief that Faculty is
Biased toward Women by Gender

	Male	Female
Agree	44%	53%
Neutral	14	18
Disagree	42	29
	(N=224)	(N=140)

Chi Square = 5.7; P < .05

these initial findings would appear to support the contention that at least a significant proportion of women report experiences that were unique to female law students.

That women experienced law school differently from males was further supported in other areas. While women at Harvard Law School report having gained greater competence during law school, they did so less often than males. Only 60 percent of these women felt that law school had made them more competent compared to nearly three-fourths, 73 percent, of male law students.

Table 6.4 Self-reported Change in the Degree
of Competency During Law School by Gender

	Male	Female
Greater	73%	58%
About the Same	17	20
Lesser	10	22
	(N=235)	(N=146)

Chi Square = 10.8; P < .01

Although they claimed a lower rate of competency gain, women reported becoming more empathetic during law school than did male students. Again, this pattern supports the previous research on gender differences that has identified a greater degree of expressivity and relationality among women.[15] A significantly larger proportion of women, 44 percent, felt they had become more empathetic since enrolling in law school than did male law students.

In interviews with women law students, many described feelings of personal alienation. The sense of marginality and of "otherness" was experienced by a number of Harvard Law School women. Many, for instance, were critical of what they saw as a male dominated form of thought and analysis promoted through their legal education. For many of these students, the emphasis that

Table 6.5 Self-reported Change in the Degree
of Empathy during Law School by Gender

	Male	Female
Greater	34%	44%
About the Same	40	41
Lesser	26	15
	(N=230)	(N=140)

Chi Square = 6.4; P < .03

was placed on objectivity and neutrality was particularly disturbing. As one second-year woman asserted:

> The first thing you realize about this whole experience is that you're judged by male standards. When you're in class you're supposed to be analytical and rational as opposed to getting down to reality. You lose sight of what's at stake. It matters to me who lawyers represent, what is at stake, and the people involved. For me, it's the process that is important. However, that is not what is emphasized here, that is not what we are supposed to be discussing.

This student was uncomfortable about learning to "think like a lawyer" with its emphasis on testing facts against one or another legal doctrine and conjuring up arguments on each side of a case. Such an intellectual approach to analyzing and resolving problems was antithetical to this student's worldview. She was much more interested in the substantive issues of what was at stake, who was being affected, and how best to settle the problem.

The focus on legal reasoning, however, and the pressures placed on women not to violate the boundaries of legal discourse tended to make many feel incompetent. One woman, who had worked as a community organizer at a women's center before attending law school, claimed to have become less intellectually capable as a result of studying law.

> I originally came to law school to become more competent to do my political work on women's issues. Since coming here I have totally resisted it [legal reasoning]. I don't like being put in positions where I have to argue things I don't believe in. I feel that my law school training has in a way disempowered me because it forces you to challenge every assumption you ever had.

Another woman reported similar feelings.

> I have been very unhappy here these three years. I don't feel as confident as I did when I came in. I feel disempowered, I trust my instincts a lot less. Some of my friends have been crushed by it.

For such students, legal reasoning is inconsistent with feminist values. These women, believing that they were being forced to compromise their integrity by arguing positions that were antithetical to their personal values, were feeling as though they were losing their ability to be advocates.

Many of these women complained of feeling delegitimized when they challenged the patriarchal foundations of law and legal discourse. Some women who confronted the normative basis of law and its relation to the reproduction of inequality spoke of receiving reprisals from their teachers. These women complained of even being "mocked" by male faculty members. One student, for instance, was insulted by her male professor when he presented her with a "baby's bottle" in front of class because of her penchant towards making what he thought to be "childish" remarks. Many of these women found little room to discuss the social context of gender inequality and subordination contained within law and legal practice.

These women also experienced derision from male students for even entertaining feminist critiques of the law. One student described an interaction she had when she challenged the gendered hegemony of law.

> I've been approached by male students who feel I'm out of line for bringing things up in class. I get criticized by students for going off on tangents.

These women were responded to negatively at times for advocating a feminist position that sought to demonstrate how law contributes to gender inequality. In some cases, feminists were even isolated by members of the law school community. One first-year student explained her experiences in the following way:

> I felt very alienated because I felt I was resisting the male orientation all the time. There was a general kind of attitude that what I had to say was unimportant to legal discussion. I felt under a steady, insistent pressure to conform. I found that people wouldn't look at me in the hallways. People would make snide remarks to me about my classroom comments. I also found out that I was on a "turkey bingo" list.[16] I was primarily seen as this fringe character.

For some, these reactions had chilling effects on the nature and degree of their classroom participation. One woman, for example, discovered that the best way to avoid contempt was to remain silent.

> I felt people discredited me after a very short while. I soon realized that I had to be more judicious about my comments or else lose my credibility entirely.

Several of these students believed that most women eventually collapsed under the weight of such an oppressive environment. Such a climate was seen as having powerful transformative effects on women's values.

These data support the contention that women at Harvard Law School not only experience law school differently than their male counterparts, but exhibit distinctive paradigms of legal discourse as well. These women, like those in much of the literature cited earlier, approached the problem of justice from an entirely different orientation. They tended to be more concerned with the actual social relations that existed in the particular cases they discussed in class. Many challenged the ideological foundations of law that included rationality, objectivity, and neutrality. Many sought to speak out against patriarchal values and assumptions in the law when they were encountered. Many of these women spoke strongly of the need to radically transform law and legal practice. However, because of their opposition, many of these women faced rejection and ridicule from the law school community.

Although these women reported having distinct experiences while in law school, it is dubious and overly simplistic to assume that such distinctions are due solely to gender differences. Not only are such explanations reductionistic, but they also underestimate the existence of contradiction within educational institutions, and threaten to compress the nature of resistance by confining it solely to male/female dichotomies. Schools do not merely "reproduce" gender hierarchies through the transmission of male-oriented values. Rather, schools provide a context through which gender identity and experience is "constituted" in relation to a student's biography and interactions within school.[17]

As was demonstrated above, many women at Harvard Law School were conscious of their shared political-sexual-class-identity and reacted toward law school in collective ways. However, they were not reacting simply on the basis of gender alone. Their rejection of the male-based values within law school stemmed from a social conscious that is only partially affected by gender. It was their interpretation, experience, and critique of dominant social relations, i.e., their particular form of feminism, that was more responsible for their perspectives on law schooling.

However, as Rebecca Klatch has persuasively argued, collective opposition to and a desire to transform patriarchal society is not the only, or perhaps even the dominant world-view of women.[18] In a world of increasing opportunities for women, the ideology of equality in the marketplace offers women a form of feminism that is quite contrary to the form expressed above.[19] Indeed, as Klatch illustrates, laissez-faire world-views among women have become quite prominent.[20] While feminists stress collective action, a second group consisting of individualist laissez-faire women place their faith in the free market and its ability to guarantee their individual equality of opportunity in the work force. This is a particularly attractive ideology, especially for those women in the middle class who have greater opportunities to negotiate their own work force participation.[21] They desire to compete with men on equal ground, not seek alternatives.

Equity Feminists and the Law School Experience

In her recent exploration of differences among women, Naomi Black offers a useful distinction that moves away from essentialist views of gender distinctions.[22] Black distinguishes between social feminism, the view that the values and institutions premised upon male orientations need to be radically transformed, and equity feminism, the perspective of equal opportunity in the market place that emphasizes individualism and equal rights. Equity feminists, unlike social feminists, seek not a social transformation of patriarchal values, but rather to establish a position of economic parity with males. Such an orientation, according to Black, unlike the orientation espoused by social feminists, accepts the dominant value system upon which the social order is structured.

In her reflections on legal education, Rosabeth Kanter asserted that the token status of women in law school represented the central reasons for the problems and pressures they experienced.[23] However, the author believed that such pressure would abate once the numbers of women in law school increased. While some seriously doubt whether the entrance of women in greater numbers will alter the core values imparted through legal education, others have predicted that as the number of women law students and lawyers increases, not only will pressures subside but the lawyering process itself will be transformed as a result.[24] Such predictions are important to consider given that women have done exceptionally well in getting admitted to law school over the past ten years. While their proportions were 10 percent less than a decade ago, the proportion of women in law school has recently soared to more than 40 percent.[25] The proportion of women entering law school today compared to 1970 has risen 500 percent.

There is little doubt that law schools are attracting a more diverse pool of women. Such a change in the sheer numbers of women attending law school has considerable effects on the range of student experiences. For instance, while the women in the above section seemed to share experiences in common, they did not represent the only "voice" articulated by women at Harvard. For instance, as many women in my sample entered law school for career reasons (money, job security, advancement) as did men. While 43 percent of the male students entered law school motivated primarily by career interests, nearly 46 percent of the women did so for the same reasons. Still, a greater proportion of women entered for altruistic reasons than did males. While only 22 percent of the male students entered the law school for altruistic purposes, more than 25 percent of the female law students indicated this as their primary motivation. The fact that women had higher rates of both career *and* altruistic interests strongly suggests the presence of gender contradiction.

As noted earlier, women generally considered themselves to have become more radical while in law school than male students. This fact remains true despite differences in their motives for attending law school. For instance, there is no significant difference among women who entered law school for career reasons and for social justice purposes.

Table 6.6 Self-reported Change in Political Views During Law School by Motivation and Gender

| | Male* | | Female | |
	Social Justice[26]	Other[27]	Social Justice	Other
More Conservative	17%	41%	13%	27%
About the Same	25	30	33	32
More Radical	58	29	54	41
	(N=36)	(N=200)	(N=31)	(N=115)

Chi Square = 12.2; P < .001

Both groups generally believed they had become more radical; 41 percent and 54 percent respectively. This is not the case, however, among male students. Indeed, while 58 percent of males who entered law school for altruistic purposes claimed to have become more radical, only 29 percent of the males entering law school for other reasons believed this to be the case. The overwhelming majority of these students, 41 percent, by contrast considered that they had become more conservative during law school.

The fact that no significant differences exist between women who entered law school regardless of their motivation, however, does not necessarily imply the existence of a common gender identity. Rather than indicating the existence of uniformity, this signifies the presence of contradiction. That the majority of women claimed to have become more radical, despite their different motivations, draws attention to the possibility that they have entirely different meanings for this concept.

There is considerable conceptual latitude over what feminism signifies.[28] Two different meanings can be derived from this singular concept. First,

Table 6.7 Self-reported Change in the Degree of Competency by Motivation and Gender

| | *Male* | | *Female** | |
	Social Justice	Other	Social Justice	Other
Greater	73%	73%	39%	64%
About the Same	13	17	22	19
Lesser	14	10	39	17
	(N=37)	(N=198)	(N=31)	(N=115)

**Chi Square = 7.3; P < .02*

because women experience the world differently than men, that is, they are more relational, women aspire to radically transform the male-oriented values and assumptions upon which social life is premised. The alternate view is one that argues that women should struggle to achieve greater parity in the marketplace as well as in the home. While these orientations often overlap, an emphasis on the latter does not necessarily imply an acceptance of the former.

There were noticeable differences between women who entered law school for career reasons and those who enrolled out of a concern for social justice. For example, the extent to which women believed they had become competent in law school was dependent on the student's motivation for entering law school. A significantly larger number of women who entered law school for reasons such as high income potential, job security, or job advancement, reported having become more competent than their altruistic counterparts. Table 6.7 demonstrates that these women viewed their legal education in ways that were distinct from altruistic women. Most career-oriented women believed they had become more competent, while significantly fewer altruistic women reported this change. This difference, however, was not reported among male students. This suggests that a significant number of women who were motivated by social justice pursuits believed themselves to have been adversely affected by their law school training. Most other women valued their legal education since it offered them essential skills to compete in the job market. Moreover, women reporting motivations different from social justice were closer to male students in this regard than they were to other women.

As this data demonstrates, women experienced legal knowledge and education not from a basis of fundamental gender-specific similarity, but rather, in relation to preexisting ideological suppositions and career goals. This finding is consistent with Freemen's recent work on corporate woman, which contradicts notions of dualistic thinking between men and women.[29] One woman who was pursuing a joint JD/MBA degree, for instance, expressed what she found valuable about legal knowledge.

> I'm here to get my ticket punched. I don't care about the esoteric issues about social justice. When I get out there doing transactions I'll be furthering some goal. I don't care whether the law is just. A lot of students come here idealistic and then become cynical. I haven't because I came in here intending to go into corporate or investment work. I've gotten exactly what I've wanted. . . . I don't think much about the law. I'm interested in learning the stuff that I have to learn and don't care about different moral views of the law.

This student's desire to move into the higher echelons of corporate life had a profound influence on her perceptions of legal knowledge. Unlike her more "idealistic" sisters, she found learning law extremely valuable.

In some cases, learning legal discourse was seen as personally empowering, particularly for those who had more traditional gender-role socialization. For women who were exposed to greater degrees of gender subordination typically found among the working class, law school promoted the enhancement of self-esteem. One woman, who grew up in the working class, described how law school bolstered her sense of confidence.

> I never saw myself going to Harvard Law School. It has changed me. It's real nice to know that I can handle it. It's been a good experience because I never really knew that. I never thought of myself as being able to understand issues and being able to think things through carefully. I have really changed in this. I really like arguing with my husband now and I never did before. Actually, I think I'm good at it. I see myself as capable of doing that. I really think that legal education can bring out people's abilities, particularly those, like me, from the working class who lack confidence.

This student experienced law not in ways that were incompatible with assumed personality traits, but rather in a highly positive sense, since it helped her overcome the subordination she felt as a working-class female. The value this student found in legal education does not mean, as some might suggest, that she was denying herself the relational needs associated with being female.[30] On the contrary, legal education offered her liberation from the oppressive combination of gender and class domination, and helped foster a new identity which promoted a greater equality with men.

The divisions among women at Harvard Law School is further evidenced by their attitudes towards poverty law. For years, women who did succeed in

Table 6.8   Self-reported Evaluation of Poverty Law by Motivation and Gender

| | Male | | Female* | |
	Social Justice	Other	Social Justice	Other
Fulfilling	50%	47%	74%	52%
Neutral	20	23	18	18
Unfulfilling	30	30	08	30
	(N=30)	(N=143)	(N=28)	(N=79)

Chi Square = 7.6; P < .02

entering the bar were often relegated to the lowest status branches within the professional hierarchy. Because of this, many career-oriented women in this sample, compared to those who entered law school with interests in social justice, tended to undervalue such low status legal areas as poverty law. Table 6.8 illustrates that while a full three-quarters of those women who entered law school for humanistic reasons found poverty law to be fulfilling, only one-half of the career women offered this evaluation. For men, regardless of motivation, there is no such difference in the evaluation of poverty law.

Despite these statistically significant differences among women, most, re-gardless of motivation for attending law school, did not worry about being successful in their careers, nor did they report being excessively grade con-scious. In both of these categories there were no significant differences be-tween men and women. However, a significantly greater number of social-justice-oriented women believed that faculty were biased toward women. While 71 percent of these students believed faculty to be biased, only about half of the remaining students agreed with this assessment.

Table 6.9   Self-reported Belief that Faculty is Biased by Motivation and Gender

| | Male | | Female* | |
	Social Justice	Other	Social Justice	Other
Agree	56%	43%	71%	47%
Neutral	19	13	16	18
Disagree	25	45	13	34
	(N=36)	(N=188)	(N=31)	(N=109)

Chi Square = 6.7; P < .03

Similarly, students with social justice orientations believed that women were systematically degraded in class for making their political opinions known. While there is no significant difference with men, social justice women com-pared to other women tended more often than not to believe that women are systematically reproached for their classroom statements.

Table 6.10   Self-reported Belief that Faculty Harass Students for
Opinions by Motivation and Gender

| | *Male* | | *Female** | |
	Social Justice	Other	Social Justice	Other
Agree	35%	23%	43%	22%
Neutral	16	14	22	16
Disagree	49	63	35	62
	(N=37)	(N=188)	(N=31)	(N=109)

Chi Square = 7.3; P < .02

These statistics are revealing because they indicate that career-oriented women at Harvard Law School were much less likely to make feminist comments in class. In fact, many of these women believed their more radical sisters to be their own worst enemies. One third-year career-oriented woman described her attitude towards women who speak out about male domination.

I haven't experienced any problems as a woman here and I don't expect to. I know a lot of women here bring these problems on themselves. They get upset when a professor uses a masculine pronoun or that the cases in the text books most often involve men. My roommate is very concerned about discrimination against women. She feels everyone is out to get women. If you act like a normal human being you'll be fine. There's no difference in the opportunity between men and women here. I think that at times she's childish.

In some cases, these women even believed male professors demonstrated remarkable sensitivity to discrimination and sexism. One second-year student who grew up in a particularly sexist community believed that she had

not felt that being a woman has jeopardized my prospects. I'm just not sensitive to sexism or discrimination here because there is so much of that at home. Here professors are so careful about what they say. They try very hard not to make gender-based assumptions.

The prestigious, masculine-oriented environment at Harvard Law School tends to bifurcate women students. Those that entered with a commitment to social justice tended to experience the school as a sexist and dehumanizing institution, while those who entered with primarily careerist goals described an aggressive but fair learning experience. They generally saw the social-justice-oriented women as creating their own problems by refusing to play by the rules.

The findings reported in this chapter do not purport to deny the alienating and oppressive experiences women report in law school. These experiences *are* real and the critique of legal education these women offer should not be minimized or disregarded. Those who challenge the gendered hegemony in law are marginalized. Many begin to feel disempowered and experience lower levels of classroom participation. Many have great difficulty with legal reasoning and do not feel as competent. However, the acceptance of this position does not necessarily imply that *all* women experience law school with unanimity. Indeed, the experiences and perceptions among women at Harvard Law School tend to diverge along ideological lines. These experiences involve "competing struggles" in which radically different views of law and law schooling occur between women.[31]

There are moments of solidarity among these women despite their differences. Most desire to overcome the subordination of women into secondary occupational roles and seemed to collectively support the value of social change. Additionally, most believed there was a need to increase the representation of women both on the faculty as well as within the legal profession. However, despite these examples of shared consciousness there was much that restricted the expression of a collective gender identity. Instead, a deep rift prevailed among women at Harvard Law School. Ideological differences regarding their reasons for attending law school had a significant effect on the experiences, perceptions, and attitudes of these women. Instances of collective struggle did inevitably occur. However, in the absence of a unifying context, the divisions among women were often substantial. Such divisions tended to inhibit the development of a unified gender critique of the institution of law and legal education.

The recognition of divisions within as well as between gender offers insight into the potential for resistance within educational institutions such as law schools. This is important, particularly in light of arguments maintaining that increased representation of women in law and legal education will lead to a transformation of those institutions. Such assumptions, however, tend to compress the nature and expression of ideological resistance in unnatural ways. While social feminists do represent one domain of resistance within law school, theirs is far from being the only reaction to the dominant discourse.[32] Indeed, in understanding such resistance it is of considerable importance to recognize that many women experience feminism in ways that lend further *support* for the dominant discourse in law and legal education.

While gender may serve as a basis for resistance, one must not lose sight of the fact that many women, particularly those oriented towards equity and economic parity, support the dominant value system. Educational institutions typically contain varying degrees of ideological struggle. Schools are political places where knowledge, values, beliefs, and social practices are continuously contested and struggled over. While some of these women do pose a challenge to the dominant values associated with law and legal education, many others, because of the expansion of opportunities (real or perceived) and their breed of feminism, invite little confrontation. Ironically, the success of the feminist movement over the past several years has contributed to a growing number of women who aspire to ascend the status hierarchy without necessarily confronting its normative condition along the way.

A social feminist critique continues to offer one possible reaction to legal education for women. The struggles of social feminists within law school and the legal profession continues to offer transformative possibilities. Perhaps more salient, however, is the reaction of women who aspire toward the material rewards of the free market and who share little in common with women who entered law school out of a concern for social justice. As the number of women increase in the legal profession and in law schools, we can expect these discontinuities to continue and possibly even increase.

◆ 7 ◆

Making It by Faking It

Working-class Students
at Harvard Law

The penetration of social class into the experience of schooling has been demonstrated by many social scientists.[1] The focus of most examinations into student life among members of the working class has traditionally been on identifying the ways that schooling contributes to the acceptance of subordinate positions in society. Rarely has there been attention directed at the experiences of working-class students who succeed in gaining access to elite educational institutions. However, one recent book by Richard Zweigenhaft and William Domhoff, *Blacks in the White Establishment*, focuses precisely on this subject.[2] In their study of underprivileged Black youth who gained admission to high status prep schools, these authors demonstrate how these schools contributed to increasing stratification within the Black community.

This chapter examines the formation of identity among working-class students in relation to the high status world in which they find themselves. I argue that the transformation of identity among these students stems from the sense of stigma they come to feel regarding their working-class background. These students experience stigma as they ascend the status hierarchy from working class to elite professionals. While upward mobility from the working class occurs far less often within elite branches of the legal profession or corporate management, a certain amount of this type of mobility does take place.[3] Working-class aspirants to the social elite, however, must accumulate cultural capital before they are able to transcend their status boundaries.[4] As a result, they experience great personal stress and react to their upward mobility in ways that distance them from their class background.

Stigmatization and Social Class

The legacy of Erving Goffman's seminal work on the subject of stigma has direct application to the lives of working-class students at Harvard Law School.[5] While stigma has generally been analyzed in relation to alcoholism, mental illness, homosexuality, physical deformities, and juvenile delinquency, the concept has also been employed in the study of gender inequality.[6] Goffman's attention to the social processes of devaluation and the emerging self-concepts of discredited individuals not only created research opportunities for generations of sociologists, but also contributed to a humanistic ideology which viewed stigma assignment and its effects as unjust. His systematic analysis of stigma as emanating from face-to-face interaction, as opposed to concrete characteristics possessed by individuals, produced a greater understanding of the arbitrariness of social typifications as well as sensitized individuals to the tribulations confronted by persons with "spoiled" identities.

One of the most vibrant research programs that emerged from Goffman's classic work has been in the area of stigma management, a concept he developed to denote the numerous strategies stigmatized individuals employ to maintain a positive self-image. A host of conceptual terms have been employed to describe the process through which discreditable individuals control information about themselves so as to minimize negative social evaluations. Concepts such as passing, deviance disavowal, accounts, disclaimers, and covering have often been used in analyzing accommodations and adjustments to deviance.[7] These tactics, while offering rewards associated with being seen as normal, frequently contribute to psychological stress. Possessing what Goffman refers to as "undesired differentness" often has significant consequences for one's personal identity as well as available life chances.[8]

While women and other social groups have been examined from the perspective of stigma, little attention has been directed toward social class, despite

Goffman's suggestion that lower social class was a potential stigma.[9] Individuals from the lower social classes often experience real or perceived devaluation and react in ways that are characteristic of stigma management. This is particularly evident within asymmetrical class interactions, that is, interactions that cross social class boundaries.[10]

Studies of working-class individuals suggest that they feel a sense of devaluation resulting from their position within the class society. Stigmatization, for instance, is implicit in Sennett and Cobb's thesis on the "hidden injuries of class" in which they explore the intersection of class and identity.[11] As these authors write, those in the working class possess a

> fear of being summoned'before some hidden bar of judgment and being found inadequate. . . . [I]t is a matter of a hidden weight, a hidden anxiety, in the *quality* of experience, a matter of feeling inadequately in control where an observer making material calculations would conclude the workingman had adequate control.[12]

The lives of these working-class individuals, as told by Sennett and Cobb, are filled with personal anxiety over their assumed inabilities when they measure themselves against those in higher social positions.

Similarly, the status frustration among working-class boys analyzed by Cohen, as well as the accommodations made by Willis' working-class "lads," can be subsumed under the rubric of stigmatization and devaluation.[13] In each case, these individuals adjusted to their uniqueness and marginality within a class society by brandishing working-class values of masculinity and toughness.[14]

Feeling Out of Place

Working-class students entered Harvard Law with a great deal of class pride.[15] This is reflected in the fact that a significantly larger proportion of working-class students reported entering law school for the purposes of contributing to social change than their non-working-class counterparts. As table 7.1 illustrates, almost one-third of the working-class students express altruistic concerns (promoting social change, interest in social justice, and/or helping people) as their primary reason for attending law school. This is twice the frequency of their more privileged counterparts.

As this table demonstrates, the greatest difference between these groups lies in the higher propensity among working-class students to be oriented towards altruistic goals.

Table 7.1   Primary Reason for Attending Law School by Class
Background

	Middle/Upper Class	Working Class
Altruistic	15%	31%
Materialistic	36	34
Intellectual	21	09
Other	27	26
	(N=335)	(N=53)

That these students entered law school with the desire to help the down-trodden suggests that they identified with their working-class kin. In fact, students often credited their class background as being a motivating factor in their decision to pursue a career in social justice. The concern about justice and inequality within society is a social identity many working-class students develop as a result of their own backgrounds.[16] Many of the working-class students at Harvard Law seem no less different from working-class students in other educational institutions who develop a political identity in relation to their own positions within the structure of class society. Although many working-class students Steinitz and Solomon studied experienced confusion and difficulty with finding careers that would facilitate their interests in pursuing social justice, many working-class Harvard law students came to law school believing that the law represented one such possible avenue.[17] Among these students, parental influences were often powerful. One third-year woman, for instance, whose father worked as a postal worker recalled her parental influence.

> I wanted a career in social justice. Law seemed like a way to do that. It seemed to me to be a good value for someone who wanted to leave this world a little better than they found it. My parents raised me with a sense that there are right things and wrong things and that maybe you ought to try to do some right things with your life.

A second-year student said he was influenced by the oppressive experiences his father endured as a factory laborer. Coming to law school to pursue a career as a labor union attorney, this student explained: "I was affected by my father who had a job as a machinist. My father believes that corporations have no decency. I would term it differently but we're talking about the same thing." Identifying with their working-class heritage and associated hardships produced not only a sense of pride but also a system of values and ideals that clashed with the informal curriculum at Harvard Law.

However, identification with the working class began to diminish soon after these students entered the law school. Not long after arriving, most working-class law students began to develop a new identity. Although initially proud of their accomplishments, they soon came to define themselves as different and their backgrounds a burden. Lacking the appropriate cultural capital, neophyte working-class students began to experience doubt about their self-worth. Phrases such as, "the first semester makes you feel extremely incompetent"; "the first year is like eating humble pie"; and "I felt very small, powerless and dumb," were almost universal among working-class students. Some students even felt embarrassed by their difficulty in using the elaborated speech codes associated with the middle class.[18] One working-class woman, for instance, explained that she was

> very aware of using "proper" English. It makes me self-conscious when I use the wrong word or tense. I feel that, if I had grown up in the middle class, I wouldn't have lapses. I have difficulty expressing thoughts while most other people here don't.

Given these pressures, it is not surprising that in-coming working-class students report significantly higher levels of personal stress than their counterparts from higher social backgrounds. More than half of the first-year working-class students reported being under high levels of stress, as compared to less than one-third percent of those students from more privileged backgrounds. Much of this anxiety came from fears of academic inadequacy. Despite generally excellent college grades and success in gaining admission to a nationally ranked law school, these students often worried that they did not measure up to the school's high standards. Nearly 62 percent of the first-year working-class students reported experiencing excessive grade pressure, compared to only 35 percent of those students from higher social class backgrounds.

In the words of Sennett and Cobb, such lack of confidence is a "hidden injury of class," a psychological burden that working-class students experienced as they came to acquire the identity beliefs associated with middle-class society.[19] While most students experience some degree of uncertainty and competency crisis during their first year in law school, working-class students face the additional pressure of being cultural outsiders. Lacking manners of speech, attire, values, and experiences associated with their more privileged counterparts, even the most capable working-class student felt out of place.

> I had a real problem my first year because law and legal education are based on upper-middle-class values. The class debates had to do with profit maximization, law and economics, atomistic individualism. I remember in

class we were talking about landlords responsibility to maintain decent housing in rental apartments. Some people were saying that there were good reasons not to do this. Well, I think that's bullshit because I grew up with people who lived in apartments with rats, leaks and roaches. I feel really different because I didn't grow up in suburbia.

Another student, a third-year working-class woman, felt marginalized because even her teachers assumed class homogeneity.

I get sensitive about what professors have to say in class. I remember in a business class the professor seemed to assume that we all had fathers that worked in business and that we all understood about family investments. He said, "you're all pretty much familiar with this because of your family background." I remember thinking, doesn't he think there's any people in this law school who come from a working-class background?

Such experiences contributed to a student's sense of living in an alien world. The social distance these students experienced early in their law school career produced considerable discomfort.

The discomfort grew more intense as students became increasingly immersed into this new elite world. Within a short span of time, working-class students began to experience a credential gap vis-à-vis other students who possessed more prestigious academic credentials. At times, working-class law students were even embarrassed by their spouse's lower status. One first-year student expressed the status anxiety produced by being married to a husband with a working-class job.

Being in law school has been difficult on my husband [and presumably her as well]. Most people I know in school with serious relationships are seeing someone else in law school or medical school. People would ask me what my husband did and I would say he works for Radio Shack. People would be surprised. That was hard. Lately, we haven't done as much with [law school] people.

Like most individuals under stress, working-class Harvard law students seek to rebuild their self-esteem through behavioral change. They generally accomplish this by learning the values, dispositions, and manners associated with the elite environment in which they find themselves. Harvard rewards such changes by replacing student insecurities with a feeling of acceptance, belonging, economic confidence, and group eminence. In general, then, as working-class students progressed through law school, they began to adopt a view of themselves as different. The recognition of this difference conse-

114

quently led them to develop techniques of adjusting to their perceived secondary status.

Faking It

The management of identity has critical strategic importance not only for group affiliation and acceptance, but also for what Weber referred to as life chances. Stigma limits one's opportunities to participate in social life as a complete citizen, particularly so for those possessing gender or racial stigmas. However, because of the visibility of these stigmas, a person's adjustment to second-class citizenship is accomplished typically through either role engulfment, in which a person accepts a spoiled identity, or through direct confrontation, where assignment of a secondary status is itself challenged.[20] Rarely are these groups able to employ the concealment tactics typical among those groups whose stigma is not overtly visible.

Unlike gender or racial stigma, however, individuals often adjust to class stigma by concealing their uniqueness. The practice of concealing one's class background is not unusual. Certainly, members of the elite frequently learn that it is in "bad taste" to flaunt their privileged background and that it is more gracious to conceal their eminent social status.[21] Similarly, individuals who experience downward mobility often attempt to maintain their predecline image by concealing their loss of status. Camouflaging unemployment in the world of management by using such terms as "consultant" and by doctoring resumes are ways that downwardly mobile executives "cover" their spoiled status.[22] Concealing one's social class circumstances and the stigma that may be associated with it assists individuals in dealing with any rejection and ostracism that may be forthcoming were the person's actual status truly known.

A minority of working-class students took pride in their origins and went out of their way to emphasize their working-class background. One first-year student who grew up in a labor union family in New York explained that "I have consciously maintained my working-class image. I wear work shirts, or old flannel shirts, and blue jeans everyday." During his first year, this student flaunted his working-class background, frequently also donning an old army jacket, hiking boots, and wool hats. Identifying himself as part of the "proletarian left," he tried to remain isolated from what he referred to as the "elitist" law school community.

This attempt to remain situated in the working class, however, not only separated students such as this from the entire law school community, but even alienated them from groups sharing their ideological convictions. While much of the clothing worn by non-working-class law students suggests resistance to being identified as a member of the elite, working-class students become increasingly aware of their difference. Although these students identify with the working class, others, despite their appearance, possess traits and life-styles that are often associated with more privileged groups. One first-year Asian woman who described herself as "radical" complained that the other law school radicals were really "a bunch of upper-class white men." Consequently, working-class students begin to feel as though they must disengage from their backgrounds if they desire to escape feeling discredited and to fit in with their more privileged peers.

Most working-class students, however, disengaged from their previous identity by concealing their class backgrounds. Just as deviants seek to manage their identity by passing as nondeviants, these working class law students often adopted identities that were associated with the more elite social classes.[23] Concealment allowed students to better participate in the elite culture that exists within the law school and reap the available rewards. Like upwardly mobile prep school students, working-class students learned how to behave in an upper-class world. In fact, these students learned that they needed to abandon their identification with their social class if they were to fit into the informal networks at Harvard Law.

This concealment requires that students mimic the dress and behavior of their more privileged counterparts. As Stone illustrates, appearance signifies identity and exercises a regulatory function over the responses of others.[24] Such cultural codes pertaining to appearance often are used to exclude individuals from elite social positions.[25] One second-year male discussed this process.

> I remember going to buy suits here. I went to Brooks Brothers for two reasons. One, I don't own a suit. My father owns one suit and it's not that good. Second, I think it's important to look good. A lot of my friends went to Brooks Brothers, and I feel it's worth it to do it right and not to have another hurdle to walk in and have the wrong thing on. It's all a big play act. . . . During my first year, I had no luck with interviews. I was in my own little world when I came here. I wished I had paid more attention to the dressing habits of second- and third-year students.

Being in their own "working-class world" forced these students to begin to recognize the importance of learning elite interpersonal skills. The recognition among working-class students that they were able to imitate upper-class students increasingly encouraged them to conceal their backgrounds. One second-year student whose father worked as a house painter boasted of his mastery of passing.

I generally don't tell people what my father does or what my mother does. I notice that I'm different but it's not something other people here notice because I can fake it. They don't notice that I come from a blue-collar background.

Paying attention to the impression one gives off becomes extremely important for the upwardly mobile working-class student.

These students were sometimes assisted in their performances by professional career counselors employed by the law school—professionals who gave students instructions on how to present themselves as full-fledged members of this elite community. Students were taught that, unless they downplayed their social class background, the most lucrative opportunities would be denied them. A third-year woman from a working-class area in Boston recalled learning this new norm of presentation.

I'm sort of proud that I'm from South Boston and come from a working-class background. During my second year, however, I wasn't having much luck with my first interviews. I went to talk with my advisor about how to change my résumé a bit or how to present myself better. I told my advisor that on the interviews I was presenting myself as a slightly unusual person with a different background. We talked about that and he told me that it probably wasn't a good idea to present myself as being a little unusual. I decided that he was right and began to play up that I was just like them. After that, the interviews and offers began rolling in. I began to realize that they [interviewers] really like people who are like themselves.

Recognizing that job recruiters seek homogeneity is an important lesson that upwardly mobile working-class students must learn to gain admission into high status and financially rewarding occupations. As Kanter has documented, supervisors differentially reward those who resemble themselves.[26] More recently, Jackell has documented how the failure of managers to "fit in" results in suspicion and subsequent exclusion from advancement.[27] Fitting in is particularly important in prestigious law firms, which tend to resemble the high status clients they represent.[28] During interviews, however, working-class law students faced a distinct disadvantage, since the interviewers who actively pursue new recruits rarely posed questions about the student's knowledge of law.[29] Most seemed intent on finding students who fit the law firm's corporate culture. The entire recruitment process itself, from the initial interview to "fly-out," represents ceremonial affirmation of these students' elite status in which they need only demonstrate their "social" competence. Working-class students typically found such interactions stressful. One third-year student explained that rather than testing her knowledge of law, recruiters

117

were "interested in finding out what kind of person I was and what my background was." Consequently, she "tried to avoid talking about that and instead stressed the kind of work I was interested in. I think that most firms want a person who they can mold, that fits into their firm."

Success begins to mean rejecting one's old social network and embracing a new social group. In speaking of her success, a third-year student on Law Review said that, on entrance

> it never occurred to me that I would clerk for the Supreme Court and then work for [a major Wall Street law firm]. But once you begin doing well and move up the ladder and gain a whole new set of peers then you begin to think about the possibilities.

Such success comes at a price, particularly for working-class students of color. Having achieved success, many of these students continued to feel like outsiders. One such student, a third-year Black man, reflected on what he considered the underside of affirmative action programs.

> I have mixed feelings about the Law Review because of its affirmative action policies. On the one hand I think it's good that minorities are represented on the Law Review. On the other hand there's a real stigma attached to it. Before law school, I achieved by my own abilities. On Law Review, I don't feel I get respect. I find myself working very hard and getting no respect. Other students don't work as hard. I spend a lot of time at the review because I don't want to turn in a bad assignment. I don't want [other Law Review members] to think that I don't have what it takes.

Students who perceived themselves as outsiders frequently overcompensated for their failings since they felt judged by the "master status" associated with their social identity. This reaction to class stigma is typical among working-class students in educational institutions. In addition to developing their educational skills, working-class students are confronted with learning social skills as well. This makes succeeding particularly difficult for these students, and a task that is fraught with the fear of being discovered as incompetent.[30]

Experiencing Ambivalence

The attempt by working-class students to manage their stigma results in what Goffman termed "identity ambivalence."[31] Working-class students who sought to exit their class background could neither embrace their group nor let it go. This ambivalence is often felt by working-class individuals who aspire for upward mobility into higher social positions.[32] Many experience a "stranger in paradise" syndrome in which working-class individuals feel like virtual outsiders in a middle-class occupation.[33] Such experiences frequently lead to considerable identity conflict among working-class individuals who attempt to align themselves with the middle class.

Working-class Harvard law students typically experienced identity conflicts on their upward climb. They often felt they had "sold-out" their own class. Like other stigmatized individuals who gain acceptance among dominant groups, these students felt they were letting down their own group by representing elite interests.[34] One third-year female student ruefully explained:

> My brother keeps asking me whether I'm a Republican yet. He thought that after I finished law school I would go to work to help people, not work for one of those firms that do business. In a way he's my conscience. Maybe he's right. I've got a conflict with what I'm doing. I came from the working class and wanted to do public interest law. I have decided not to do that. It's been a difficult decision for me. I'm not completely comfortable about working at a large firm.

Another student, who grew up on welfare, expressed similar reservations about his impending career in a large firm.

> I make lots of apologies. I'm still upset about the fact that my clients are real wealthy people and it's not clear as to what the social utility of that will be.

Like the previous example, this student experienced a form of self-alienation as a result of his identity ambivalence.

Those students often experienced a sense of guilt as they transcended their working-class backgrounds. This guilt was typically dealt with in ways that allow working-class students to accept their new reference group, thereby reducing the status conflict they experience. For working-class students, adjusting to upward mobility required secondary strategies of accommodation in personal attitudes regarding their relationship to members of less privileged social classes. Secondary identity adjustments were critical in helping students mitigate the ambivalence they experienced over their own success and subsequent separation from the working class. These identity adjustments used by working-class students as well as other law students will be explored in greater detail in chapter 9.

Suffice it to say here that many of these working-class law students did not simply abandon their working-class values and interests in helping those they left behind. Nor did they just adopt the material interests associated with success in the higher classes. For instance, 63 percent of the third-year working-class students expressed an increased desire to engage in public service work, while 80 percent claimed to had become more interested in pro bono legal services. However, in interviews most also became increasingly uncertain about the actual feasibility of promoting the cause of social justice as lawyers. Such pursuits are complicated by the opportunities for material success available to them. As one working-class male student who expressed a desire to work for the labor movement explained:

> I'm worried because when I come to my class reunion in ten years, what will I be doing? Maybe I'll go out there with big ideas for the world and get disillusioned like other people. Who knows, maybe I'll find out I want a Mazeratti.

Despite the potential for great material success, some working-class students did graduate with their public interest praxis ideals intact. These students generally relied on communities outside the law school for support. One student went through his entire law school experience by "trying to remain as far away from the law school as he could," and by relying on his identification with America's Hispanic community to keep his public interest ideals alive. Another student claimed her involvement in liberation theology helped her sustain public interest ideals. This sustained her despite the fact that she found very little sympathy for her religious views in law school.

> I don't do the kind of lefty things others do here because I have a different motivation [religious] which is not respected here. I don't find that the left in this law school is very supportive.

Another student commented on how family support aided in his decision not to practice corporate law. This student, whose father was a union organizer in a factory, said:

> I told my father that I wasn't going to be taking a corporate job and he said, "Good, you're not working for those bloodsuckers."

Most working-class students, however, seemed to develop greater interests in large law firm employment. While 40 percent of the first-year working-class students expressed an interest in large firm work, almost all third-year working-class students communicated this career path. In some cases, working-class students took corporate jobs *because* they continued to feel a sense of obligation to help others. One third-year woman from the working-class, for instance, explained that taking a job with a large New York law firm would allow her to help her family, who was experiencing significant economic hardships. Most working-class students adjusted to their upward mobility and opportunities for great material reward, as well as to the related ambivalence they experienced, by adopting new definitions regarding the pursuit of social justice that minimized the need to feel penitent about their status transformation.

The stigma that working-class students experience in elite schools is considerably important to comprehend in analyzing the difficulties upwardly mobile working-class youth face as they ascend the status hierarchy. Research that has sought to explain the formation of identity as it intersects with social class has generated important insights into understanding stratification as a "constituted" experience.[35] Much of this work presents a less rigid, monolithic view of social class as causing behavior, and instead sees class as a social construction. According to Steinitz and Solomon, "individual members of a class construct their interpretations of social class through their actions in specific contexts and times."[36] Understanding how individuals interpret and experience social class as well as grasping how situational vicissitudes alter these constructions is important to gaining greater awareness of the relationship between class and identity.

The recognition that social class is an "experienced" and constructed reality offers insights into responses to stigma. Over the years, a plethora of stigmatized groups have directly combatted attempts to relegate them to a secondary status within society. Certainly, women and racial minorities have fought against the unjust system of devaluation which restricted their opportunities, reduced their humanity, and forced them to make adjustments such as covering, passing, and careful disclosure for the benefit of dominant groups. The willingness of these groups to confront critical social typifications came directly from their growing realization of the arbitrariness of such evaluations.

However, in regard to social class, the ideology of meritocracy serves to legitimate devaluation of the lower classes. Because class position is frequently seen as the outcome of individual talent and effort, the assignment of stigma to lower socioeconomic groups is not seen as being based on arbitrary evaluation. Given the legitimacy of the meritocratic ideology, is it any wonder that upwardly mobile working-class students choose not to directly confront the devaluation they experience, but rather to forge a new identity which effectively divorces them from the working class and the values associated with it? It is not surprising to find, for example, that the movements to reform law and to make it more accessible to persons of lower economic status emanated not from working-class intellectuals but from elites who were sympathetic to their plight.[37]

Upwardly mobile working-class students at Harvard Law School interpret and experience their social class from the perspective of stigma. However, since the stigma of being a member of the lower classes is thought to be just, upwardly mobile working-class students frequently construct identities in which they seek to escape the taint associated with their affiliation. Overcoming this stigma is therefore considered an individual rather than a collective effort.

Such an outcome is similar to that identified by Steinitz and Solomon, who found that some upwardly mobile working-class students tend to see themselves in ways that undermine their solidarity with the working class.[38] These students vigorously tried to overcome their sense of difference by assimilating the traits associated with their more privileged counterparts. Such attempts to fit into the elite culture within Harvard Law School, however, sever working-class students from their original desires to pursue social activist law and push them toward careers in corporate law firms. Although their elite credentials help them overcome their class disadvantage, they learn they must abandon their ties to the working class.

As was demonstrated by the above data, the efforts to overcome class stigma often involve managing one's identity in the ways that Goffman outlined. However, like those described by Goffman, upwardly mobile working-class students often end up living a double life, in which they feel increasingly alienated from both their previous as well as their new social class. The tragedy of this is that not only do these students redirect their altruistic desires into places where their concerns will not be appreciated, but that even as they try to achieve upward mobility, they feel they need to abandon any identification with their working-class background. Such a reaction would be predicted by Zweigenhaft and Domhoff's conclusions about inner-city Black youths who gained admission to elite prep schools.[39] While some remained partially connected to the working class to the extent that such identification affected job selection, most others abandoned their working-class background and values. As I will demonstrate in the next chapter, given the culture of eminence that prevails at the law school, it is unlikely that many students with social activist inclinations will pursue career options other than employment in large, commercial law firms.

♦ 8 ♦

Learning Collective Eminence

The Social Production of Elite Lawyers[1]

I
t has been well-established that there is a placement hierarchy among American law schools. Graduates of the most prestigious schools, whom Kilmer labels the "Brahmins," generally obtain the most eminent positions within the legal profession, while lower rated schools place most alumni in less prestigious positions.[2] Analysts have characterized the post–law school placement process as "a large number of employers competing fiercely for a small proportion of the student pool, and the rest of the student pool competing fiercely for whatever they could get."[3]

However, despite the many descriptions of this "bifurcated bar," analysis of how elite law schools prepare their students for prestigious futures is poorly developed.[4] An implicit assumption reigns that training people to accept subordinate positions in the social hierarchy is problematic and therefore must be analyzed, but that it is natural for those with the opportunity for advancement to wish to join the power elite.[5] In reality, students must be taught both to desire prestigious jobs and to have the social qualifications necessary to fulfill elite positions. These lessons constitute an important part of Harvard Law School's informal curriculum.

Elite schools produce "eminent" graduates through several processess, including recruitment of already eminent students, as well as teaching elite styles and dispositions to those who lack them upon entrance.[6] Meyer stresses the importance of a school's "charter," a prestige image arising from the institution's eminent history and name recognition.[7] Cookson and Persell demonstrate that class privilege is transmitted in prep schools by well-established placement networks, through alumni prominence, and because the school provides an education oriented toward future command.[8] Van Alstyne, Julin, and Barnett identify all of these factors as contributing to the eminence of law schools, and add that faculty prominence, the school's financial resources, its postgraduate programs, and educational innovations also help establish a prestige image.[9] Harvard Law School, which has top ratings on all these factors, bestows a mantle of eminence upon all its alumni.

Much of Harvard Law's eminence comes from the extreme difficulty of obtaining admission. To be chosen from the huge number of applicants to this elite training ground requires extraordinary personal talents and academic credentials. Those selected generally are highly competitive individuals who have bested their less talented or less aggressive undergraduate peers.[10] However, while less distinguished institutions often promote competition in order to elicit the best in their students, Harvard Law School diligently pursues a sense of cooperation and fellowship.[11] In sharp contrast to the "paper chase" myth of vicious competitiveness at Harvard Law School, students develop a sense of solidarity that prepares them for their elite futures.[12] They learn that success comes from working with their peers rather than competing against them.

One goal of all elite educational institutions is to develop a sense of cohesiveness. As Cookson and Persell illustrate, students are socialized away from a personal identity and toward a collective one almost as soon as they arrive at elite private schools.[13] Elites are held together not only by wealth but by a collective sense of mutual respect and shared values.[14] In the words of Keller,

> Elites must be capable of developing self-images that stress their communality and their uniqueness. They must consolidate their identities, images, and aims around ideologies that justify and at the same time illumine their specialized, autonomous roles in a joint destiny.[15]

Education in this leading law school has less to do with learning technical abilities than with providing an opportunity to cultivate contacts and develop an elite collective identity.

Research on elite education has consistently demonstrated the school's role in fostering a sense of collectiveness among its graduates, while, in contrast, working-class schools block the formation of collective identities.[16] However, little empirical examination has been performed on the process of collective identity-formation within elite schools. This is particularly true in postgraduate education. An exploration of the dynamics within Harvard Law School can tell us much about the ways that law school training shapes the elite professionals of the future.

This chapter explores the micro-politics within Harvard Law School that creates in most students a sense of shared eminence that points these students toward elite legal careers. Consistent with recent approaches to the study of educational institutions, I view the development of collective identity as a constitutive process that enables Harvard law students to make sense of the social reality they experience, and to do so in ways that direct them into elite careers within the legal profession. This chapter focuses on the experiences of Harvard law students and the process through which they develop collective eminence; the view that they are members of a distinct group and occupy a privileged position within society.

Pre–law School Competitiveness

Many Harvard students attributed their law school admission to their aggressively competitive nature. They frequently characterized themselves as having always been driven to outperform their peers. One typical first-year student, for example, reflected that

> While all my friends in high school were out screwing around I was studying. I worked hard to get into this place. The reason that I'm here and they're at some other lesser law school is because I worked hard. They could be here too if they were willing to make the sacrifices that I did.

In most cases, newly admitted students expect Harvard Law School to be the greatest competitive challenge of their lives and come prepared for the worst. They feel nervous about the prospect of competing against some of America's most brilliant and aggressive students. One student recalled

> I had seen *The Paper Chase* and was worried that Harvard Law School would be terrible.

Another first-year male reported that

> I had read *One L* and I thought it was going to be real competitive. I thought
> that I would be swamped with work twenty-four hours a day. I thought that
> I had to be careful about what I said.

The imposing architecture combined with omnipresent oil paintings of famous legal scholars conveys a sense of the law school's eminence and, in so doing, strengthens in-coming students' belief that it will take every ounce of skill and dedication to live up to the university's standards. One first-year woman explained how she felt during her initial days at the law school.

> When I first came here I was impressed by all the columns and pictures and
> thought, "my god, I'm at Harvard Law School—the best!" Once a week for
> about three months I would walk around the campus with my head in the
> clouds and think about actually being here. I was intimidated by the whole
> idea of being here. I remember being more nervous than I thought I would
> be, competing with all these smart people. I was worried whether I could
> keep up.

Other institutional messages reinforce this combination of exhilaration and fear. For example, among a variety of registration materials stressing the eminent company to which they have been admitted, students read:

> As president of the Harvard Law School Alumni Association it is a pleasure
> to join in welcoming you as you begin your student years in the legal
> profession at the School. You join a long succession of men and women who
> have benefited from their studies here and have made significant contribu-
> tions to the welfare of society, both in law and in the areas outside law, in
> the United States and in over 100 countries abroad. Graduates of the Law
> School have been richly diverse in backgrounds and in accomplishments, and
> our alumni include, for example: one president of the United States; such
> distinguished jurists as Oliver Wendell Holmes, Louis Brandeis, and Learned
> Hand; such public officials as Archibald Cox, Elliot Richardson, William
> Coleman, Patricia Schroeder, and Elizabeth Dole; and —for good measure—
> James Russell Lowell and Archibald MacLeish. You have the very best wishes
> of those who have preceded you, and you have our high expectations for the
> future.

Students fear that they will experience difficulty living up to the lofty traditions associated with the law school.

However, almost immediately, these students receive messages that competition is not the key to law school success. While their competitive ambitiousness helped these students procure admission to this top law school, it is their emerging sense of collectiveness that will help establish them as elite professionals.

The groundwork for developing a collective spirit is cultivated within days of their arrival on campus. For instance, students are greeted not with intimidating authority figures but with a round of relaxing social events such as a get-acquainted boat cruise and seats at a Boston Red Sox game. Students participate in small group orientations during which second- or third-year students create an atmosphere of comraderie and esprit de corps. During these "O-groups" new students are introduced to the collective spirit within the law school.[17] A woman in her second year commented that

> I really liked the orientation groups. It helped me make a few friends and deal with this mass of students. I was able to develop a bond with a few of these students. My "O-group" leader was great. He told us that we didn't need to compete with each other. He had parties at his house and I liked that.

Students are told that Harvard's curriculum and faculty are superior to the "lower-ranked" schools and that they should not worry about being average within such a talented group. As one student explained,

> Our group leader was reassuring. He kept saying, "law school is easy and you're going to have a great time." He told us not to worry about anything. The thing I kept hearing over and over again was reassurance, it's going to be all right, everyone does fine, don't worry. Some friends of mine are at Alabama Law School and their orientation process was, "you all have to work and put out." The *One L* and *Paper Chase* was my impression of law school when I came here. After being here awhile I laugh about those books.

Orientation week is capped off by the dean's welcoming address. The dean praised those who were about to embark on their three-year journey through law school, assuring them that they were worthy inheritors of Harvard Law's eminence, and urged them to share it collectively. The graduates of Harvard Law, he pointed out, are not ordinary, but rather include heads of foundations, presidents of universities, and leading politicians. Among the ranks of law school graduates were three 1988 presidential candidates: Bruce Babbitt, Michael Dukakis, and Pierre du Pont, as well as three U.S. Supreme Court justices William Brennan, Harry Blackmun, and Antonin Scalia. As an aside, the dean informed students that Justice Scalia would preside over this year's Ames Moot Court competition.

In his address, he charged them with the burden of elites. Harvard does not turn out merely technically proficient corporate tools. "Your predecessors," he pointed out, "have played heroic roles in the quests for racial equality, for arms control, for childrens' rights, for environmental protection, and for international human rights." Harvard Law School, he instructed, would be "good training for such roles."

> There is no school in the country where major issues about the role of law and legal education are being debated with more energy. . . .There are crucial questions about whether and how the law can be an instrument of a just society and they concern us all. If you find yourself worrying about such issues, you are in good company. If lawyers who build their livelihoods on those processes are not morally obliged to serve as their guardians, who does have that obligation?

Harvard Law is not a place to prepare oneself to merely become rich. Students are expected to devote themselves to the higher task of constructing a better world. This sense of duty and obligation to use one's eminent position for the betterment of society has commonly been associated with social elites as well as legal elites. A leadership position and associated social ameliorism is the "burden" carried by elites that acts to justify their privileged position within society. This is a community to be embraced, not competed against.

In sharp contrast to the orientation speeches at less elite law schools, the dean reassures law students that there is no need for competitiveness.[18] Attempting to release students from any anxiety, he tells them

> The fact is that you are not competing with each other. Your life at the School and your life as a lawyer will be happier and more satisfying if you recognize that your goal is to become the best possible lawyer so that you can serve your clients and society with maximum skills. . . . Although you will experience frustrations from time to time, I think that rather than the *Paper Chase* you will see the School as much closer to the image invoked in a letter we received some years ago from a Japanese lawyer who had just been admitted: "Dear Sir: I have just seen the movie *Love Story* with Ryan O'Neal and Ali McGraw and I am looking forward to a very romantic time at the Harvard Law School.

In-coming students' mailboxes overflow with reassuring symbols of their newly acquired status. Fine local clothing stores send tasteful cards announcing their willingness to aid in projecting an appropriate image. World famous faculty members extend invitations to attend cocktail parties. Knowing that students will soon be flying frequently at corporate expense, travel agencies compete for the students' good will. Such materials begin to define for students their collective position within society and help construct elite dispositions of distinction, superiority and self-confidence that are associated with leadership. That all Harvard law students receive these messages serves to promote the growth of a collective identity. There are enough rewards for all, so there is no reason to compete.

Students soon have their emerging sense of collective identity bolstered by the discovery that many outside the Harvard community hold its students and alumni in awe. A first-year student reflected on an experience that occurred within days of his arrival on campus.

> The thing about Harvard Law School is that it's instant prestige. The credential here gives you every opportunity coming out. It's not only for jobs, it's everything. I called my insurance adjuster last week because I was involved in an accident that required surgery. I called and he said, "Oh Richard, I understand you're from Harvard Law School. That's wonderful." That guy was great and insurance adjusters are usually assholes. It's things like that that make you realize that this place is magic.

Even before they have attended their first class, students have begun to enjoy the material and psychological rewards bestowed upon them as a result of their association with such an eminent group.

Producing Collective Eminence in the Classroom

At first, the classroom experience challenges the emerging sense of collectivity. As one first-year student recalled,

> During the first two weeks of class I think everyone here felt like they had to say something intelligent. I spoke three or four times the first two weeks of class and then went more than two months without speaking. A lot of people like to show off at first.

Despite encouragement to cooperate with others and forge a collective identity, many continue to fear being thought incompetent and tend to be skeptical of the cooperative messages they had received during orientation. Regimentation within the first-year classes is seen as further confirmation of the essentially

129

competitive nature of the institution. Students are typically assigned to seats alphabetically, frequently addressed as Mr. or Ms., and occasionally are called upon by a professor looking at a seating chart.

It appears at first as if Harvard Law is really the place portrayed in *Paper Chase*. One first-year student reported:

> I was humiliated the first year by the professors and some of the other students' knowledge of the subject. My perception of myself was challenged. I was an "A" student at Columbia and I was getting "B's" for the first time in my life. That was hard.

The fear of exposing one's inferiority leads many new students to restrict conversation to reassuring small talk on subjects that do not reveal weaknesses. As one first-year student explained,

> You can't expose yourself because you're always being judged by your peers. People generally don't talk about what law school is doing to them for fear of exposure. I know I feel this way. You have to watch your guard around here. Most people just end up talking about working in law firms. This is a safe topic.

To students who have always excelled, the sense of being simply one of the crowd creates substantial stress. One student explained how difficult it is at first to accept that you might only be mediocre even in such a distinguished group.

> I had a problem with my sense of myself the first year, my sense of my ability to do the work to my own satisfaction, and my sense of working hard for very little results in terms of grades. It was frustrating to have worked very hard and ended up only average.

This stress often leads to personal crises that are dealt with by Harvard Law School psychiatric staff who refer to this syndrome as "wounded narcissism." In the words of one staff psychiatrist,

> All these people come into law school being at the top of their class and they now have to deal with being one of the many.

One Harvard Law School professor calls students so affected the "walking wounded." Students learn to take pride in the capabilities of their peers, rather than see them as competitors. The emergence of a collective sense that they are part of a superior group rescues students from their feelings of personal inadequacy and insecurity.

Relative mediocrity is acceptable in such a talented group. One student described the collective superiority of Harvard students as follows:

> I find the teaching and the classes really boring but I like the community. It's like a fraternity or a sorority. Although there are some dregs here mostly everyone else is incredibly bright and creative. Everyone here graduated at the top of their class in college, so Harvard is able to select the best students.

Superiority is proclaimed by association with elite classmates rather than by individual excellence.

Students begin regaining self-esteem and building solidarity through their symbolic rejection of the distinctive characteristics and authority relations of the law school. They learn self-confidence and group pride through this symbolic resistance, feeling that they have personally triumphed over a stressful, demeaning and pretentious environment. Such experiences in common help foster the collective identity students soon develop.

The school facilitates such rejection. The classroom experiences of students involve only mock severity. In sharp contrast to the popular image, students are allowed a "no hassle pass."[19] Those who wish to avoid class participation are also free to sit in unassigned seats at the rear of the classroom; a practice known as "backbenching."

Once students learn to enjoy their shared eminence, it becomes possible for them to cooperate. As one second-year student explained,

> Most people quickly find out that if you do most of the work yourself, it's redundant and senseless. Most people end up realizing that it's better to share outlines with everyone else.

Students begin to focus on ways to manage the work load instead of trying to outdo their peers. One second-year student explained,

> For a good part of the first year I was intimidated. There was a point, however, that I realized that going to law school was more a matter of doing the work. Once I realized that I became more comfortable and didn't feel the pressure to show how smart I was.

As their collective identification develops, all expressions of competitive individualism in the classroom come to be defined as impolite or even neurotic. For many, the sense of cooperation that emerges within the student culture serves as a sign of proof of Harvard's distinctiveness. One second-year student illustrated this perspective:

> Our section was very cohesive, we all got along well. No one stole notes or ripped pages out of law reviews. We all borrowed each other's notes. What I have found is that what people think happens here doesn't really happen. A lot of people think we're all cut-throats. There's no need for that, that's why this place is so elite. There's no need for me to tear out another student's throat. I would imagine that the level of competition must be much higher at other schools that aren't as good.

"B" grades, the most common grade received by Harvard law students, are redefined as not being indicative of merely acceptable work but are considered to be superior to top grades anywhere else. This homogeneity of grades, in fact, contributes to collective identity by downplaying differentiation and uniqueness. Students aggressively proclaim their averageness. Some wear T-shirts proclaiming that "grades are random," and hold grade-burning rallies to illustrate the neuroticism of competition within such a homogeneous collection of high achievers.

The few remaining highly competitive individualists are punished for attempting to disrupt the collective bond that is being established. One third-year student referred to these "gunners" as "psycho-nurds" and not "the kind of people you want to spend time with." Those who persist in being competitive are subjected to ridicule through such activities as "turkey bingo."[20]

This tendency to discourage competition permeates the law school community. More than half of those returning the questionnaire, 57 percent, described Harvard Law as not being very competitive. This sense of personal security encourages them to embrace the group. Seventy percent of the students reported never worrying about being a success and nearly 90 percent expected to have little trouble in finding a good job after graduation. Only 24 percent of the students reported experiencing high levels of stress during law school. As one third-year student explained,

> I think that here there is not that much pressure on grades. There is some competition early on but the sense of competition stays with you for only part of the first year. This is because most people have this idea that you are at the top of your class so you want to stay there. However, because everyone is so bright, you just can't continue to be competitive. There's no need for it. Second and third year it seemed to me that there is virtually no pressure on grades and it seemed to me that the difference between working hard and not working at all is the difference between a B+ and a B−.

In fact, students become so nonchalant about their grades that many, after their initial year, begin to skip classes. As one third year student reported:

> I've pretty much stopped going to classes. Every semester I go to a few classes. Last semester I went to one class three times and another class four times. A lot of people do this. I generally do all the reading but I don't go to class. I tend to get grades like everyone else here, mostly B's.

This is possible because most students freely share notes, participate in study groups, and circulate outlines. In many instances, a non-hierarchical division of labor is set up whereby a student is responsible for one section of the course and then shares the outline with others. In some cases, the whole class may collectively participate in the construction of course outlines. One third-year student debunked the "paper chase" myth in the following manner:

> Things are pretty democratic. There are lots of outlines around, even by people on Law Review. The legal copy center circulates outlines now. When I was a first-year student I got access to a Law Review property outline. The legal copy center institutionalized the circulation of these outlines.

Professors' questions come to be resented rather than feared since they offend the collective sense of superiority. Rather than seeing their classes as helpful in preparing them for legal practice, students come to see their teachers as an annoyance. As one third-year student explained,

> What irritates a lot of people here is that you're treated like a child. Although no one gets grilled the professors try to embarass you in front of all these people. People get real angry with this. Most people after a while do as little work as possible.

Affirming Collective Eminence through Recruitment

The most important confirmation of collective eminence comes through the recruitment process. In fact, the eminence these students begin to feel is so strong that they often question the necessity of a third year in law school. As one third-year student remarked,

> After the second summer I think you're as capable as any attorney and I think
> third year is unnecessary in the concrete and measurable sense. By this time
> we have a lot of confidence.

The process of law firm recruitment does much to build a sense of eminence
and distinction. With representatives from over eight hundred large national
law firms interviewing second-and third-year students on a daily basis during
October and November, law students soon witness the power of a Harvard
Law School pedigree. A second-year male reflected on his first year:

> I was incredibly nervous the first year in class. I just didn't talk. Although
> students are really supportive of each other there's still a lot of uncertainty.
> That's where the job recruiters play a big role because they really want you
> to work for them and unless you've done really well in class you don't know
> if the law school really wants you. There's not a lot of ego-stroking in class
> whereas the recruiters really do that. It's like realizing that you're still really
> competent in spite of how the classes made you feel. The recruiters are willing
> to fly you around the country and put you up in the best hotels. It's like
> instant gratification.

The task of selecting a suitable firm from among the plethora of choices is
made as easy as possible for Harvard students. Each student receives an
employment bulletin containing a listing of firms that interview at Harvard,
complete with demographic breakdowns on the racial and gender characteristics of partners and associates. This compendium lists other vital statistics such
as areas of practice, starting salaries, and the types of pro bono work, if any,
offered. Telephone books from all major metropolitan areas are located on
nearby shelves, as are student evaluations of their summer experiences working
for these firms. Students may use any of the available telephones in the
placement office to place collect calls to the law firms.

During recruitment season for second- and third-year students, collective
eminence is forged by the requirement that recruiters talk with every second-
and third-year student who signs up for an interview. A sense evolves that
students are choosing firms rather than competing for scarce slots. Two of
the Harvard respondents reported receiving more than ninety interviews. This
is not a sign of the particular desirability of these two individuals, only of
their stamina.

Social events arranged by recruiters, ranging from mere cocktail parties
to elaborate barbeque parties like "Texas Night," further contribute to the
formation of collective eminence. As one third-year student explained, "You
can literally eat your way through recruiting season by going to the different

receptions every night." Being wined and dined by the legal elite provides ceremonial affirmation of their new status. That everyone can participate reinforces the message of collective eminence.

The building of this collective prestige is cultivated by informal ties that will prove helpful to these students throughout their careers.[21] Many interviewers are former graduates demonstrating their loyalty to the institution. Ultimately, it is Harvard's social network, not necessarily a student's individual achievement or legal skill, that has opened so many doors. One second-year male unabashedly noted the value of being at Harvard Law.

> Here I have the opportunity to meet five hundred people during my first year, in addition to the opportunities to work in the best corporate law firms. These are important factors—not necessarily the legal education one receives.

As part of the recruitment process, firms finance "fly-outs" after the on-campus interviews. These trips bring students to the law firm to allow hiring partners a closer look at the propective job candidate.[22] However, they also teach the desirability of elite perspectives, life-styles, and dispositions. Students are often astonished by the lavishness of their fly-out. One third-year student reported:

> It's incredible! When I first started on the fly-out routine I tried to save the firm money by arranging for a few interviews in the same city. I then got a call from this partner in an LA firm that I was going to interview at and he asked whether I was bringing a guest. I told him I would stay with some friends just outside LA and he asked me why I wasn't staying at a hotel that they would pay for. Here I was trying to save them money! I couldn't believe it.

Students often take fly-outs simply to enjoy the luxury. One second-year student boasted that

> The second-year interviews were great. Everyone was after my ass. I knew I was going to get anything I wanted. On campus I had about twenty-five interviews. I flew out for about fifteen of those. They were real cushy. In New York I really didn't care that much. I just flew out for the hell of it.

Academic endeavors take a back seat to the enticements of the recruitment ritual that offers to students a glimpse of "life in the fast lane." A third-year woman discussed her experiences:

> I got a lot of fly-outs and spent a month on the road raking up my frequent flyer points on the Eastern shuttle. . . . I missed weeks of class, but it's more important to make a decision about your job than attend anti-trust for three weeks. You can always cram.

Recruitment offers dramatic confirmation that everything the students have been told about their superior status is true. They feel deserving by virtue of the fact that they are so desired. Still, it is clear that their eminence is collective, not individual. As one student commented,

> The second year I was blown away. I couldn't believe it. It [recruiting] was beyond by wildest dreams. There's plenty of students here that I wouldn't trust to carry out my trash, but they can get great jobs just as easily as I can because they're from Harvard. It's an incredible feeling to be sought after so intensely.

Indeed, the collective bond students share is greatly enhanced by the similarity of their recruitment experiences. Through this process, students develop a sense of poise and sophistication associated with being socially polished.

This celebration of students' worldliness promotes collective identity by emphasizing the importance of learning social skills appropriate to their elevated status. Like pupils at other elite schools, Harvard law students learn the importance of cultural capital.[23] Recruiters, for instance, rarely pose questions to students that test their legal knowledge. Rather than focusing on a student's abilities and intellectual potential, interviews are more a screening device whereby a firm evaluates a student's social qualities. A woman in her second year at the law school explained that

> I prepared myself for a technical discussion. I thought they would ask me about strict liability or something. They didn't ask me any legal type of questions. They were mostly interested in how I would fit in with their firm. . . . I can't believe that a law firm would pay so much for a first-year student who really doesn't know much about law.

Most recruiters simply probed to see whether a student would fit into the firm's corporate culture. The casualness associated with the recruitment process sends a resounding message throughout the law school that confirms the validity of their feelings of collective eminence.

A recent American Bar Association report concluded that personal characteristics were ranked among the most important traits recruiters look for when hiring new legal associates.[24] The placement office recognizes this fact in its manual, which suggests that students being interviewed focus on personal attributes such as their best trait or their knowledge of French cooking. Possession of cultural capital is critical for success, particularly within the elite law firms that most often handle the legal affairs of high status individuals.[25]

Students learn that proper mannerisms, not necessarily superior academic performance, are required to gain prestigious jobs in the large law firms. As one woman in her second year demonstrated, collective eminence is built not only through interactions with recruiters, but also through the interactions with peers, who themselves are beginning to experience elite status.

> The big thing for me was seeing the second- and third-year students in October going through the interview process. They bring the information to other students. They told us about the perks, the pay, the benefits. For instance they told us that it was important to make a good impression. They told us to emphasize social skills. That what these places want are people who will fit in.

Many respondents report that degree of social polish is a key distinguishing characteristic, since everyone at Harvard Law can be assumed to be intellectually capable. One first-year female commented on the importance of such traits.

> I have really begun to see the value of having good social skills. I think that this is one way that law firms weed out people. Everyone here graduated at the top of their class in college. We are all about the same, high achievers. But in order to get the best jobs, you have to have those social skills. I'm real conscious of this when I go out on interviews now.

Twenty-three-year-olds become nonchalant about staying at fine hotels and dining in four star restaurants. A second-year male noted:

> I've learned how to dress, how to hold a drink and not look twice when I walk into a very fancy hotel. I've learned to accept this as given. It's the life-style of a corporate lawyer. While this was all new to me, I found that I could adapt.

The collective eminent spirit among students even reduces potential social class divisions. As one working-class student commented,

> I'm from the Midwest and didn't go to prestigious schools. I was surprised though because there didn't seem to be much pretentiousness here. I was surprised by how many Yale and Harvard people there were here. I have a lot of friends here now that I've forgotten they went to Harvard College. It

used to be that I would look up to a Harvard graduate and now I don't. I'm here, they're here, and we're all equal and that's a good feeling.

By the time such working-class students graduate and take legal positions within America's elite law firms, they will have assimilated many of the values and behaviors of the elite. Wealthy students are happy to teach their peers from less privileged backgrounds elite behavior and norms. Working-class students are anxious to learn that they can "pass" as elite.[26]

Threats to Collective Eminence

Still, not everyone accepts this ideology. Two groups of students challenge the growing spirit of collective eminence. Those on Harvard Law Review threaten the value of collectiveness by being superachievers, while "The Counter-hegemonic Front" scoffs at the ideological pretensiousness of the school's eminence.

While competition among students for academic honors persists, the most successful law students take pains to conceal attempts to outdo their peers. Although competition is minimized because Harvard has several student run law reviews, there is a sub-elite composed of the editorial board of the most prestigious: the *Harvard Law Review*. The fact that only forty students can be invited on to the Law Review assaults the sense of shared eminence. Those who will have the opportunities for the most prestigious judicial clerkships are likely to be on the staff.

Yet, despite their elevated status, even these students abide by the collective spirit that pervades the law school. In order to minimize the challenge to collective eminence that the Law Review represents, mention of one's affiliation to non-members is kept to a minimum. One student explained that

> You just don't talk about it [being on *Law Review*]. I think there's a lot of resentment. We do get more clerkship opportunities than anyone else here. People defer to you when you've got *Harvard Law Review* as a credential. Some people do let others know they're on *Law Review*. I think this upsets people. But you really can't blame *Law Review* people. We're all people who like to think of ourselves as very smart and we like other people to think we're smart.

Another Law Review member described it as a "taboo" subject; "you don't want to be perceived as gunning for it—no one wants to be perceived as being real competitive." These students go to great lengths not to appear arrogant or be too obviously strivers. This combination of cooperative, modest manner and quiet determination to excel is ideal preparation for those destined to serve at the highest rungs of American society.

A small minority of students reject the top law firm path prescribed by collective eminence. "The Counter-hegemonic Front," a loose collection of approximately twenty students who challenged the elitist orientation of the law school, is highly visible on campus. Activities of this group include picketing corporate recruiters, inviting speakers with radical viewpoints on the legal system, and making posters urging students not to "sell-out" by joining large law firms after graduation. However, this group's principal form of resistance involved attempts to expose the pretentiousness implicit in collective eminence through such activities as covering the portraits of prominent legal scholars that line the law school's corridors, altering faculty name plates from "Mr." to "White Male," and publishing a newsletter, *The Reptile*, that lampooned the law school.

Such blatant mockery of the law school drew criticism from most of their peers. Fellow students frequently described those who directly assault the collective spirit of eminence within the law school as childish, foolish, and even self-interested. In fact, the storm created within the law school by the limited resistance of this small group reveals the strength of collective eminence. In interviews with students, most were very aware of the activities of this group, despite the fact that few knew who was affiliated. The group also received considerable negative media coverage in the law school's newspaper, *The Harvard Record*. That such a small group of resisters could elicit such a collective outcry evinces the psychological importance of the feeling of shared eminence.

More activist resisters staff the Labor Law Project, the Students for Public Interest Law program, and the Harvard Legal Aid Bureau. Still, even these radicals are sometimes unable to resist the power of collective eminence. For instance, one second-year student reported:

> I was in housing court the other day and this judge began lecturing me about being late. I felt like telling him that "Who do you think you're dealing with, I'm from Harvard Law School."

Even among students who seek to resist developing this elite identity, the overwhelming majority come to accept the rightness of large, urban, prestigious law firm membership. Students commonly disparage other types of practice such as working directly for corporations, for small firms, or doing plaintiff's law. As one second-year student explained, "although family law is interesting, no one does it because it's not seen as being that difficult." Even joining a less prestigious midsized law firm is considered deviant. As one student complained, "People have treated me badly because I'm working for this smaller firm. I get razzed a lot for it." Even employment in a corporation as an in-house counsel is considered beneath students. As one student told me that "they [corporations] don't pay the going rate. They're looked down upon." Students at Harvard Law School are not merely "corporate tools," but rather are destined for greater responsibility. One student explained the lower status associated with corporate work.

> In a corporation, the legal department is considered staff and are never really involved in the important decisions. In a large law firm, the lawyer is primarily concerned with important facts of the operation—with the business, the profit, and decisions of the firm. Any time you decide to go into a corporation you eliminate yourself from the important work and you end up as simply a staff worker.

Although collective eminence channels most students into high paying law firm practices, it carries with it a sense of obligation to promote the public good, not only to maximize individual gain. However, for the most part, students adopt the view that such goals are best facilitated by working at highly prestigious law firms and volunteering one's time to remedy the problems that concern them. As one student explained,

> I think it's a moral and ethical responsibility of every lawyer to help make positive social change. Coming into law school I didn't have a favorable view of corporate law firms and corporations. But since I've worked there I realized that corporate law firms are positive. I think I'll have the opportunity to be a more effective advocate for the poor or the homeless.

Programs such as Code Critical, in which students on fly-outs stay in less lavish surroundings and donate the savings to worthy causes, teach that the best way to do good is to divert elite resources to the less privileged, not work with them directly.

Although 70 percent of those returning the questionnaire described public interest law as personally rewarding, even those most committed to social activism come to see this type of work as an ineffectual way of doing good. Despite student beliefs in helping others, the assimilation of the values associated with collective eminence makes it extremely likely that they will serve the interests of the corporate elite rather than other individuals and groups who are in need of talented lawyers.

The Result of Collective Eminence

Throughout their schooling, Harvard law students are initiated into a culture of shared privilege. For those who, because of their background, already possess a predisposition toward eliteness, Harvard Law School cements their sense of eminence and class pride. For those who have not been exposed to such elite dispositions in their earlier lives, Harvard Law School offers both a psychological and material path of least resistance into America's higher circles.

Further research into this process is important not only for the development of an understanding of how professional elites are trained and recruited, but because it provides insight into the often bemoaned maldistribution of legal services. Harvard law students learn that to refuse jobs in elite law firms is to abandon the collectivity. Having learned this, they find it appropriate to join a social network that eases entry into top law firm practice. This sense of collective eminence reproduces itself when it leads powerful alumni back to Harvard Law to recruit future lawyers.

The promotion of collective eminence, the collective attitude students develop about their superior position and responsibilities within society, has significant implications regarding the career decisions of Harvard law graduates. Despite the fact that large numbers of Harvard law students express interest in settings other than large law firms, few embark on such careers upon graduation. While 60 percent of the first-year Harvard law students report being primarily interested in law practices other than large law firms, the great majority upon graduation join large, urban law firms.

While this suggests that student interests might lie elsewhere, most feel compelled to accept prestigious positions within large corporate law firms. Only 5 percent of Harvard Law's class of 1986 entered either government service or public interest work.[27] Of the 11,000 graduates of the top eight law schools between 1983 and 1987, only 243 went into public interest jobs upon graduation.[28] There has been considerable evidence over the years that while many students enter law school with public interest goals, few graduate with these commitments intact.

Administrators in the most elite law schools have become increasingly concerned about the restricted career track taken by their graduates. These occupational decisions made by law students are mistaken as simply going where the financial rewards are the highest. This belief has led many of the most elite law schools throughout the country to establish loan forgiveness programs in order to promote greater willingness among law graduates to accept alternative legal positions, particularly those in public interest law.

While these programs are too new to evaluate fully, this analysis suggests that the success of such programs will be minimal because they neglect the ideological dimension of identity production among elites. As I have demonstrated, elite law school education involves a great deal more than simply learning the law. It is an introduction to a culture in which a student's rightful position in society is constructed.

For many of these students, however, the decision to enter large firm corporate practice poses considerable conflict. Most students construct a set of justifications that legitimizes their decision to enter these law firms. The next chapter explores the ideological conflict students experience and the ways that such conflict is resolved.

♦ 9 ♦

The Dilemma of Job Selection

Ideological Work Among Harvard Law Students

This chapter explores the job choices of activist-oriented Harvard law students and how they adjust to the dilemma of having decided to enter a corporate-style law firm. While many students enter law school with social activist ideals of helping people and promoting social justice, few graduating law students take jobs in public interest law. As I shall demonstrate, this occurs despite the fact that many Harvard law students believed they developed greater degrees of social consciousness and concern. Ironically, the very contradictions that students live out and resolve in their day to day lives often end up supporting institutions and ideologies that they may themselves oppose.[1] Ideological work represents a crucial component of an elite education that serves to justify the elite occupational positions they come to occupy and the power they wield.[2]

143

Professional Work as Ideological Work

Social psychologists have generally established that most people experience contradictions in their lives. While some have referred to this phenomenon as cognitive dissonance, more recent investigators have described the contradictions people experience as ideological dilemmas.[3] Dilemmas are social experiences "arising within a particular common sense, as people debate about the common sense which they share."[4] Research on dilemmas have focused on people's contradictory attitudes about poverty,[5] minority groups,[6] and politics.[7] The contradictory nature of ordinary life reveals that people possess contrary linguistic repertoires for talking about their social life.[8]

In most cases, personal dilemmas must be resolved or managed so as to reduce the tension they produce.[9] This is particularly apparent among professionals who often experience conflict between the organizational goals they serve and their own personal values.[10] Corporate managers, for instance, must resolve the moral dilemmas they confront in favor of organizational goals if they are to achieve material success and professional respect.[11] Professionals often confront dilemmas as part of their everyday practice and experience ambivalence over the roles they perform.[12] In many cases, they resolve such dilemmas by focusing on the technical aspects associated with their work, by appealing to professional ethics,[13] or by becoming cynical.[14]

In one examination of the dilemmas professional workers face, Schevitz explored the ways anti-war scientists and engineers involved in the production of bomb sights during the Vietnam War managed the contradiction that arose from this activity.[15] Despite their opposition to the war in Southeast Asia, these professionals continued to be involved in the production of weapons of mass destruction. So long as these engineers maintained their political views *and* continued working on weapons contracts they experienced an ideological dilemma. As a way of resolving this dilemma, most of these engineers desensitized themselves from the implications of their work.[16] These engineers came to define themselves as separate from the interests they served by engaging in a variety of activities that included rationalizing their work, focusing on the technical aspects of their labor, and attempting to organize opposition on the shopfloor. Similar to Burawoy's findings on factory workers, such practices allowed these workers to remain ideologically separated from the consequences of their work.[17] This adaptation strategy allowed these workers to successfully integrate and make consistent the seeming contradiction between their public and private lives.

The practice of resolving the embedded contradictions within professional labor is a form of "ideological work."[18] According to Berger,

Ideas are human creations, and *they are created for purposes, in contexts, and are definable in time and place*, by living people who invested themselves in *these* [rather than *those*] ideas for discoverable reasons. . . . "Selling-out," "struggling," and "accommodation" are seldom unambiguously self-evident *while they are occurring*. Ideologies are usually sufficiently ambiguous that these terms are actually interpretations of events they ostensibly describe or summarize, and the interpretations are likely to serve the interests of the groups who make them. . . . They also, when they have to, accommodate their ideas to recalcitrant circumstances, while at the same time they attempt to maintain some semblance of consistency, coherence, and continuity in *what they believe they believe they believe. That is what ideological work is about.*[19] (emphasis in original.)

The insight offered by Berger's study in the "microsociology of knowledge" focuses attention on how "local social contexts" interact with their "larger environments" in ways which allow individuals to "accommodate" beliefs from "recalcitrant" practices. In this context, the management of dilemmas professional workers face, like the internal contradictions within some religious movements, constitutes ideological work that helps these individuals minimize the conflicts they experience.[20] Such ideological work involves the construction of a common sense that justifies contrary behaviors.

Schooling and Ideology

Recent advances in social theory have focused on ideology as a lived experience. Contrary to orthodox Marxist perspectives, which characterize the concept of ideology as a system of illusory beliefs and false ideas that distort the true interests of the dominant class, a focus on ideology as a lived experience takes as its unit of analysis the episodes of situated activities in which dominant meanings and beliefs are constituted within the processes of social interaction.[21] From this perspective, ideology is best understood not as a reflection of social structure but as a medium through which individuals make their social world "meaningful."[22] It is in this sense that the concept of ideology cannot be reducible to preexisting "structuralist" readings of Marxist epistemology.[23]

Drawing upon the interpretive sociologies of interactionists, phenomenologists, ethnomethodologists, and cultural anthropologists, recent studies of educational institutions have focused attention on how daily activities within schools contribute to building a logic upon which a larger structure of social relations is reproduced. Unlike conventional notions of socialization, this literature focuses on the social processes within schools that produce subordinate and dominant identities.[24] The view that schooling contributes to the production of these identities has received considerable support. Prep school students, for instance, construct a collective ideology regarding their own eminence to justify their dominance in society.[25] Working-class students interpret schooling in ways that justify their academic failures and the subservient work roles they assume.[26] Women in schools produce an ideology that serves to ensure their acceptance of subordinate social roles.[27] Minority students construct an oppositional ideology in school that sometimes limits their educational attainment.[28]

Lived ideologies in school do not simply mirror material forces within society; nor, however, are they unconstrained by these conditions. These ideologies are always situated expressions of beliefs and common sense. They are localized practices which give meaning to individual experience and whose expression often produces and reproduces existing patterns of social relations. One does not merely "know the rules" in the Goffman sense, nor is one molded by them in a Durkheimian way. Rather, strategic action takes place in bounded situations whose outcomes contribute to producing patterns of social organization. The active construction of ideological work represents an element of that strategic action.

Ideology is constituted within everyday life in educational institutions such as law schools. Indeed, norms, values, beliefs, dispositions, justifications, and "practical consciousness" are all elements of ideological hegemony produced in schools. However, unlike mechanistic reproduction metaphors, ideologies often emerge out of the contradictions students face in the course of their schooling. Students construct ideology when they resolve the dilemmas they experience in the course of their schooling.

Ideological Work at Harvard Law School

During my fieldwork I had occasion to visit a legal services clinic supported by Harvard. This center provides free legal services to Boston area residents who are unable to afford attorney fees. On one such visit, I spent an entire day with a second-year law student that I had interviewed several times. After discussing with him the elements he found rewarding about working at the clinic, reasons that included actual client contact, making a difference in someone's life, and helping people who really needed legal help, I asked whether he saw himself doing legal services work in the future. "Unlikely," he said, "you really can't accomplish all that much, you have few resources, and the pay is pitiful. I'm going to work at a corporate law firm in Philadelphia." Concerned about how he viewed himself in relation to his career choice I inquired, "does that make you a corporate tool?"[29] Slightly taken aback by the nature of the question, he responded:

> I hope not. I don't consider myself a corporate tool. A corporate tool is more than just a person who works at a corporate law firm and besides, you would never see a tool working at a legal services clinic.

The social identity many Harvard law students strive to present is one that reflects liberal and leftist values. Many, upon entering the law school, claim to be interested in pursuing either social activist or small firm legal practice where they intend to pursue social justice and to do, as one student explained, "socially meaningful work." In my sample, more than half of the first-year students returning questionnaires reported that their most likely initial law job after graduation would be in a social activist or public interest area of practice. In addition, half of the sample, 51 percent and 49 percent, respectively, reported becoming more concerned with social change and public service during law school. Fifty-two percent reported finding poverty law fulfilling, while another 76 percent found public interest law personally rewarding. As noted earlier, in a separate survey conducted by students at the law school, 70 percent of the first-year class in 1986 reported having desires to practice public interest law.

As students progressed through law school, however, they increasingly gravitated toward large corporate-style law firms. One student commented that the typical wisdom is that everyone comes in saying they're interested in public interest and everyone leaves doing large firm corporate work. While less than half of first-year students anticipated entering large, corporate law firms upon graduation, almost all of the third-year students expressed the desire to work in one of these law firms. Accommodation to large law firm work, however, created personal conflicts for students who had to begin to reconcile the contradiction between their altruistic values and their material interests. Students began to aspire to the material rewards available through large firm employment, but did not wish to appear as though they had "sold-out."

In the general lexicon of American culture the concept of "selling-out" connotes the conscious exchange of one's personal and political ideals for monetary gain. Born out of the 1960s struggle over being politically conscious and upwardly mobile, soul-selling is a metaphor used to describe the abandonment of ideals, beliefs, and commitments. While students who entered the law school with unabashed desires to work in corporate-style law firms experienced none of these conflicts, the concern with "selling-out" was of particular concern to many of those Harvard law students who entered with altruistic concerns. One student, a third-year male, commented that

> It's a difficult choice. The bottom line is that I came in with a vague notion of wanting to do good work but then everyone around you is selling-out. It becomes, for them, more important to gain prestige than represent someone they care about. I have reservations about my career decision. Should I have spent more time looking for a public interest job, should I be working for twenty-five thousand dollars instead of seventy thousand? I've made my choice and it's not doing public interest. My reservations about this stem from my concern with selling-out.

These students often demonstrated a nonchalant and even hostile attitude about financial success. They frequently criticized those students who appeared unabashedly interested in financial rewards. Such students were avoided and were the subject of scorn and ridicule. As one second-year male law student explained,

> I think most of the people here see themselves as on the left. There are some people though who are really conservative, you know, the Joe Corporate type. These students are plugged in for success and making it into [major law firms]. It's not only working a lot but having it [success] as your conscious goal all the time. They have just sold themselves to any corporation that makes asbestos or produces deadly pharmaceuticals. They're just in it for the money and no other reason. I try to avoid them as much as possible.

A third-year student registered similar contempt for such students.

> Some people come here and say, "I want to practice corporate law and make big bucks." I remember seeing one of these guys in my first-year section about the third week of school clutching one of the 2L and 3L [second- and third-year law student] placement manuals. He said, "Peter, look at this, this is where the bucks are." There are some jerks around like this, but you can avoid them.

Thus, overzealous commitment to large law firm work, corporate values and financial reward was viewed negatively, if not as deviant by many of these students.

It is common within schools for students to generate classifications of deviance.[30] The social construction of deviance within educational institutions represents one of the processes through which acceptable social roles and practices are communicated on a daily basis. Students who violate these acceptable roles and practices are subject to degradation. At Harvard, most students accepted lucrative jobs in large corporate law firms, but did not wish to be perceived as materialistic. Minimizing the importance of financial gain was critical in lessening the contradiction students experienced over accepting employment in a corporate law firm. This was typically accomplished through rationalizations, justifications, accounts, and disclaimers, which were all used to avoid the encroachment of a "corporate tool" identity. Such accommodation strategies, when successful, exonerated students from culpability of having "sold-out."

Strategies of Accommodation: Coping with Job Choice

Accommodation strategies are commonly employed by people who wish to manage a potentially spoilable self-image. Offering "accounts" to justify and explain inappropriate behavior is often done to avoid stigmatization.[31] Accounts may be conceived as a "vocabulary of motive" that explains social conduct so as to neutralize any discomfort associated with being implicated in the activity.[32] Strategies of accommodation are commonly found within the ideological work law students use to resolve the contradiction they experience during law school.

Resolving the contradiction students feel is typically accomplished through the degradation of others. Pejorative categories are created by these students to revalidate personal self-images. Within the Harvard law student culture, the "corporate tool" represents the most visible deviant classification. The term is used to describe those students who are viewed as comporting themselves in ways that support corporate interests. The term is generally reserved for those who possess the following traits. First, it refers to someone who expressly desires to work in a corporate-style law firm in order to reap great material benefits. One student, a second-year female on the Harvard Law Review, who had been often described as a corporate tool, commented:

> What is a corporate tool? Anyone like me. Anyone who would go to work for Cravath.[33] I've been called this quite often. It's used to describe anyone who goes to work for these big firms for money and prestige because that's what they really want. The fact is that everything comes down to money. The corporations have money, so they're the ones who will get you money.

149

In addition, "the tool" is seen as possessing a willingness to work on either side of a case without regard for any interests save the ones he/she is hired to represent. This corresponds to the proverbial "hired gun" label that altruistic-oriented students pejoratively apply to "tools." As one student explained, corporate tools are

> just cogs in the capitalist wheel and don't really think about what they're doing. They don't have any social consciousness. They just want to be hired guns for industry.

Such students are described as being functionaries for corporate interests, or as one student put it, "soldiers for capitalism," who unquestionably serve the interest of wealth and power.

Thirdly, the label is applied to those who register for courses like "corporate tax," "corporate finance," "mergers and acquisitions," and "secured transactions." A third-year student commented:

> There are certain corporate tool classes, like corporate tax, corporate finance, commercial transactions. I was in a corporate tool class this Fall, real estate planning, and didn't know it was a corporate tool class until I was in it. I should have known because I didn't know anyone in it. They're the ones going to the large law firms and not having doubts about it.

Finally, tools are seen as "drones" in a bureaucratic wheel that extracts a great expenditure of time from individuals, making them conservative, narrow, insular, disaffected, and boring.

It is not surprising to find that most students seek to distance themselves from such a dubious classification. The term denotes not only parasitic and greedy intentions, but also represents a criticism of the bureaucratic ethos associated with life in a large firm. The construction of this negative social type suggests that a law student's identity is negotiated through subtle attempts to avoid stigma. Defining oneself or others in relation to the "corporate tool" is a form of signification that represents a collective activity carried out within the social context of a law student's education. Applying the label to others and avoiding its application to oneself constitutes a central feature of the underlife of student culture at Harvard Law School. This disassociation helps altruistic students handle the dilemma they experience over entering such law firms.

Students neutralize the dilemma they experience through ideological work. The ideological work practiced by these students is varied and involves separate strategies of accommodation. These include making appeals to autonomy, personal conflict, loan debt, professional development, affinity, good firms, effectiveness, and even resistance. For students who employ these strategies, a corporate tool is not simply anyone who enters into corporate-style legal practice, but is one who wholeheartedly and unquestionably accepts the role of a hired gun. By disavowing the corporate tool identity and maintaining one's ideological distance from corporate interests, a student is relieved of much of the conflict that is associated with corporate law firm employment. *What changes during schooling is not necessarily a student's "values" but a student's definition of the reality to which the values are applied.* While these strategies are diverse, they are not mutually exclusive. Students often use several of these accounts to justify their decision to enter a large corporate law firm. In the interviews, students were asked how they as well as other students resolved this conflict. In the overwhelming majority of cases, students reported that both they as well as their classmates employed these strategies when explaining their job choice.

1. The appeal to loan debt

The most common accommodation strategy involves the offering of accounts that are related to financial pressures. Fifty-eight percent of the students mentioned the importance of loans in making corporate law firm job decisions. Many of these students expected to have loan debts of approximately thirty thousand dollars upon graduation. This debt provides many with a rationale for seeking employment in large commercial law firms. Indeed, the opportunities to make high salaries are extremely attractive. In many firms, students have the prospects of earning more than one hundred thousand dollars five years out of law school. Students express amazement over the salaries available in the larger commercial law firms. One second-year male student from a small midwestern town commented:

> My idea of lawyers prior to law school was the small town lawyer. The lawyers I saw at home didn't seem to work too hard, which is really different than the lawyers who work in large cities. I knew that being a lawyer was a well-paying profession but I had no idea of the range. I thought lawyers made in the high twenties or in the thirties. I had no idea that the big time lawyers made as much as seventy thousand to start. That blew my mind.

Many students conclude that working at a large firm is necessary to pay off their school debt. As a mechanism of adaptation, however, these debts shield students from the status of "toolism." Many believe that they will leave commercial practice and enter the "public interest sector" after their debts have been relieved. As one first-year student commented,

> I think that I would like to do some public interest work, but I have to pay off my loan debt, so I will probably go with a large firm for a while.

Another student, who entered law school to be a criminal prosecutor, commented:

> I decided to work in a large law firm in San Diego. All through law school I didn't give any real thought to doing corporate work. I wanted to be a prosecutor because I was interested in violence against women. I found this prosecutor's job out on the west coast but they were only willing to pay me $29,800 to start. So I decided not to take that job but rather took a job with a firm that will give me a starting salary of sixty thousand. I don't intend to stay there very long, just long enough to extinguish by debt.

The financial burdens these students have accrued pose real pressures. Although there does not appear to be any correlation between the amount of money law students owe and their occupational decisions, these debts weigh heavily on the minds of Harvard law students.[34] Despite these burdens, the focus on their debt serves a useful accommodation strategy. Ideological work does not rest upon "false" ideas. Rather, the success of ideological work hinges on the plausibility structure associated with the account.[35] In the case of heavily indebted law students, it is certainly plausible that they could resume there search for public interest practice after they have paid their school debt. The important point here for the analysis of ideological work is that students feel forced to join large law firms to pay their debt. Students believe their decision reflects financial realities, not ideological preferences.

There is some question as to the actual importance of student debt. In many cases, a focus on debt covers a student's desire to earn a lucrative salary. Some students even realize the deceptive nature of being debt conscious. One public-interest-oriented student who had accepted a job in a large firm commented:

> I don't think that loans are a meaningful thing. You can take a government job and still pay your loans. The question is the social pressure to make a lot of money. Everybody leaves here making lots of money and you get evaluated by others on that basis. . . . I remember interviewing with this one firm and their were people there making $750,000 a year. Being rich is better than being poor.

More than simply relieving debt, high incomes become a measure of social worth. Such incomes signify to students the meaning of success. Furthermore, high incomes are seen as allowing the student to live the life-style of eminence that is prevalent at the law school. Covering these desires by focusing on their debt, however, protects students from the contradictions they might experience over their job choice.

2. The appeal to effectiveness

Another common strategy, and perhaps the most ironic, is the belief that large firm work allows students to more effectively pursue public interest causes. More than half of the students interviewed, 56 percent, reported believing that one could be a more effective advocate of social change by working at a corporate law firm. Students adopt the view that political action and social change activities are most effectively carried out from a position of power, as opposed to a position working within grassroots organizations. Obtaining prestigious positions within large commercial law firms, therefore, becomes seen as compatible with social reform. While initially hostile to working in these settings, most students redefine the utility of such employment. Such strategies are consistent with Derber's notion of "ideological cooptation," in which workers come to minimize the ideological distance between the law firm's interest in profit and their own altruistic values.[36] Rather than a product of shifting sympathies or political ideology, changes in career decisions "appear to involve shifts in the student's perceptions concerning the extent to which the jobs in question would allow an attorney to do public interest work."[37]

Thus, one way in which law students make sense of their decisions to join large commercial law firms is by constructing an ideology that places these firms at the forefront of progressive social change. One third-year student, who felt that his public interest work during a summer job was futile, commented:

> In 99.9 percent of the cases in poverty stuff the results are limited. I don't anymore see that change will come this way. The thing I care about is the distribution of wealth. Nothing on the state level is going to do much. It's going to have to be a federal program that starts a negative income tax. The question for me is how you go about pushing it. You don't do it by working for legal services, you don't do it by working for a state agency, you don't do it by becoming a staff attorney at the Department of Health and Human Services. I can see working for a senate staff. To do this it will be helpful to get a job with a large New York or Washington law firm that has connections to the government.

Working within the elite levels of corporate law firms becomes seen as the most effective way to bring about social change. One student, stating his reasons for choosing a prestigious Wall Street law firm, commented:

> I wasn't originally interested in working for a large firm but I have decided that it's probably the best way to accomplish what I'm interested in.
>
> Q: When did you begin to experience this change? When did you begin to see corporate firms as a viable alternative?
>
> Well, my first summer I worked in a public defenders office and it was terrible. I don't think you can really accomplish much of anything working someplace like that. The next summer I worked at [a large firm] and the thing that sold me was that they weren't all conservative Republicans. This firm was even active in opposing Bork. They were concerned about the same things that I was.

Despite his altered career plans, this student continued to maintain an idealistic self-image.

> I think that since I've been here I've become more interested in social change. I've done more reading about people doing social change stuff. I'm still an idealist. Someone put together an argument for Brown that won nine to nothing. You can do it. To see how it was done was empowering. This was a damn correct decision and that lawyers did it, to me was great. Lawyers are the movers and shakers of change and I think law firms are a good place to do that. I'm still interested in poverty stuff and will do some pro bono. While my view is to make change on a larger scale you have to do the incremental stuff at times.

Such ideological work is especially common among law students of color and those from the working class who are motivated by political interests in increasing racial harmony and equality. These concerns, however, are often juxtaposed with interests of financial success and professional respect. In many cases, family pressures often support their kin's upward mobility. One woman from a working-class background who was interested in public interest law commented:

> There is a lot of pressure on me to get up there with everyone else. To make less money than my father will just break his heart.

The ideology of upward mobility is particularly strong among these students. While these students often adhere to public interest values and ideals as neophyte law students, they typically resolve their ideological conflicts in favor of corporate law firms. A Black law student who came to law school with what he characterized as a "strong personal commitment to public interest law" illustrates this conflict.

I get slammed for being a corporate tool, both by the Black and White left. They feel that I have sold-out. I'm irritated by that. I think that I can be more effective making deals than by doing public interest law. There are these people who, because I'm taking urban finance and banking regulations, think I'm a corporate tool. I don't think I am. For years, Blacks have been treated as slaves, sharecroppers, or porters. So I think that whether I want to be a partner at [a major New York law firm] or to be an NAACP defense attorney, either of these positions are politically correct because I'm just saying I'm going to do what I want, I'm going to be free. People should understand that. We need Black people with money and power. I see that there is a real risk to pursuing the corporate path. It's possible not to ever again have any contact with my community and live the good life. Or I could use my money and position to advance the position of Black people. I think I can make significant contributions to Black causes.

While this student may engage in public service activities as a corporate lawyer, it is unlikely that such activities will threaten the values of corporate America.[38] Students consequently redefine the value of large corporate law firms for the opportunities such positions provide in contributing to social change. Many come to believe that such positions offer the only real opportunities to have a positive effect on society. They are often assisted by the recruiters themselves, who likewise uphold such views and seem enamored with similar ideals. One third-year student explained how his views of social change had been transformed through interactions with elite lawyers.

I used to think that social change would come about by being an activist. That's why I originally wanted to do public interest law. But you really can't accomplish much by doing this. The hiring partner at [a major New York law firm] convinced me that this is the only way to get things done. He served as Undersecretary of State in the Carter administration, and when he was younger he was with Johnson. He made good sense when he told me that if I wanted to contribute to social change I had to become an important person.

The certification implicit in such conversations is particularly important in light of the fears and anxieties that public-interest-oriented students experience.

3.   *The appeal to affinity*

Thirty-nine percent of the Harvard law students interviewed explained that they had significantly changed their attitude about corporate law firms and the people employed in such firms. Direct exposure to corporate lawyers provides students with this accommodation strategy. During their first and second years in law school, students often receive high paying summer internships with large commercial law firms. Not only do large law firms reward students with high salaries, they offer an assortment of other amenities. The fact that many students have these opportunities *before* they have even completed their second year of legal study sends a powerful message to law students, that effectively makes taking what many students describe as the "path of least resistance" particularly attractive.

The experience that students reported during their summer internships offer further insight into the ways they redefine social reality and consequently desensitize themselves from the ideological conflicts they experience. The ability to redefine and construct reality lies at the heart of ideological work. Students frequently reported having changed their impressions of corporate law firms as a result of summer internships. Initially hostile views of corporate law gave way to "more tempered" views. Summer internships communicate to students that the corporate world is not an evil world but, instead, one that needs to be understood and sympathized with. One second-year woman, who entered law school with social activist inclinations, explained:

> I came in here and remembered asking a friend of mine who was working at one of those big corporate firms, how she could work for them. She told me that it's not as black and white as it seems after you're here for a while. I have come to see that she was right. I used to believe that those people were the enemy. Now I really see that there is this huge legal apparatus, secured transactions, trade, all this stuff that needs lawyers to do it. It's not always black and white that all corporations are bad guys. Sometimes corporations try to screw each other so you have to try to figure that out.

Instead of seeing such firms in the service of "corporate fatcats" who victimize people, she redefined corporations as potential victims and could sympathize with their plight.

Sympathizing with corporate law firms and their interests is one of the most distinct learning experiences students receive during their summer internships. During internships, students begin to identify with the personalities of corporate attorneys. Returning law students typically describe the attorneys for whom they worked as "nice people." The realization that corporate lawyers are "just like them" is often startling to students who had negative impressions of law firms and corporate attorneys. A second-year student, for instance, described his summer experience as follows:

> The law firm people are really nice. I found a lot of people there who were like me. They had many of the same political views I do. I remember working with this one attorney and I was telling him how I really didn't know if I wanted to work for a large firm, that I was interested in public interest law, and that I was active in public interest things at school. He told me that I reminded him of himself when he was in law school.

Another student explained how his summer experiences altered his opinion of corporate lawyers.

> The people at the firm were really nice. It's not the image I had of these people. I thought they would be all grinds and ogres. Most of the people were pleasant and interesting. They were good people and many of them did pro bono and charity work.

Summer internships are the subject of considerable conversation among Harvard law students. Most of these conversations focus on the "social" characteristics associated with large firm practice. For these students, summer internships represent more a cultural experience than a skill-building one. As summer interns, students are invited to participate in the affluent culture of the law firm. Students describe with great vigor the various social activities that they participated in during their summer internships, activities that often included boat cruises, attending the theatre, and going to assorted parties. One student even described a benefit known as "dream night" in which the firm alloted students one thousand dollars for an evening's entertainment. Such experiences introduce students to the cultural capital of corporate law firms.

4. The appeal to good firms

In addition to realizing the value of large firm practice in promoting social change, law students begin to discriminate between "good" firms and "bad" firms. Thirty-five percent of the law students interviewed made these distinctions. As students start to entertain serious notions about large firm employment, they simultaneously undertake a process of searching out law firms that do "good" work. This is an important step in a student's conversion to large firm work. For instance, first-year law students were often appalled by legal cases in which companies willfully exposed consumers to danger. During the early stage of law school, many students viewed corporate law firms with an eye of skepticism. Many characterized these law firms in negative terms. Yet, as students began to accommodate themselves to the likelihood of large law firm work, their initial characterizations underwent a radical shift. Only the most "heinous" firms, such as those representing pharmaceutical industries or engaging in union-busting practices, were defined as "evil." Students began to define specific incidences of legal work as objectionable while viewing the vast bulk of corporate practice as "neutral." The subtlety of this process is exemplified by one third-year "public-interest-oriented" student who had accepted a job with a prestigious commercial law firm in New York.

> I would never want to litigate for something like Dow Chemicals. I just don't think I could do that. It's against my principles. That's why I want to do corporate law versus litigation. The evil thing about corporate law tends to be litigation; defending tobacco companies, defending pharmaceuticals. Some might say that if you're helping Robbins buy Union Carbide then you're not helping mankind, but upholding their right to make asbestos or another Bhopal [India]. To me, it's a neutral thing, rich people moving their money around.

Other positive attributes were also sought out as students tried to balance their personal identity with their career choices. One third-year woman explained,

> I'm working for a large firm in San Diego. I never really thought I would go with a corporate firm but I am excited about this one for two reasons. One is that it's 50 percent women and second it does some plaintiff's sex discrimination. I feel that I could be happy at this place. It's a good firm.

Students who failed to accept the legitimacy of these distinctions were often subject to reprisal. Those who persisted in their condemnation of corporate law firms were ultimately avoided and marginalized. Students failing to made adjustments in their views became sources of irritation. As one student explained,

> I don't fit in anymore because I've said some inflammatory things about corporate firms in class. I believe that all corporate firms are bad and I let people know. I'm not always the most friendliest of people to talk to. It tends

to make people not think much of me. Around here you're expected to let people rationalize their decisions for working at corporate law firms. I don't and that pisses people off.

Such rejection occured even among the most committed students. During a public demonstration in which a small group of law students picketed recruiters from notorious union-busting firms, this became apparent. Approximately twenty students [and myself] marched in front of an elegant Cambridge hotel where recruiters were conducting interviews with students. In the course of the demonstration, each student took turns leading the others in protest chants such as, "Fulbright and Jaworski you can't hide, we charge you with prolicide."[39] During this demonstration, one student assumed command of the public address system and used the occasion to vehemently denounce all corporate law firms. Within seconds, he was relieved of his post by another student who latter described him as "a little crazy" and as a "liability." Following the demonstration, the silenced student commented:

> I just refuse to accept the idea that some commercial law firms are good. The people who sell out believe they can go to firms which they can be comfortable in. The left here is really confused. People think I'm crazy for condemning all corporate law firms. They think that I'm too extreme but I think that one corporate firm is as bad as the next. It's fine to oppose some on the grounds of their union-busting policies but I think that we should oppose them all. There are incredible contradictions that I just can't handle. I have a friend here who sees himself as really radical. He has found himself a job in a firm where there are about ninety lawyers but five do only labor law. He'll be making about seventy thousand to start to do pro labor law. The other lawyers, however, do this terrible corporate law where they represent horrible people. I'm not willing to be homeless but I am willing to make sacrifices.

In some cases, friendships are dropped because of the failure to accept redefinitions of corporate law firms. For students whose original commitments lie in the area of public interest, the accommodation of corporate practice can be particularly embarrassing, causing some to disassociate from those who remained committed to public interest practice. One student explained how his decision to do corporate work affected his relationship with his public interest friends.

> It is so taken for granted here that you can take these high paying corporate jobs and still be a good person. The people who aren't reinforcing this message make me uncomfortable now. Frankly, that's why I no longer associate with [a student run public interest group]. They remind me of my

guilt. I suppose that if I really wanted to remain committed I could have surrounded myself with people who would have supported public interest but I guess I just got hooked. My first year I was conscious of my public interest goals and I fought the corporate stuff all the way. I was proud of myself when I made it through the first year with my public interest goals intact. I guess I let my guard down.

5. The appeal to professional development

Students at Harvard often feel ill-equipped to practice law. Many reported tremendous anxiety about handling cases, believing they did not know enough about legal process and, in some cases, considered themselves incompetent, particularly in trial proceedings. Nearly 30 percent of the students interviewed explained that they had accepted a large law firm offer because of the need to develop their skills as an attorney. One typical student who used this strategy commented:

> I don't think that I really know all that much about law. I wouldn't know what to do if I had to go into court and argue a case. This really frightens me. I need to work in a large firm for a few years to get some skills.

The apprehension these students experience about practicing law provides them with an account for not pursuing public interest jobs. Students come to believe that they must join a large law firm for a while in order to develop the necessary lawyering skills. One third-year student explained why he was joining a large firm.

> It's hard to go directly into public interest jobs because you don't have much experience. They don't have the time or resources to train you. The large firm, on the other hand, gives you all this training. Some places even have special programs set up so they can train new lawyers. I think it's important to get a couple of years of good training after law school.

Students begin to feel that their professional development will be adversely affected should they choose not to accept an offer form a commercial law firm. While law students no doubt require further training in clinical settings in order to become accomplished professionals, the amount of training one receives during the first two years in a law firm tends to me minimal. New associates have little client contact, spend few hours in court, have minimal autonomy, and are generally relegated to the task of doing legal research.[40]

This point, however, is of little matter in the performance of ideological work. What matters is that a student comes to believe in the legitimacy of this reasoning. *Indeed, the character of ideological work is not contained in the truth or falsehood of a belief.* Ideological work can only exist where there are strong beliefs that are used to legitimate action. For these students, working in a large commercial law firm is not perceived as an indication of their ideological preferences. They see their affiliation as an extension of their law school training. Such practice is defined by some as their "clinical years." Seen from this perspective then, law students struggle less with their decision to enter corporate law firms because it reflects not upon their identity but upon their lack of skill, a fact that students believe necessitates they work in a commercial law firm.

6. The appeal to autonomy

Another appeal offered by Harvard law students to reduce the conflict between their social activist ideals and their career decisions is to assert their relative autonomy from the corporate interests they will serve as lawyers. Nearly 28 percent of the students used this reason to explain their job choice. For instance, one student, who had accepted a job with a prestigious Wall Street firm, explained he was not a corporate tool because he was intending to maintain his autonomy.

> I don't believe I'm a corporate tool. I'm working for a large firm but I don't think it's against my principles, which are left-oriented. People are a little surprised when they find out I'm going to a big firm because my activities on the Civil Rights/Civil Liberties journal and other left-leaning things. People who are corporate tools are politically right wing and have a vested interest in upholding that power structure. Corporate tools seek to uphold that power structure in an affirmative way and come here to learn to do that. I'm not a corporate tool. I intend to work on the right side of the cases I'll be involved in. I'm going to make deals, not fuck people over.

While this student recognized "a little contradiction" between his values and his practices, he was not disturbed by it, since he had not "bought into" what he described as a corporate orientation. He perceived himself to be socially progressive and even a little rebellious, despite the fact that he had chosen to practice in a large prestigious law firm on Wall Street. His continued identification with liberal and left politics allowed him to neutralize the conflict that he periodically experienced.

Students also make appeals to their autonomy by drawing fine distinctions between the types of law that divide the "tool" from themselves. This is a particularly effective strategy of neutralizing conflict. One student described why being a corporate attorney is not the same as a "hired gun."

> I wouldn't want to be a corporate litigator because they're just tools. The myth is that all corporate firms are cut-throat. That myth comes from litigation departments. As a corporate litigator you have to take the side that your client is on, regardless of what it might be. In corporate transactions lawyers are mediators, they bring people together. Corporate lawyers aren't like corporate litigators. They're not charlatans. I don't think I'm a corporate tool. I think you're a corporate tool if you do corporate litigation, not corporate law.

Students holding social activist ideals but who intend to enter corporate practice, are deeply offended when others label them as tools. Not unlike Sykes and Matza's techniques of neutralization, these students rejected those who condemned their decisions by perceiving such students as childish and immature.[41] A twenty-eight-year-old student, who entered Harvard to do environmental law but had decided to work at a large commercial law firm in Seattle, commented:

> I don't like the term "corporate tool" because it carries with it the notion that there is only good and bad work—good work is public interest work and bad is doing corporate work. The term corporate tool could mean that you've given up your ideals and are just doing work. I think most people who know me would not see me as a tool because I still have ideals. The people who are critical of what I'm doing are a bit naive. I'm really offended by them. They don't even really know me and they consider me a tool. I haven't given up on my ideals and I don't believe that working for a corporate law firm will alter those ideals either. In fact, I think that I can be a voice of reason for some corporations.

Such appeals to autonomy are common strategies among students who continue to identify with activist goals but have chosen to work at large commercial law firms. The belief that they have retained their political ideals and can remain independent from corporate interests helps neutralize the conflict these students experience.

7. *The appeal to personal conflict*

Some students accommodate corporate interests by offering apologies and by seeking public forgiveness from others. Nearly 20 percent described how making the decision to practice corporate law involved great personal conflict.

Students develop a vocabulary of contrition to justify their career decisions. Such justifications are not only a critical part of one's own ideological work but have important implications for collective practices. Students are drawn together by the activity of account-giving, thereby building a community that is held together through the collective expression of remorse. Repentant roles are particularly effective neutralizers of guilt.[42]

The vocabulary of contrition law students use to explain their career choice relinquishes them from any individual responsibility associated with their job selection. In fact, students are sometimes expected by others to present "reasonable" justifications for entering a large law firm. One student explained,

> It's a painful decision to make between doing public interest work and law firm work. I didn't feel comfortable about doing law firm work until I came to terms with it. It's been painful but I think I've made the right decision. I have a friend who is going through the same process. She originally wanted to be a prosecutor but has decided to go into a business firm. I had a tough discussion with her and I was pressing her [with questions like], "Is this good for you? Are you planning on staying? Will this further you? Is there an opportunity to do good work?" What I was asking her to do was to rationalize her decision which is what I did. It's important that people feel good about their decisions.

In justifying their decisions, students employ a series of motives and strategies that explain themselves. Indeed, it is this justifying activity that differentiates these students from students whom they would classify as "corporate tools." The very fact or at least appearance that their job choice poses a significant conflict suggests to themselves and others that they are not "tools." The expression of conflict disavows students from any association with corporate toolism. Students often seek understanding and sympathy from their fellow classmates. A second-year student committed to public interest work explained that

> People come up to me all the time at parties and confess their sins about not doing public interest work. People who are of liberal-left persuasions come up and tell me that they're working for a big firm and they feel terrible about it. They say that they have big loans to pay off. It's a little sad. People aren't fully approving of what they're doing in their own minds.

Another student, a third-year male, reported having similar experiences.

> A lot of people come to me as someone who has made the decision never to go the large firm route. Some people come to me who have decided to go

163

the corporate route and they want to explain themselves to me. There's a lot of guilt that people experience.

The conflict students experience is neutralized by publicly announcing their guilt, only to offer a series of accounts to justify their decisions. One student publicly expressed her disturbance with the decision to do corporate law: "I talk to a lot of people here about how hard and difficult this decision has been for me." This public expression of guilt is part of the collective ideological work carried on within the law student culture. Students offer social apologies in order to demonstrate their "real" identity and disclaim the identity of the "tool." A third-year Law Review student commented,

> Most people have doubts about what they're doing. I'm not real happy about going to a firm. I make lots of apologies to other students. I'm still upset about the fact that my clients are real wealthy people and it's not clear as to what the social utility of what I will be doing will be.

Very often students rely upon the same types of accounts and apologies. This suggests that strategies of accommodation are part of the stock of knowledge within the student culture. The exchange of accounts that takes place within the law school student culture provides a release from the tension associated with their career decisions, by producing an atmosphere in which collective acts of contrition are expressed. One second-year student summed this up by saying,

> There's a tendency for each person here to reinforce the next. It's OK to go to work in this atmosphere [a large firm] instead of a public interest one because everyone else is doing it and they all feel the same guilt that I feel. They all justify as much as I do. They all give the same reasons.

8. The appeal to resistance

One final strategy of accommodation that students use involves resistance. While fewer than 15 percent of the students employed this tactic, it demonstrates the subtlety of the ideological work they perform. In recent years, the concept of resistance in schooling and its consequence has gained considerable interest.[43] Derived largely from critical ethnographies of schooling, research has sought to gain an understanding of how activities of resistance may paradoxically contribute to the maintenance of the status quo. As Apple points out, "whatever reproduction goes on is accomplished not only through the acceptance of hegemonic ideologies, but through opposition and resistances."[44] Ironically, the forms of resistance that reside within educational institutions may ultimately tend towards the production and reproduction of dominant social relations.

With regard to Harvard law students, resistance is reproductive when practices and beliefs justify one's accommodation of corporate law firms. Many students, for instance, engage in symbolic acts of resistance even as they accept legal positions within corporate law firms. One student "resisted" by taking a job in a large firm where he would practice labor law. Seeing himself as being on the side of labor, as opposed to management, made this student's decision less difficult, since he believed he was resisting the corporate emphasis. Another third-year student, who originally entered law school with a desire to do civil rights litigation, resisted the elitist orientation within the law school by taking a large firm job but in a non-prestigious city. He explained his resistance in the following way:

> I don't think that I'm a typical Harvard law student. I've tried to stay away from this place as much as possible. There are so many people here who are just interested in making lots of money. That really bugs me about this place. Fortunately, I have been able to avoid all that. I'm not going to be herded off to New York, Los Angeles, or Chicago like most people here. I have chosen an alternative path. I've decided to go to a law firm in San Antonio. It's a big firm but it's not like the ones in those other cities. I'm actually proud that I haven't gotten caught up in the Harvard syndrome.

The accommodation to large law firm practice made by this student is significant. During law school, he was active in a number of political activities, including opposition to apartheid and Harvard's investment in South Africa. He was outspoken in his opposition to United States' involvement in Latin America, and was an active member of a student organization that provided legal assistance to the poor in Cambridge. He considered himself on the "far left" and had original intentions of practicing public interest law. Ironically, however, his opposition to the elite culture of Harvard Law School was used as a strategy to accommodate the very form of practice that he was opposed to. In his very last days of law school, just before his final exams, his intolerance over the elitism of the school had grown to a feverish pitch. He felt that he had been permanently damaged by his experience at the law school. He had "no respect" for his classmates who were all taking "the path of least resistance" by joining large commercial law firms in Los Angeles, Chicago, Washington, or New York. Because he maintained a view of himself as having been spared the negative aspects of elite culture, he experienced little conflict over his decision to join a large law firm.

This chapter has demonstrated that job choice among Harvard law students poses ideological conflict, which is resolved through strategies of accommodation that justify their immediate career plans. This ideological work prepares students for large corporate law firms by helping them neutralize the contradiction experienced by accepting such employment. Consequently, students develop the self-serving ideology that there is no ideology involved in their job choice. For these law students, such choices, while appearing contradictory, actually reflect practical needs, temporary arrangements, or perhaps even greater insight into where one can best contribute to social reform.

Given the class background of these students and the intense materialism of the 1980s, it is little wonder that they constructed ideologies that conveniently directed them towards America's giant law firms. The enormous salaries offered by most of these law firms, as well as the status and prestige that adheres to such firms, are extremely seductive. The seductiveness of these jobs is no doubt stronger at elite schools like Harvard, due to the relative ease in gaining access to such firms. The social networks between Harvard Law School and the giant firms are so embedded that it is often more difficult for a student to get a lower paying public interest job. This structural linkage between the school and these law firms provide the social context under which students practice ideological work. The ideological work carried out by these students on a daily basis is directly related to the placement of the law school in the larger social structure.

Today, law schools play a major role in directly allocating students to positions within the legal hierarchy. Students in the most elite schools have direct exposure to large law firm practices throughout their professional training. In fact, for most law students, actual law firm work has become a central component of their educational experiences. The direct intrusion of corporate interests into law schools such as Harvard has increased exponentially since the mid-1970s. Students in law schools during this period witnessed a growing intimacy between legal professionals and the corporate elite. As a result, there were dramatic shifts in patterns of employment and practice. The relative number of sole practitioners has consistently fallen over the past three decades, while the number of lawyers employed as associates in law firms has increased significantly.[45] Indeed, there has been a significant growth of large law practices over the past decade alone. According to a recent *Wall Street Journal* article,

> Many law firms . . . expanded at incredible rates. Gibson Dunn more than tripled in size to about 700 lawyers in 1980 to 1,221 in 1990. An annual survey of firms ranging from 69 lawyers to more than 1,500 showed annual growth of 9% or 10% between 1985 and 1988.[46]

As Derber has recently pointed out, professions and business in contemporary society have established a mutually beneficial bond.[47] This bond will no doubt contribute to some forms of "professionalism" that are compatible with corporate and entrepreneurial interests.[48] Although initially disinclined toward corporate legal practice, these law students effectively redefined these firms in ways that were compatible with their own ideological and emerging professional interests. The contradiction they experienced in their schooling was resolved by constructing a rationality legitimizing their job choice. Such practices illustrate the ideological work many professionals use to adjust to the imperatives of the workplace.

Ideological work, however, is often quite tentative. Dilemmas can often become so great that no amount of ideological work will create a sense of symmetry and coherence. Under those conditions, radical personal decisions are made. Despite the enormous salaries corporate attorneys receive, many appear to be dropping out of this type of legal practice. One corporate lawyer who resigned from a large law firm after several years of practice explained that he was "tired of the deceit" and disturbed by the lack of concern placed on social justice.[49] His decision to leave may illustrate the fragile nature of ideological work. The practice of ideological work involves an ongoing struggle. Dilemmas like the ones faced by these law students are never completely resolved. Breakdowns in ideological work often result in significant change in an individual's life-style. Understanding the fragile nature of ideological work among corporate lawyers may give greater insight into the difficulties many of these individuals seem to experience throughout their professional lives.

◆ 10 ◆

The Public Interest Law School

An Alternative Challenge or the Illusion of Difference?

To what extent can educational institutions promote alternative visions and practices in their students? Can a school be oppositional to the dominant paradigm so as not only to represent a counter-hegemonic initiative, but also to succeed in producing students that are fundamentally different from those receiving hegemonic forms of education? Within recent years, there has been a groundswell of theoretical interest in the possibility of resistance and radical pedagogy. Of central concern to these theorists is the promotion of alternative public spheres so as to provide the conditions for the development of transformative intellectuals. As Aronowitz and Giroux assert, the starting point of any radical education is

> an understanding of how knowledge and patterns of social relations steeped in domination come into being in schools, how they are maintained, how students, teachers, and others relate to them, and how they can be exposed, modified, and overcome, if possible.[1]

168

Such alternative educational institutions and pedagogies would, however, not only strive to critique the dominant paradigms of power relations, but would also foster collective empowerment among students so as to encourage oppositional practices and principles.

This chapter examines the history, social organization, and internal contradictions within one such "alternative" law school in order to investigate whether its design and emergent culture produces greater numbers of social activist lawyers. This law school provides a unique opportunity to explore the emergence of an oppositional educational institution, pedagogical efforts that encourage transformative possibilities, and the internal contradictions that threaten to undermine its alternative vision.

Northeastern University School of Law: Alternative to Convention

Across Boston's Charles River and the spacious confines of Harvard Law School lies Northeastern University School of Law. Housed in an austere four-story concrete edifice, the School of Law is located at the westernmost edge of Northeastern University's urban campus. In contrast to Harvard's tranquil surroundings, the law school at Northeastern occupies a small corner building that is flanked on two sides by congested city streets. Subway trains from the Massachusetts Bay Transit Authority's "Green Line" regularly pass along the front of the law school, and their horn blasts often disrupt students studying in the library or concentrating on class lectures.

The physical atmosphere of the law school is noticeably leftist. Walking into the law school one is immediately greeted with a display of books that reflect liberal and left political interests. Most of these displays deal with social problems such as racial discrimination, environmental issues, labor and women's struggles, poverty, and social inequality. On walls that stretch along the narrow corridors are posters and announcements advertising an assortment of left-oriented political issues, including gay and lesbian meetings, fundraisers and benefits for Nicaragua and South Africa, National Lawyers Guild and Critical Legal Studies meetings, and statements criticizing policies from the law school to the White House.

1. The early days

Initiated through the activities of the Young Men's Christian Association in 1898, the school was originally part of an effort by elites to ease the transition of "worthy" working-class immigrants into American society. Like many other major cities during this period, immigrants had come to occupy a large segment of Boston's population. By 1899, the largest concentration of Boston's population was foreigners.[2] Although advanced education was available in Boston at the time, few opportunities existed for those unable to shoulder tuition costs. The Boston YMCA, founded in 1851, was the first in the nation, and was soon followed by others. Dedicated to a goal of promoting men of moral character for the purposes of "americanizing" them, the YMCA offered working-class men the opportunity for physical, social, and intellectual development. Bible classes were taught alongside gymnasium activities. Language courses were provided, as were courses in bookkeeping, algebra, music, penmanship, stenography, and electricity.

In addition, special courses were instituted. One such special course was in law. On 3 October 1898, Robert Gray Dodge, one year out of Harvard Law School, launched what was to become the Boston YMCA Law School with a lecture on "property." Dodge had been hired by the Boston YMCA to coordinate courses in law. The courses were all conducted at night, thereby allowing students to work by day while studying law at night.

The part-time evening law schools that emerged during this period were subject to intense criticism. Unlike the Suffolk Law School evening program, which was considered a maverick among the elite legal community, the Boston YMCA Law School received favorable treatment from the legal establishment.[3] This was primarily due to its relationship with elite law institutions. Begun as a colony of Harvard Law School as well as Boston University Law School, the faculty at the "Y" was often composed of the very same persons who offered law courses across the river. James Barr Ames, Harvard Law School dean and a first-generation descendent of Christopher Columbus Langdell, as well as other distinguished faculty members such as Louis Brandeis, left their ivy-trimmed towers of Harvard to travel to the spartan halls of the "Y" to offer instruction in law.[4]

The law curriculum was very conventional. Courses in pleading, property, criminal law, contracts, and torts were offered four evenings a week.[5] Within six years the program of law at the Boston YMCA had grown in tremendous proportion, so that by 1904 the school boasted of having had 662 students enrolled since its opening. Forty-two men had been graduated in the two classes of 1902 and 1903, and thirty-seven of those graduates were admitted to the bar. The success of the school was officially recognized in 1904, when the Committee on Education of the Massachusetts Legislature granted the school the right to incorporate and confer degrees in law.[6] Twenty degrees were awarded in 1904 and 1905 to evening students, whose occupations included merchants, bookkeepers, and salesmen.

Many of those attending the YMCA Law School were men who possessed good academic credentials from Brown, Harvard, Boston University, and Amherst College.[7] The fact that many of its students were from respectable social backgrounds, as evidenced by their advanced degrees, explains why the school received a favorable reception from the legal community.[8] However, despite the number of students who attended local and national colleges, most were not college graduates.[9] Over time the student body grew, so that by 1926 enrollment had reached 2,440 students. Extension programs were established in Worcester, Springfield, and Providence, and in 1938 day classes were initiated.

Over the next fifteen years the Law School achieved nominal recognition. Now officially affiliated with Northeastern University, the Law School boasted that 25 percent of all Massachusetts judges were among its alumni, as were several bank presidents and assorted local politicians.[10] Despite this success, the Law School faced fierce competition from an overdeveloped market. By the early 1950s, faced with increased competition from other area law schools, and with the burden of having to increase expenditures in order to retain certification, a decision was made to discontinue the School of Law. In April of 1953, the Board of Trustees of Northeastern University voted to close the school. No entering class was accepted for the following September, and the last graduating class received degrees in 1956. Shortly thereafter, the school, with its library and other materials, was sold to the University of Puerto Rico, thereby removing any trace of the school from the university.

The decision to close the Law School, however, was never one that was accepted by its alumni, who felt that they had been abandoned. In 1961, after only a brief hiatus, the Law School Alumni Association communicated requests to the university that the Law School be reopened. While no commitment to reestablish the Law School was given, Northeastern University president, Asa Knowles, was willing to consider the proposal. In his communique to these alumni Knowles wrote, "I want you to know that this whole matter is very much on my mind."[11] Although hesitant to make a firm commitment, Knowles suggested that the alumni establish a committee to investigate the amount of support there was for reopening the school.

On Knowles' suggestion a committee of Law School alumni was formed, and by the spring of 1964 it had procured $150,000 in pledges toward reopening the school.[12] This overwhelming response and support from the alumni were received favorably by Knowles, so that in 1965 he introduced the idea of reopening the school to the Board of Trustees. The board, concerned about the costs of reopening the school, requested that alumni raise a sum of one million dollars to help defray expenses. Within a year and a half, after organizing Law School alumni throughout the country, a substantial portion of the total sum had been raised. On 13 May 1966, with $500,000 already in sight, the Board of Trustees resolved that: "A School of Law be hereby authorized and established at Northeastern University."[13]

Although the necessary sum had been raised and a commitment from the Trustees given, obstacles still remained. The Board of trustees would only reopen the Law School on the grounds that it conform to the style of education that had come to characterize Northeastern University. In short, the school would have to incorporate a "cooperative" educational plan consisting of rotating academic and on-the-job schedules. A four-year program was initially decided upon, but it was soon discarded for fear of losing students to traditional three-year law schools. With hard work and frequent interaction with the American Bar Association regarding its standards, the Law School's first dean developed a plan that limited the course of study to the conventional three-year period. Such a plan called for overloading the first year of study with one extra course, condensing another first-year course into three months, and offering a summer semester. With most of the bugs worked out, the School of Law at Northeastern University reopened in the fall of 1968. Twenty-three students, mostly from the Boston area, were admitted into the program leading to a JD, the first such program in the United States to offer a Cooperative Plan of Legal Education.

2. *The rise of an "alternative" law school*

From its inception, the newly reopened Law School at Northeastern University was unique. While being the first law school in the country to admit equal or even larger proportions of women and having a curriculum that included mandatory clinical experience, the school represented a clear alternative to conventional law schools. Most of the faculty hired by the school had received their law degrees from Harvard Law School, thereby reaffirming the historical connection that once existed between the two schools. Of the fourteen-member faculty in 1970, 64 percent had graduated from Harvard Law School. This fact is significant, since much of the unique character of the new Law School was based upon a rejection of the type of legal education these individuals experienced while at Harvard. The criticism of traditional methods of legal instruction, as well as of its orientation to forms of practice, is evidenced in the school's statement of purpose, outlined in its 1970 program catalog.

> The purpose of the Northeastern University School of Law is to train lawyers who can meet the challenges and obligations cast upon the profession by contemporary society. The school was founded on the conviction that traditional legal education inadequately approaches this goal, and that law schools

172

have not altered their programs quickly enough to match the pace of change on the world and national scene. The most frequently remarked shortcoming of traditional law school training is the neglect of the practical side of a lawyer's work. The consequence of this omission is that newly graduated students are poorly equipped to pursue their profession until they have been exposed to a period of apprenticeship. In this respect they suffer badly in comparison with their contemporaries who enter other professions. *Even more serious is the failure of law school curriculum to reflect a genuine concern for the urgent problems of American society. Although our society leans heavily upon lawyers for solutions to its social, economic and political problems, the narrow training afforded by a conventional curriculum does not equip the lawyer for these tasks. To a remarkable degree, the typical course of studies appears to be based upon the narrow assumption that most graduates seek to enter very large law firms where they are likely to work chiefly on the problems of large corporations and financial institutions.*[14] (Emphasis added)

The unique character of the new Law School, as expressed by this statement, was both practical and ideological. Cooperative legal education at Northeastern was unfavorably received by the legal practitioners in the Boston establishment. Few area practitioners were willing to employ students from Northeastern. Elitism and the hegemony of the Harvard model posed difficulties for Northeastern. Recognizing this resistance, the Law School faculty began to call upon friends and alumni. As one law professor commented, they began to "twist the arms of everyone they knew" in order to successfully place their students. Through the use of their strong tie networks in small practices as well as public interest clinics, students received placements in various locations throughout the country.

The story behind this school goes much further than a pedagogical challenge. A second feature of the newly developed Law School, and perhaps the most important, was ideological. Energized by the spirit of the late 1960's, the New Left student movement, the feminist movement, and the establishment of the O.E.O. Legal Services program under the Johnson administration, the Law School sought to overcome the elitist and corporate orientation of most traditional law schools. The ideological role of the Law School was to be consistent with the values reflected by 1960's social activists; students would be trained for the goal of providing legal services to the poor, minorities, and oppressed social groups.

Reviewing the program of studies for first-year students in 1971, the ideological character of the Law School is plainly visible. In their constitutional issues course students were to study "draft resistance" and "de facto segregation," while in their economic justice course they would explore "the potential use of the tax mechanism to effect social change." In their criminal justice course they would examine issues of "search and seizure" and "wire-tapping," as well as spend time studying white-collar crimes. Students studied socialist conceptions of property in their land ownership and use course, while in torts students would examine the "availability of tort remedies for wrongful conduct against disadvantaged persons," as well as consider the "economic and social realities" of "current proposals for social distribution of losses." The ideological mission of the newly constituted Law School was to emphasize the progressive values of economic and social justice.

The School of Law at Northeastern presented itself as an ideological alternative to traditional forms of legal study. Individuals who wished to play a role in promoting social change could find sincere commitment and competent instruction. Its commitment to social change and democratic values also lead the faculty to shape a school culture that reflected those values. Letter grades were eliminated in all courses, and a pass/fail system with written evaluations became the standard measurement of a student's progress. This practice abolished the system of class ranking that existed within most traditional law schools. In addition, the Law School's departure from traditional programs was found in the faculty's unwillingness to support a Law Review, for fear it would lead to increased competition among students. Indeed, the Law School at Northeastern reflected a political and cultural alternative to the conservative and corporate values promulgated within most schools of law.

The Current Reality: Who Attends Northeastern?

The Northeastern University School of Law is characterized as a "special" place and its students as "extraordinary" people.[15] This emphasis on the extraordinary character of the Law School has, over the years, served as its principal marketing strategy. Being the most recent law school to emerge in an already crowded law school market in Boston, Northeastern Law School has sought to elevate its status by tapping an untapped market. By emphasizing high academic standards while offering a mixture of practical and humanistically sensitive instruction, the Law School at Northeastern sought its niche within the legal education marketplace.[16] The school is presented as a place where students can achieve personal growth and professional competence without having to sacrifice their ideals. Unlike traditional schools, the Law School at Northeastern communicates an image of community, diversity, equality, and idealism.

Analysis of student motivations for attending Northeastern indicates that they choose to attend for two primary reasons: the school is practical, and it is politically significant. In most cases, however, the students interviewed fell into two distinct groups. While many attend the Law School because of its political image, and see its practical emphasis as better preparing them to be activist lawyers, others are attracted by the emphasis on practical experience, which they believe will help them acquire jobs in commercial law firms. The distinction between these two groups and the conflict that this difference creates is a central feature of student life at Northeastern.

1. *A law school for radicals*

Among the reasons students listed for attending Northeastern School of Law, concern with social change, achieving social justice, and helping people all rank high. Nearly 43 percent of the students reported being motivated by these interests. Such a high percentage seems to attest to Northeastern's ability to attract students who are oriented towards social activism. One student, for instance, commented that

> I thought law school would give me the skills to help people. I was interested in family law and thought I could be a lawyer/counselor. I came to law school because I thought it would be the best thing for what I wanted to do.

Some expressed interest in helping a specific population—

> I wanted to work for abused and neglected kids, and some delinquency work. I was concerned about how decisions are made about kids' lives. I was interested in giving kids a voice, empowering them because they are under-represented.

—while others entered with more general advocacy concerns:

> I'm 42 and have spent most of my work life in community non-profit groups in a range of human services and advocacy. I came to law school to learn how to better promote those interests.

As was true at Harvard, several Northeastern students had chosen law school because of their interest in social change. A former labor organizer, who spent time working among California grape-pickers, reported:

> I was working in the United Farm Workers Union in the 1970s. I was exposed to labor conflict and it made me conscious of how law effects labor,

and I became interested in law. I came to law school because I wanted to change the system.

Another student, a former social worker who worked with abused women, offered similar reasons for attending Northeastern.

> I had been working in social work and I decided that I would make a better advocate for clients as a lawyer. I wasn't interested in money, but in social change.

A great deal of pre–law school idealism regarding law and legal practice was evidenced by these students. A third-year female student who had grown up in a major metropolitan area where she witnessed "bad things happening to people," explained that

> I thought that all lawyers spent their times in court. I had no idea that most lawyers never go to court. I thought that if you came in with "just" ideas and what was right then you would win. I always thought law would prevail.

This student's concern for resolving problems drove her to law school with the hope of playing a role in promoting social justice. Such was the case with another student who, having a previous career in social work, wanted legal training to assist her with her "humanistic" activities.

> The law I thought was a structure we live by, standards we set. I thought of law as effecting the way people live. I saw it as a system that you have to live in but one that could help people. I came to law school to be a better advocate for people with problems.

For many of these students, Northeastern was their first choice among law schools. In several cases, students had been working in social service careers or had engaged in various forms of political work, and became aware of Northeastern's leftist reputation through their networks. Students often reported becoming interested in law school only after hearing about Northeastern's political orientation. As one student explained,

> After college I went to work for Nine to Five. I was interested in empowering women. After a while in that organization I became a little discouraged with it, and I thought about how I could have more power in changing things related to working women. I was never really interested in law school, but one of the people I worked with was going to Northeastern and she told me about program. The public interest orientation was really attractive to me.

Similarly, another student commented that she learned about Northeastern's reputation through her activist friends.

> I was involved in political work after receiving my graduate degree. A lot of things that I was involved in doing seemed to be related to law. I really didn't want to be a lawyer because of the image they have, but then my friends told me about Northeastern. I hadn't heard about it, but it seemed best suited for my political interests.

Another student, whose activist credentials included a period of time working as a union organizer, offered a similar account.

> Coming from an underdeveloped country I have always had a perspective on law and capitalism. I was exposed to labor conflict and it made me conscious of how law effects labor. I became interested in law. I didn't really want to be a lawyer because they are corrupt, particularly in my country. I heard about Northeastern through my contacts in organizing and thought that it fit with my philosophical viewpoints.

These students all felt that Northeastern would further empower them as social activists. Indeed, these students had chosen the Law School for the explicit purpose of entering public interest forms of legal practice upon graduation.

2. A law school for the career-minded

A second group attending the Law School, however, possessed little interest in public interest law. Nearly 30 percent of the Northeastern sample reported being motivated by interests such as monetary gain, job security, career enhancement, and social status. These students often reported having been unfamiliar with the political reputation of Northeastern, and having chosen it solely on the basis of its "co-op" program.[17] As one student explained, "I chose Northeastern because the amount of practical experience would give me a leg up on other law students in the area."

These students often selected Northeastern after being rejected by higher status schools. Most reported having applied to other area law schools first. Forty-seven percent, for instance, reported having applied to Boston University Law School, while only 23 percent reported being accepted. Similarly, 40 percent reported that they applied to Boston College Law School, with only 25 percent being accepted. In addition, 20 percent applied for a seat at Harvard Law School, with only one student having reported being accepted.

By contrast, of the 31 percent of the Northeastern students who applied to Suffolk University Law School, a school whose reputation is considered below that of Northeastern, all but one student reported to have been accepted. A similar pattern exists for those students who applied to New England School of Law, a proprietary law school, whose reputation is evaluated below that of Suffolk. Of the only 11 percent of the Northeastern students applying to this school, all were accepted but chose not to attend.

These statistics suggest that for many students the decision to attend Northeastern was based upon their failure to gain entrance into a "more prestigious" law school. As one second-year student commented,

> Northeastern wasn't my first choice but my third. I wanted to go to [another law school] but was rejected. When I got accepted at Northeastern I looked into their "co-op" program. I found that really attractive.

Another student, a first-year Black male who unabashedly expressed financial reasons for choosing a career in law, stated:

> I grew up in poverty and spent six years in a boy's home. Upward mobility is a key for me. I wanted to be successful for my ego, my family, and any children I might have . Being a lawyer is the epitome of success. I applied to Harvard and didn't get in. I also got rejected at a couple of other schools. Northeastern was the best school I got accepted at. The fact that it has a co-op program though will help me advance my career. It will give me the experience to get high paying jobs.

For students who chose Northeastern for financially rewarding careers, public interest work was hardly an option. While many of these students were sympathetic to public interest goals, few were attracted to it. One first-year student commented,

> I want to make money and live a fairly comfortable life so public interest work is out of the picture for me. I'm not sure I want to work at a large firm because you'll probably end up by screwing people. I want to help people in my legal practice, not screw them.

Internal contradictions

As was the case at Harvard Law School, students at Northeastern organized themselves around the individualist/altruist polarity within law. While several students selected Northeastern Law School in order to promote social justice,

178

others attended for strictly careerist reasons. This bifurcation created considerable tension within the student culture at the law school. Students who gravitated toward the altruistic side of legal practice expressed concern with what they believe to be the encroaching commercialism at the school. Over the years, the Northeastern chapter of the National Lawyers Guild has attempted to pressure the administration into maintaining the school's commitment to public interest. Some students have even proposed that school officials limit the number of "corporate"-oriented students they enroll each year. However, most feel they are fighting a losing battle. One third-year woman, reflecting upon the struggles she has witnessed, commented:

> I don't like the bad feeling in this school. Because there's no clear sense about what kind of school we should be people just rip each other up. The school is really changing. I've seen that over these past three years and I don't like it. It's no longer a public interest school. They tell us that there aren't many public interest types applying anymore. I just don't believe that. Northeastern has built its reputation on public interest law. I think that they have begun to go after more conventional types of students.

The bitterness and dissatisfaction that these students feel is, at times, great. Although most reported having had positive experiences, largely as a result of associating with other public interest students, they often reacted strongly to both students and faculty who did not appear oriented towards the altruistic pole within law. In one course, students organized a boycott against a teacher who they believed failed to adequately confront issues concerning racism, sexism, and poverty. Students found one class particularly egregious. The legal problem involved equal protection under the first amendment, and whether women had equal protection against inequitable welfare benefits. During his discussion of the case, a student raised the following concern:

S: Why can't we just make a commitment about the fairness of welfare that people should live above the poverty level?

T: How would you decide that?

S: Statistics could give you some idea of what people need and you could just make sure that people didn't fall below a certain level.

T: What kind of statistics? Most statistics are contradictory and therefore not of any value. Plus statistics are used to define things in different ways. They can't be trusted.

179

S: But there should be at least a minimum level so people can live.

T: What kind of minimum level? How would you determine it? Most people would agree that statistics don't relate to poverty. How would you do it? I agree with you from a philosophical point of view but I don't think a judge can just do it. What would you order? If you're going to argue these cases you're going to have to be pragmatic. If you order housing, where?

S: Instead of reforming a bad system why not have stricter rules on something like campaign contributions, because powerful elites dominate decision-making about welfare benefits.

T: Well, things are related but I would rather stick to the issue.

As is the case at Harvard, the legal instruction at Northeastern places an emphasis on pragmatism, and often views legal problems as self-contained issues that are unrelated to a larger social context.

A number of students expressed deep frustration and anger with this teacher's unwillingness to articulate a social justice orientation. While these students were primarily concerned about the injustice of poverty, the teacher seemed only interested in exploring technical issues. Neither did he appear willing to consider the argument that "poverty is unjust," or that legal remedies to poverty should go beyond the immediate issue by altering the process of political participation and decision-making.

In another class, this seeming unwillingness to challenge the foundations of legal ideology was again challenged. The teacher posed a hypothetical case which directly involved three individuals whose actions resulted in the death of a fourth person. The teacher presented the following scenario:

> An employee of the Acme company was injured on the job. The employee's supervisor instructed a second employee to drive the injured man to the hospital as quickly as possible, thereby encouraging the driver to intentionally violate traffic laws. In route to the hospital the driven went through a stop sign and was struck by another motorist who was speeding. While neither driver was injured, the man being taken to the hospital died.

After outlining the fact situation, the teacher asked students where they would assign criminal responsibility for manslaughter. Students were told that there was no correct answer; they only needed to explore the various legal issues. For the most part, class discussion focused on trying to determine which of the three individuals should be charged with negligent homicide. However, one student, a particularly vocal left-wing student, voiced an alternative view.

S: What about going after the company. It could be demonstrated that the company knowingly subjected the injured man to a dangerous situation.

T: OK, the company was perhaps wrong but what can you do? The issue is are they guilty of manslaughter. Even if you could find the company was reckless it is difficult, because of the issue of cause. For instance, the supervisor acted recklessly by instructing the second employee to drive as rapidly as possible.

S: Well, using the Model Penal Code, why couldn't you go after the company?

T: You need the court to see the link between what they did and what happened is sufficiently close enough to establish proof beyond a reasonable doubt. The causality problem is the issue here.

S: [Continuing with his point] I still think that you can go after the company. You could show that the company had a history of neglect and numerous safety violations. [As the student spoke, several other students began getting restless with his argument.]

T: [Noticing the restlessness in the class] Well, the problem is one of causality. If you would like to continue this, we should talk after class. [The teacher went on discussing the assignment of criminal liability for the three individuals.]

When I was discussing the matter with the student after class, he expressed anger and frustration. "This is what I really don't like about this so-called public interest school," he complained. "They portray themselves as being an alternative place when in fact they are very conventional."

Experiences like these take a toll on activist-oriented students. In spite its alternative reputation, Northeastern University School of Law still represents a "professionalizing" institution. Because of this, the latitude of discourse within the pedagogy is severely restricted. Indeed, the role of the school is to train lawyers who are competent enough to pass a state bar examination. In so doing, Northeastern law students, like their Harvard counterparts, must acquire the skills and knowledge associated with the legal profession. In spite of its alternative image, the school must teach students to "think like lawyers." Moreover, in order to maintain its academic legitimacy, the school must conform to a professional image so as to continue to attract students and receive accreditation. Unless the school can train students to pass the bar exams and participate in the professional community, its legitimacy as an institution would be seriously jeopardized.

This, however, creates a serious dilemma for many of the Northeastern law students. In a group conversation with three first-year law students at Northeastern, just a few months into their legal training, the tension they were beginning to experience was apparent.

> What really bothers me about this whole process is that there are never any answers. One judge argues this way and another argues differently. I thought law had something to do with justice, but I think now that it's all about making a good argument, a good justification. [twenty-four-year-old female]

> I know what you mean. What really bothers me is that I am finding myself being able to make strong arguments for positions that I am opposed to and consider irrational. I can construct rational arguments for irrational positions. That is disturbing. [twenty-six-year-old female]

> What bugs me is that it's affected my personal life. I get into arguments now with my wife or friends and I can really cut them up because of the logical inconsistencies I find in their arguments. I think in terms of rigid fact patterns, organization, and outcome. I have become too rational. I respond to things now on a cognitive level as much less of an emotional one. I feel that I have lost that side of me. [twenty-four-year-old male]

The fact that a number of altruistic-oriented students at Northeastern were disturbed by the type of instruction they received offers insight into the limited range of discourse articulated within the school. Although there are instructors who, as one told me, "try to be subversive," there is not a consistent message that supports social activist ideals. For social activist students, such limitations posed serious problems. Very often these students were critical of the school for what they perceived to be a shift in its ideological mission. As one first-year public interest student complained,

> This isn't a radical law school, it's not a public interest school. I think the school is really changing. I had heard that this was a real public interest place, but in many ways it's conservative. They're pushing for a more corporate emphasis. The administration tells us that they think it's a good idea if we get training in a large firm to see what it's like. I don't have any interest in what a large firm is like. Also, they teach the same courses that are taught everywhere else. There's very few, what I would call, real public interest courses. Many of the faculty don't have any training in public interest law and they often teach law from a non-public-interest perspective. Even our oral argument [18] doesn't relate to a public interest issue. It was basically a business dispute on a relatively small scale, but I wouldn't call it a "public interest" problem.

Students complained that the Law School disseminates a mixed message, one that praises the virtues of public interest law, while simultaneously encouraging large firm practice. Ironically, many of the administrators were proud of Northeastern's entrance into the larger firms, believing it signified proof of the school's success. One third-year woman complained that

> The school is really confused. You have some people who are committed to teaching law from a radical perspective, but then you have others who teach class and talk about their sailboats and going out for fancy meals. A lot of the students believe Northeastern is changing. There are a lot of confused messages going around. The dean gives messages about doing public interest, but that view isn't really consistently shared among the faculty.

The fate of idealism at Northeastern

In recent years, the school's ability to maintain an activist focus among its students has become increasingly difficult. In 1986, for instance, only 10 percent of its graduates entered public interest practices, as compared to 1978 when 22 percent of its graduates went into practices such as legal services. Only a meager 4 percent of Northeastern's graduates accepted legal aid positions in 1986.

While the trends at Northeastern tend to correspond to those occurring at Harvard, there are some major differences. Perhaps the most startling difference is that while Northeastern students similarly defined themselves as being on the left, there are indicators suggesting that students tempered their committments over time. Like Harvard students, Northeastern students believed that they had become more radical while in law school. Nearly 53 percent of the Northeastern sample reported having become more radical during law school, while only 20 percent claimed to have become more conservative.

Students, however, began to perceive themselves as less radical over time. As Table 10.1 indicates, while 53 percent of the first-year class believed to have become more radical during law school, only 36 percent reported

Table 10.1 Self-reported Shift in Political Attitudes by Year

	More Radical	Same	More Conservative
First	53%	38%	9%
Second	33	43	24
Third	36	32	32
	(N=34)	(N=30)	(N=16)

Kendall's Tau = .20; P < .01

this in their third year. By contrast, only 9 percent of first-year students reported becoming more conservative, compared to 32 of those in their third year.

This pattern appeared again when student interest in public interest law was examined. First-year students reported significantly greater interests in this area than did their third-year counterparts, 53 percent and 24 percent, respectively.

Table 10.2 Self-reported Interest in Public Interest Law by Year

	More	Same	Less
First	53%	30%	17%
Second	38	38	24
Third	24	20	56
	(N=32)	(N=23)	(N=25)

Kendall's Tau = .30; P < .001

There is a general trend away from the radical spirit of the school as students move through the program. The majority of first-year students, 69 percent, claimed to have become more interested in pro bono legal services, compared with only 44 percent of the third-year students. Moreover, students reported having become significantly less interested in resolving social problems and in fostering social change. Sixty-five percent of the first-year class believed themselves to have become more interested in resolving social problems, while only 32 percent of the third-year class reported this. Over 71 percent of the first-year class indicated having become more interested in social change since coming to law school, compared to only 44 percent of third-year students.

Table 10.3 Self-reported Interest in Pro Bono by Year

	More	Same	Less
First	69%	26%	5%
Second	38	38	24
Third	44	32	24
	(N=43)	(N=25)	(N=13)

Kendall's Tau = .23; P < .009

Table 10.4 Self-reported Interest in Resolving Social Problems by Year

	More	Same	Less
First	66%	20%	14%
Second	55	20	25
Third	32	24	44
	(N=42)	(N=17)	(N=21)

Kendall's Tau = .22; P < .002

Table 10.5 Self-reported Interest in Social Change by Year

	More	Same	Less
First	72%	14%	14%
Second	48	38	14
Third	44	36	20
	(N=46)	(N=22)	(N=13)

Kendall's Tau = .20; P < .04

During law school, students often began to believe that the opportunities to promote social change through law are exceedingly limited. One student commented with remorse:

> I came in to law school thinking it would be possible to make social change. In law school I began to realize that it's much harder to effectuate social change. You get real frustrated. You can maybe, maybe deal with small problems, but there's little that you can do to enact social change. I don't think you make social change in the legal context.

Coming to Northeastern Law School in her first year, this student recalled being excited about the possibilities of using law to advance progressive change. Though she didn't know how she would contribute to social change, she was interested in using her law degree to "do something about human suffering." However, instead of concentrating on social problems, she found a focus on individual concerns. This emphasis constitutes the core of the "case method" of legal pedagogy that prevails in law school. The case method, she complained is "so individually-oriented. All we studied for three years was one person fighting against another." This orientation to individual issues, however, had become a world-view that undermined this student's social change orientation. Similar to her counterparts at Harvard, this student explained, "I think I had a naive view of the law. You really can't change society through the legal context. It's too complicated."

Another third-year student, a twenty-eight-year-old female, feeling disenchanted with the limitations that law imposes upon efforts to bring about social change, offered similar reflections.

> I came to law school really interested in social change, particularly involving women's issues and criminal justice. I thought my first year here was positive. After awhile I became really disenchanted with the whole process. As I went along I learned that you never really accomplish much. I began to realize that you can't really accomplish much real social change with law. I think law is less fulfilling now because I recognize this. You really can't change much through legal analysis.

Although this student lamented over what she saw as the limitations of the judicial system, she nonetheless had grown to accept the legitimacy of the legal paradigm.

> I think there is value in helping individual clients though. You can't just go out and change things. I used to think that if something was unjust, well, change it. There are legal procedures that you have to follow and although this may prevent me from doing what I think I would like to do, legal procedure is important. We need it, otherwise there would be chaos. So I think that any change that will take place will have to be done on an incremental basis. I still believe that I can do good work, but I don't take it that seriously now.

Like so many of her activist counterparts at Northeastern, this student had accomplished an ideological redefinition of law and legal practice. No longer was it feasible to think that injustice could be rectified through law.

While many students at Northeastern generally held social activist forms of legal practice in high regard [63 percent, 75 percent, and 74 percent consider poverty law, public interest law, and civil rights law to be challenging and personally rewarding], there was a tendency for this to wane among second- and third-year law students. While almost half of the Northeastern students started their law school careers with a public interest consciousness, many experienced a dramatic transformation. Indeed, as tables 10.6 and 10.7 demonstrate, many students developed a greater interest in commercial areas of practice.

There was also a statistically significant pattern among these students to become increasingly more interested in corporate law firm settings. More than 73 percent of the first-year students in the Northeastern sample reported

Table 10.6 Self-reported Student Attitudes toward
Business by Year

	Favorable	Same	Unfavorable
First	6%	47%	47%
Second	14	57	29
Third	32	44	24
	(N=13)	(N=39)	(N=28)

Kendall's Tau = −.27; P < .05

being oriented toward non-corporate style forms of legal practice. While a small proportion of these students expressed interests in community law firms and in teaching, the overwhelming majority listed their most likely future practice as being public interest or social activist law.

The expression of a public interest orientation was highly visible within the first-year class. Most students expressed varying degrees of commitment to public interest practice. As one first-year student commented when asked about her future practice,

> It will definitely be in public interest, probably having something to do with women's issues. I don't think I would have come to law school if I couldn't do public interest law. That's what I'm going to be doing when I graduate. I've told everyone not to depend upon me for seventy thousand dollars. I just want enough to live on. I'm just not one bit interested in commercial stuff. Maybe it would be OK for a summer, but anything more than that is just unthinkable.

However, there was a significant increase among second-year and third-year students to entertain employment in large commercial law firms. While only 26 percent of the first-year students expressed an interest in large commercial firms, nearly three-quarters of the third-year class, 71 percent, reported that

Table 10.7 Self-reported Student Attitudes toward Tax
Law by Year

	Favorable	Same	Unfavorable
First	24%	8%	68%
Second	20	20	60
Third	44	22	34
	(N=19)	(N=10)	(N=34)

Kendall's Tau = −.24; P < .01

they anticipated their most likely and immediate future law practice would be in these settings.

Table 10.8 Anticipated Future Practice by Year

	Large Firms	Other
First	26%	74%
Second	31	69
Third	71	29
	(N=37)	(N=50)

Kendall's Tau = −.35; P < .001

This suggests that despite the pervasive public interest orientation that characterizes first-year students at Northeastern, students become significantly more oriented to commercial legal practice during law school. This growing interest in larger commercial law is also reflected in the internships students choose. A greater proportion of students choose large firm internship during law school than public interest ones. While public interest internships have remained relatively constant over the past few years, the number of students selecting large law firm internships has been steadily increasing. In addition, a greater number of students select multiple large firm internships than do students choosing multiple public interest internships. Between 1984 and 1988, approximately 33 percent of each class at Northeastern had selected more than one large or medium-sized law firm internship, compared with only 14 percent of those choosing multiple public interest internship placements.

Despite Northeastern's public interest orientation, increasing numbers of these students select positions in commercial law firms upon graduation. One third-year student who entered Northeastern with the intention of practicing public interest law, but who had taken a job with a large commercial law firm, explained:

> I came to law school because I was interested in union organizing. I have decided though to take a large firm job. I think I'm a typical Northeastern law student who comes in here fired up to do public interest but leaves here not doing that. I know that I really won't have very many opportunities to do the things I wanted to do when I came to law school, but I think that maybe I can be the voice of reason in the management side. I don't think that I'll always be working to try to screw the unions or break them. When I took the job I felt uncomfortable about it. I've come to terms with it. I'm not unhappy with the job, but I'm not vocal about it around school.

The strain in this student's words is obvious. She has convinced herself that she will not be "always screwing" the unions, but recognizes that her role will involve doing just that. She reported not being "unhappy," yet was uncomfortable about discussing her decision with her classmates. With utter contradiction, she was thrilled by the opportunity to work at a large firm, attesting to what she believed to be her hard work and adroitness as an attorney, yet remorseful over not choosing public interest work. She was entering legal practice with noticeable reticence and a sense of alienation.

Transforming the Mission

Perhaps the most salient conclusion that may be drawn from these data is that while most students enter Northeastern University School of Law with public interest aspirations, few maintain their commitments. There seems to be a general decline in a public interest "spirit" as students go through their legal education at Northeastern. Indeed, by their third year, many students feel disspirited by their experiences in law school. By contrast, few non-public-interest students feel the same disspiritedness that angers those with social activist orientations. How are these findings to be explained? In this final section, I shall address the cultural and ideological factors prevalent within a law student's experience at Northeastern that contribute to these patterns.

The lack of cohesiveness among students at Northeastern is a central factor in the movement away from the school's alternative mission. During the mid-1970s, as Northeastern's student body grew in size, most of its students accepted "coop" and permanent jobs in small private law firms, government, and public interest jobs. In some cases, students from Northeastern even started their own legal clinics in unpopular areas such as Alaska. By the beginning of the 1980's, however, the occupational culture of Northeastern began to change. One noticeable change occurred in the area of public interest employment. While over 22 percent of the students selected public interest jobs in 1978, fewer than 17 percent did so in 1981, and by 1986 no more than 10 percent of the Northeastern students were choosing public interest jobs.

By contrast, larger law firm placements were experiencing dramatic increases. In 1981, the largest percentage of graduates accepted positions in small law firms. Such small firms were the main staple for Northeastern graduates for years. In that year, 37 percent of the Northeastern graduates accepted jobs in small firms. Less than 10 percent received employment in law firms of over thirty attorneys. By 1985, however, the number of students entering larger firms began to increase. While 24 percent of the 1985 graduates chose a small firm practice, nearly as many, 22 percent, entered a large firm of over fifty attorneys. In 1986, this pattern was repeated. Twenty-three percent of the 1986 graduating class took positions in small firms, while 22 percent entered large law firm practice. Also, of those students entering larger firms, 42 percent took positions in firms of one hundred attorneys or more.

The recent success graduates of the Law School have achieved in gaining access to larger law firm practices has produced a change within the school culture. Although the majority of Northeastern Law students are still unable to receive large law firm offers, a growing number of students in recent years have succeeded in breaking into the large firm market. In addition, most students, while perhaps not receiving permanent large firm job offers, did receive "coop" placements in several of the largest Boston area law firms. Some students received large firm "coops" in other metropolitan areas as well.

At the present time, there are Northeastern graduates who are employed at prestigious law firms in downtown Boston. Relying on the strong tie networks, former graduates become "coop" supervisors for current Northeastern students. Graduates of the school employed in these firms are invited back to discuss with students the opportunities and "myths" of large firm work. In one such large law firm discussion, students were encouraged to "go for" large firm work. Students were told that opportunities for Northeastern graduates had greatly improved over the years and that "partners like the fact that students can hit the ground running." In addition, student "myths" about large law firm practice were eased. "You don't have to sell your soul," one graduate told these students. "There are plenty of opportunities to do good at a large law firm." This meeting was well-attended and, in fact, significantly outnumbered a public interest discussion group that was advertised as "How to Practice Law without Selling your Soul." The belief that Northeastern students have an advantage resonated among many students. One second-year woman who was interested in working at a large firm described what she saw as the benefits of her coops.

> I haven't had any problems getting large firm coops. I'm working for one this summer. It's one of the top five firms in Pennsylvania. The place I interviewed at, although they didn't know of Northeastern, hired me. I can walk in and give them billable hours, whereas if you get someone from Boston College or Boston University you're going to have to pay them a lot of money while they plod their way along.

There is other evidence of the intrusion of larger commercial law firms into the culture of Northeastern. Students from non-elite college backgrounds often felt the need to boost their image in order to compete with students educated at elite institutions. Indeed, many first-year students, concerned

Table 10.9 Self-reported Perception of Student Competition by Year

	High	Low
First	11%	89%
Second	17	83
Third	39	61
	(N=20)	(N=73)

Kendall's Tau = −.23; P < .007

about the prospects of larger firm practices, began carefully planning coop jobs in order to appeal to prospective large firm employers. This process of credential building and concern for status mobility introduced a competitive dimension to the spirit of cooperation initially experienced among Northeastern law students. Permanent and coop job offers were publicly posted on what students referred to as the "wailing wall." While the vast majority of students at Northeastern found coop and permanent jobs, there were few "quality" jobs available to students. While the first-year experience for most Northeastern students was a non-competitive one, the atmosphere changed significantly in subsequent years. As table 10.9 indicates, the level of perceived student competition among third-year students increased dramatically.

This increase in reported levels of competition occurred in conjunction with other changes between classes as well. As tables 10.10 and 10.11 illustrate, the degree to which students attributed pecuniary interests to their classmates, and the importance students placed on receiving good evaluations fluctuated across classes. The introduction of a larger law firm focus into the student culture undermines the cooperative spirit the school seeks to foster. While public interest jobs, as one student commented, are "easy to get," the desire to acquire large law firm jobs increased the level of competition within the school and altered the way students interacted.

Table 10.10 Self-reported Belief that Students are Motivated by Financial Interests by Year

	High	Low
First	9%	76%
Second	14	81
Third	32	40
	(N=15)	(N=53)

Kendall's Tau = −.26; P < .005

191

Table 10.11   Self-reported Belief in Importance of
Evaluations in Securing Good Jobs by Year

	Very Important	Not Very Important
First	25%	54%
Second	45	45
Third	68	24
	(N=36)	(N=35)

Kendall's Tau = −.30; P < .001

First-year students are cooperative because they don't go through the job process. There's a lot of sharing. Second-year people begin to realize that to get a good job you have to work really hard. The jobs change the whole thing. People are tense. Thirty people will apply at [a large law firm] and only five people get an interview. It's all done in public, so you see who's getting the jobs and who isn't.

For many students, acquiring a position in a large law firm is confirmation of the student's competence. One thirty-two-year-old woman who had entered law school to do public interest law described her large firm job as the great American success story. "It makes me proud," she said, "to know that I'm good enough to be hired at a large law firm like this."

Ironically, the transformation of the occupational culture within Northeastern University School of Law is a trend that many of the faculty and administrators support. Although still considered a "public interest" law school, many of the schools's staff endorsed the corporate push. Indeed, the fact that students from this "renegade" law school had gained access to prestigious law firms was taken by many to be a sign of success. Administrators took pride in the fact that many of their graduates were finding opportunities in law firms that once excluded them. The administration now routinely encourages its students to take large firm coops in addition to public interest ones.

The fate of idealism among Northeastern law students does not occur in their political values and occupational shifts alone, but also in the ways in which students come to define law. Like altruistic students at Harvard Law School, most law students at Northeastern developed high levels of cynicism. Fifty-one percent of the students reported having become more cynical while in law school. The greatest degree of cynicism, however, was reported by those students who were among the most idealistic. Sixty-two percent of the students entering law school for social activist reasons reported having become cynical, compared to only 45 percent with materialist interests.

The cynicism that these students reported closely resembles that of Harvard

Law students. Despite the pedagogical differences between the two schools, the intellectual style of strategically constructing arguments on either side of a case is deeply embedded in Northeastern's curriculum. For instance, in a trial practice class, which utilized mock trials and student presentation, this ability was fostered. In one case a man's wife had been struck down and killed by a passing motorist. The husband was suing for emotional damages he sustained through the course of his wife's death. The central question posed by the teacher was whether to admit into evidence a picture of the deceased woman taken at the time of the accident:

T: Why would you want to admit the picture?

S: Because it verifies that she was struck by the car?

T: I think you could use it more strategically. This woman was an attractive young woman and would be considered more valuable than an ugly old one. Juries take that into consideration. You don't tell the jury this, but you suggest that because she was vibrant and young he deserves compensation. If you're on the plaintiffs side you want the picture admitted as evidence. You could say something like, "doesn't he deserve compensation for this murder of his wife that took four long agonizing days to complete while she lay in the hospital? [The teacher and students laugh at her performance.] If you're on the defense side you would, on the other hand, try to prevent the picture from being admitted, since it would hurt your case.

Like the Harvard students, these students developed a "game-like" approach to the law. One third-year student, initially interested in public interest law, but who had decided to work in large law firm, explained:

I see it [legal reasoning] as a game. At first it bothered me but I began to enjoy making a variety of arguments. It's a real form of power. I can make any kind of argument now, whereas before I would tend to make only those that I believed in. In a way, law is not real to me. It's all abstract and the professors are just teaching us a technique. I don't think of it in ethical ways anymore.

Such redefinitions of the law, similar to those at Harvard, occurred very early in a law student's career at Northeastern. A twenty-six-year-old first-year student, just three months into her education, had already become acclimated to the necessity of the "game," while continuing to possess reservations.

I see things differently now. Things that go on in everyday life. Oh, that could be a tort problem, that's a contracts' issue. It's definitely affected my thinking pattern. I try to outwit people now. I never did that before. Thinking on both sides is important. It's like a game. When I initially agree so strongly one way, it's hard to think about an opposing argument. I think though that I'll eventually be able to do this. I just hope that I don't lose my sense of self or my ethics. This shouldn't happen because I have learned that it is possible to make arguments that you really don't believe in because it's all just a game. I think I'll be alright.

Like students at Harvard, many of the Northeastern law students reported losing their sense of idealism they brought into law school with them. One thirty-three-year-old woman who "grew up in the sixties" and came to law school "fired up about doing public interest" commented:

It's a game. The fact is you can take the same exact person and put them on one side and they argue that, and you put them on the other side and they argue that. I don't know what's right anymore. I mean, I can argue both sides of anything. I have begun to lose track of what I believe in. I've always seen the world as black and white. In law school though, everything is gray.

Although this student had decided to take a large law firm job, she experienced a conflict; she had decided not to pursue public interest law, but continued to have sympathies in that direction. However, this conflict abated the more she saw law as a game.

I'm on the side of management now and the employees are really and truly just looking for benefits that they feel they deserve. If I were on their side [as a legal representative] I would feel strongly that they were getting screwed. But on the other side, I say, "well wait a minute, what kind of precedent is this setting?" As a person what do I care about a fucking precedent. These people are trying to make a living, they're working hard so they should have their benefits. But as a lawyer on the other side I can't say this. Even if I don't want to be adversarial to the employees, and I don't, as a lawyer I can't help it. I guess I just have to continue telling myself that it's just a game that lawyers play.

The cynicism students reported corresponds to a pluralistic view of the world in which a multitude of self-interested individuals are seen as competing with one another. The moral basis of this vision is premised upon the value of possessive individualism. With such a world-view, it is natural that students come to see social relations as game-like. This world-view forms the ideological core of the American legal profession that believes that there are no beliefs, that maintains the vision that there are no visions, and that applies the principle that there are no principles. It is a perspective that is, even at an "alternative" institution, firmly entrenched in law school pedagogy.

Still, as was the case at Harvard, some law students persevere and enter public interest practice. Although seemingly moving in a conventionalizing direction, graduates of Northeastern enter public interest jobs each year at a rate that is above the national average. Like those who remained committed to social activism and public interest practice at Harvard, these students most often perceived law in dramatically different ways than their cynical counterparts. A forty-two-year old third-year student with a history of experience working in human services, and who had just recently taken a legal services position on the west coast, commented:

> I don't think I have become cynical with legal thinking. I think it's a useful skill. You can't make your best argument unless you know the best arguments coming at you. That doesn't mean though that you can go out and represent any despicable corporation. It's a tool. It's a way to be the best representative and particularly beneficial if you 're going into public interest, where people haven't typically gotten representation. The ability to manipulate and construct is very powerful.

Similarly, a third-year Northeastern student with a long history of work as a labor and community organizer explained that

> I chose law school because I used to be a community organizer and I thought that law could give me the tools to change society. This is why I came. I don't have any problems with there not being answers. It's part of social change. I see it [legal reasoning] as a positive skill. It is a tool. I want to go after corporations and government to keep them in line, a whistle-blower. When an injustice has been done you can do something about it and at the same time limit what corporations and governments can get away with. Having the tools to do this is important. I just keep reminding myself that I'm acquiring skills to do what I think is right.

Maintaining strong political views such as these, however, required hard work and constant vigilance. Students at Northeastern, like those at Harvard, who were able to maintain their commitment to social activism needed substantial and continual support. Many students found support for their views in the small networks they established within law school. Students who were able to maintain their political views of law and practice created an oppositional force within the Law School. The collective struggle to preserve the mission of the Law School helped these students maintain their commitments.

However, because there was such a strong need for these students to be oppositional, they were often perceived by others as pushy and cliquish. One woman, who saw herself as initially public-interest-oriented was "put off" by the public interest community at the school.

> During my first year I began hanging out with conservative people. The people that I ideologically agreed with were not the people I hung out with. After a while I realized that their comments were too much of a knee-jerk reaction. I think they're too rigid and I don't really enjoy being with them. It was the other group that tags itself as more conservative that I began to hang out with. When I go into the voting booth, I still vote the same as the public interest students, but I just don't like being with them. It's a social thing. I hung out with people who played basketball on Friday afternoons and would go to [a local bar] afterwards to hang out and watch the World Series together. I enjoyed these people. I kind of resented the public interest people even though I agreed with them a lot.

Another student, a second-year woman who had entered law school to do public interest work but had made the decision to "go after a large law firm," had similar complaints about such students.

> I think the radicals here are the most closeminded people I have ever met. They really don't want to discuss things. In civil procedure there was this case that involved a woman who stopped payment on a stove and the corporation tried to repossess it. Suddenly, in the minds of people the stove became a political symbol. People were saying that this was the only way she could heat her apartment for her eleven children. They totally changed the facts. There are some things about these people that I agree with, but I really began, for the most part, to dislike them. They are just too rigid and unpleasant.

It is difficult to assess whether or not the fact that the Northeastern Law School culture is becoming more conventional has caused some public interest students to be increasingly aggressive. Many of the most active public interest students were deeply disturbed by the trends occurring within the Northeastern community, and organized efforts that sought to promote a radical vision of law and legal practice. What is apparent, however, is that the activities of radical students, both individually and collectively, remain offensive to a large portion of law students in the school. The lack of an intersubjective world-view contributes to extreme disharmony within the student culture at Northeastern.

Although it is only speculative, it appears that the more marginalized radical voices become at Northeastern, the less credibility they receive. The more law students at Northeastern feel as though *they* must maintain the school's public interest reputation and resist the intrusion of corporate interests, the more rejection they will elicit from their peers.

There is a cultural and ideological struggle taking place at Northeastern University School of Law. This struggle presently involves the forces that seek to further conventionalize the Law School, and those that seek to maintain the school's commitment to social activism. Students at the Law School are locked in what is at times bitter confrontation with each other and with the faculty.

The school is presently at a crossroads. Whichever direction the school takes will be greatly influenced by the job market, the students it attracts, as well as the preferences of the faculty and administrators. At present, the administration has accepted the dual yet contradictory tendencies within the school. The school is at once concerned about its decreasing numbers of public interest graduates, while at the same time proud of its increasing number of students entering the more "prestigious" echelons within the profession. School administrators would like to think they can have it both ways. They would like to think that they can offer a successful alternative to traditional forms of legal education, attract students interested in pursuing careers in large firms, and still train students for legal positions in the public interest. From the analysis provided here, this may be a dubious assumption. A public interest law school needs a uniform student culture and a curriculum that reflects this commitment.[19] At present, neither exists at Northeastern.

◆ 11 ◆

Legal Education and Professional Powers

Reflections on Theory and Practice

T his book has explored the visions of law and legal practice students construct while in law school. I have asserted that the "sense-making" activities carried on by these law students mediate their occupational orientations towards large urban law firms. Orientations students develop towards law and practice are not independent of the identity production processes occurring within school.[1] Students do not simply internalize the ideological and occupational orientations communicated within a school's "hidden curriculum," but rather are themselves actively involved in the collective constitution of these orientations. From this perspective, schools should not be thought of as institutions of power because they reflect functional necessities of class, race, gender or professional domination, but because they provide a situated context within which dominant and subordinate identities are constituted on a daily basis.

However, not unlike Karl Marx's famous remark in *The Eighteenth Bru-*

198

maire that individuals create their lives but not under the conditions of their own choosing, students in school are actively involved in creating as well as being created by the structures of inequality that exist throughout society.[2] To say that students undergoing a legal education create and are created by social structure is by no means new. The insight that law and legal practice are related to and "bounded" by external realities is central to the social theories of Karl Marx and Max Weber. To Marx, lawyers represented nothing more than bourgeois servants to capitalist domination. Weber, less convinced that law and legal professionals were servants to class rule, asserted that self-interested market concerns drove lawyers to create and recreate visions of law and legal practice. While these theorists offer conflicting perspectives on the role of the legal profession, each saw law and legal practice as constrained by external social forces.

In her classic book on the rise of professionalism, Magali Larson synthesizes Weberian and Marxist traditions.[3] Larson uses the concept of the "collective mobility project" to describe the process whereby professionals engage in self-interested efforts to achieve market control and exclusionary rights to practice. However, this collective project to establish professional dominance in society is not directed, according to Larson, at undermining capitalism. While many have asserted that the rise of the "new class" of professionals would, under the right conditions, pose a threat to capitalist control, Larson believes that the privileges offered to professionals actually integrate them into capitalist society. While the labor of these experts exists autonomously from capitalist control, professionals are less likely to subvert the interests of dominant economic groups. Although it is certain that "new class" professionals at times do resist capitalist demands, it is also the case that their resistance tends to be more often reformist than oppositional. This is particularly true among elite professionals, who are seldom the champions of equality and social justice.

In this concluding chapter, I will move beyond the empirical material and explore the implications associated with the knowledge, status concerns, and ideology law students develop. Like Larson, I will focus on how each of these aspects of the professionalization experience effects the structure of social inequality. The knowledge, status concerns, and ideology developed by members of the legal profession are geared towards dominant economic interests. I do not mean to imply that lawyers are simply an arm of a dominant class. The professionalism project carried on by lawyers grants them autonomy from ruling interests. However, while not controlled by dominant groups, lawyers directly benefit from such association. Such an association makes lawyers, particularly those elite members of the profession, unlikely advocates for subordinate groups who might challenge those in power.

Knowledge as Power

It has been frequently observed that knowledge represents an instrument of power.[4] The expert knowledge held by professionals is inextricably linked with power. Those individuals and groups who, because of the cultural authority they possess as experts, are able to define, classify, categorize, punish, and treat, wield great power in modern society. Professionals have the ability, as Charles Derber claims, to construe truth to serve their own self-interests.[5] Moreover, expert truth, be it medical, legal, or therapeutic, constitutes social life by the symbolic boundaries it creates. Professionals gain and maintain cultural authority through these abstractions, and by their ability to control the uncertainty and indeterminateness associated with modern life.[6] Because of this, professionals possess great opportunity to set themselves apart from and above the remaining population by creating images of social life that have lasting influence.

Professionals produce visions about social order that possess greater authority than other more pedestrian visions. In this regard, professionals are conceptive ideologist who constitute social reality. Professionals, however, do not constitute any reality, but ones that are consistent with dominant values and assumptions. For instance, teachers at times disseminate knowledge that legitimizes gender subordination.[7] Journalists construct the news in ways that minimize the extent of popular opposition to national policy.[8] Engineers and managers help rationalize and legitimize corporate control of labor in the name of science.[9] Lawyers construct images of conflict that downplay class, racial, or gender oppression.[10] Psychiatrists, therapists, and doctors erect diseases and images of normality that subordinate marginalized groups.[11]

If the substance and application of professional knowledge constitutes power, so does its form. The manner in which lawyers come to "make sense" of the social world has significant implications for the power they wield and the inequality they legitimize.

The legal knowledge constructed by students attending each of the law schools I have examined increasingly separates them from the social problems that confront society. In both law schools, students grew to perceive the world from a position of detached cynicism in which they purge themselves of their original principles of justice. For most students, the problems people face are reduced to the level of gross manipulation and gamesmanship in which *legal* justice is sought. By upholding legal justice, lawyers construct an image of equality that neither significantly empowers subordinate groups, nor threatens dominant ones. Students, for instance, learn that the value of advocacy is great, while leaving aside the merits of what is being advocated. As Jerome Auerbach points out, the legal mind is one that "can think of something that is inextricably connected to something else without thinking about what it is connected to."[12]

This disposition towards legal justice as expressed in its gamesmanship, coupled with the fixing of symbolic boundaries upon images of justice, serves to constitute reality for students in ways that make them dubious advocates for less powerful groups in society. The interpretive activity of law students within the context of legalism leads them to define legal subjects as a collection of Hobbsian individuals struggling over respective self-interests. The constitution of this world-view in law school consequently pulls law students to the center of the ideological spectrum. Such a disposition, while making it unlikely that these law students will dedicate themselves to substantive public interests requiring deep personal commitment, encourages them to sell their services to the highest bidder.

The constitution of social life through legal consciousness, however, is never complete. While the majority of law students "make sense" of legal knowledge in ways that reduce justice to a game, others forge alternative interpretations that openly challenge the dominant meaning attributed to law. Students who contest visions of legal justice tend to define law and its relation to larger society in uniquely different ways than their classmates. Such students see law as a tool to be used in advancing substantive visions of social justice to which they are personally committed.

Status as Power

One leading perspective in the sociology of education holds that the principle role of schools is to allocate status to those who attend them. In fact, Randall Collins asserts that status accorded through academic credentials is more important to professionals than the knowledge they acquire.[13] As Collins writes,

> the value of any particular kind and level of education came to depend less on any specific content that might have been learned in it, and more and more upon the sheer fact of having attained a given level and acquired the formal credential that allowed one to enter the next level.

The possession of elite prep school credentials, for instance, dramatically increases one's chances of entering an elite college or university as well as elite occupations.[14]

While allocation theories that assign a functional necessity to educational differentiation have been soundly criticized for their reductionist emphasis on class reproduction, few would challenge the basic premise that educational institutions confer statuses upon students.[15] John Meyer, for instance, has argued that this is largely due to the fact that different schools possess different "charters" through which students learn roles appropriate to the status the school confers on them.[16]

The differential status conferred upon individuals by law schools is well-known. However, law schools do not merely produce external differentiation between lawyers and non-lawyers, they also produce an internal stratification within the bar.[17] Indeed, a lawyer's position within the hierarchy of law practitioners greatly depends upon the law school from which he/she graduates.

This suggests that law schools possess distinct "charters" within the profession. Law schools foster differential ties with social networks through the collective cultivation of personal characteristics, i.e., cultural capital, as well as through the personal contacts organized by the school. The professional contacts students make while in school play a significant role in a student's career trajectory.[18]

There are important consequences of status allocation and the networks developed in law school. The social status conferred through law school and the values associated with this status often are incompatible with developing commitments to less eminent areas of legal practice, such as those associated with public interest law. Students at Harvard Law School, for instance, build collective identities within law school that all but guarantee that they will become members of America's power elite. The habits and tastes developed by these students direct the vast majority away from lower status legal positions. In fact, affiliating with the social network at Harvard demands that students gravitate toward positions in large urban law firms, in spite of the reservations they may harbor.

For those students most unlike the social network to which Harvard Law School charters them, particularly women and working-class students, law school creates special pressures. Despite the potential challenges these students represent to the dominant orientations to law and legal practice, their lived experiences in school contribute to the acceptance of the hegemonic perspectives within the school. Although they express interests in helping the downtrodden, working-class students at Harvard Law find they are able to gain access to the school's elite network only after they abandon their identification with their social class origins. Though ambivalent, the pressures attached to such acceptance often drive them to do so. Women choose to challenge the structure of legal practice not by carving out new areas of practice, as some have suggested, but by enhancing their own individual status and equity through large law firm employment. In each case the ability to overcome their marginal status by gaining entry to elite positions in society encouraged the acceptance of hegemonic forms of legal practice.

At less eminent schools where the social networks are much more restricted, students often must rely on the local contacts developed by the schools and on their own personal networks. Students at Boston's Suffolk University School of Law, for instance, have often relied on their personal contacts with politicians and family members in acquiring work upon graduation. Those graduates who succeed in gaining admission to prestigious Boston law firms, although minute in number when compared with Harvard, generally do so by specializing in areas of the law not traditionally covered in law school.[19] Such schools are often status-conscious and seek to enhance the reputation of the school by placing their students in high status jobs after graduation. Such status anxiety seems to be leading Northeastern University Law School away from a program dedicated to public interest law.

Ideology as Power

All professional groups employ self-legitimizing ideologies to justify the relationship of the occupation and its members with the larger society.[20] In part, the justificatory schemes associated with professional ideology protect these workers from the self-serving nature of their practice, thereby helping preserve their power. As Geison suggests,

> Professionals have usually constructed their ideologies unself-consciously and sincerely. . . . [W]hatever deception may be embodied in professional ideology and rhetoric is partly a matter of self-deception.[21]

The accounts professionals offer to justify their relationship to the larger society have important implications for the work they perform.[22]

The ideology constructed by law students during the course of their legal education is one that effectively exonerates them from any dishonor associated with their failure to seek public interest jobs. It is ironic that while much about American law may be conceived of as justificatory schemes, law students themselves engage in an endless exercise of justifying their occupational decisions. During their legal education, law students develop the rudimentary ideological parlance upon which the legal profession is based. Potential employers tell students they need not be disturbed by their choice to practice corporate law, because they will have the opportunity to do pro bono. Faculty members and administrators often talk about the duty to public service without ever really promoting it. Older law students frequently tell neophytes that they need not sacrifice themselves for the cause of public interest.

In both Harvard and Northeastern law schools, few students believed themselves to have radically changed. Students continued to believe that they were concerned with injustice and inequality. But most, particularly at Harvard, came to believe that large law firm work represented the most effective way to contribute to social change. Such an ideology, while extremely functional in alleviating any apprehension about "selling-out," constitutes a powerful legitimation of large law firm practice. While many of these students experienced real discomfort with their occupational decisions, their service to the power elite was obscured through a patina of ideological work.

Practical Implications

Writing in the *National Law Journal* in October of 1990, Irving Kaufman, former chief judge of the 2d U.S. Circuit Court of Appeals, commented on the idealism within the legal profession.[23] Referring to a report on job satisfaction released by the ABA stating that only one-third of lawyers surveyed were "very satisfied" with their jobs, Kaufman wrote:

> I do not view the unhappy findings of the ABA survey as symptoms of terminal depression. On the contrary, the mounting frustration within the legal profession may indicate healthy undercurrents of idealism. A desire to serve permeates the profession. Many lawyers whose work denies them the opportunity to contribute to the greater good are dissatisfied. Regardless of the towering heights their salaries reach, they feel their work is of little consequence.[24]

He goes on to say that as law firms reach their saturation point, thereby signalling the end of private firm domination, graduates from law schools will begin to drift towards public interest law.

In an attempt to make it easier for law students to enter alternative forms of practice, several law schools provide loan forgiveness incentives. Begun in 1978 at Harvard Law School, these programs have now expanded to include more than thirty law schools throughout the country. Similar to loan forgiveness programs in some medical schools that endeavor to redistribute physicians into rural areas of the country, loan forgiveness in law school is designed to encourage graduates to pursue careers in public interest law. In addition, law schools have raised money in the form of fellowships offered by large corporate law firms such as Shadden, Arps. In February of 1990, the Harvard

Law School began a one million dollar fellowship program for graduates who go into public service instead of heading for well-paying corporate jobs. Administrators at Northeastern Law School have also been active in raising money for public interest jobs. Moreover, students in various law schools, including Harvard, have taken it upon themselves to collect donations from their classmates to be used to fund public interest internships. At Northeastern Law School, a number of students organized a musical concert called "Jammin' for Justice" to raise money for public interest jobs. Although there has been a great deal of activity in the area of fundraising, there is little hard evidence to assert that such efforts accomplish their goal.

In addition to financial incentives, some law students have proposed a mandatory public interest program. Such programs, not unlike the proposed mandatory pro bono programs that have been debated in the legal profession for years, would require that all law students donate a particular amount of their time during their legal education to doing poverty law. Students on the Harvard Law School Council have urged the Law School administrators to require that all students devote a specified number of hours to pro bono work and take courses in public interest law. Mandatory courses and work in public interest law during law school are designed to promote an ethic of caring among law students for those with lower incomes. According to the Council's report on public interest law,

> Law students are most impressionable during their first year, yet it is during that year that courses in public interest law are virtually absent from the curriculum. To overcome this bias against public interest law, Harvard should create a first-year elective requirement that will allow students to choose one of several substantive law courses that lend themselves to public interest work—courses such as poverty law, family law, civil rights law, housing law, immigration law, environmental law, and consumer advocacy. . . . The law school should develop teaching materials so current first-year courses can systematically incorporate the perspectives of low-income people in legal study. Finally, Harvard should sponsor a national curriculum conference to study ways to make law school curriculums more responsive to the legal crisis afflicting America.[25]

Some law schools, such as Tulane and CUNY, have already attempted to build a community of public interest commitment by structuring into the curriculum public interest practice requirements.

Such programs have, however, encountered stern opposition from many students and practitioners alike, who believe that mandatory pro bono would interfere with the voluntaristic spirit associated with the profession.[26] Mandatory pro bono programs have also been opposed by many social activist lawyers who fear that such programs would simply produce increased representation at the expense of quality advocacy. Those required to offer pro bono services against their will would more than likely expend as little time and energy on these cases as professionally possible.

At the present time, there does not appear to be a shortage of law students who are interested in pursuing alternatives to private firms. In the words of Ronald Fox, the former director of the Public Interest Counseling Center at Harvard Law School, "in any given year about 40 percent of the first-year class express some level of interest in public sector law. That figure drops to 12 percent after the second year and about 6 percent following the last year in law school.[27] The data presented in this study support this general trend.

Louis Brandeis once proclaimed that lawyers have a duty to be more than adjuncts to the major corporations. Whether or not tomorrow's lawyers will uphold this duty is hard to say. From the evidence provided here, doing so will probably require more than mandatory pro bono programs and the offering of financial incentives. While curriculum reform will no doubt produce some favorable outcomes by sensitizing law students to the legal needs of the poor and other under-represented groups, as well as by encouraging law students to identify with the powerless instead of the powerful, and by placing greater emphasis on client service, such reforms may fall short of their mark.[28] While perhaps some of the experiences documented in this book are isolated events related to the tremendous expansion of large firms during the past decade, many others are all-too-often an outcome of legal education itself and the introduction into professional culture. The orientations towards law that students develop encourage a sense of cynicism that all-too-often undermines any idealism a student may possess. The orientations towards legal practice developed through legal education encourage all but a handful of law school graduates to take jobs that will minimize their opportunity to provide needed services to vast numbers of the population. The status concerns associated with the legal profession, particularly among those members within the elite ranks of the profession, make them unlikely advocates for subordinate social and economic groups.

Encouraging alternative practices among law school graduates will require efforts on the part of law schools and the legal profession to build identities of commitment among law students. Such a community of commitment to alternative practice within law school could facilitate greater numbers of public interest graduates. This would no doubt involve making significant changes within the law school environment, as well as within the values of the profession itself. However, such change may be limited, due to the ways in which lawyers attain their status. High status within the legal profession is typically associated with complex legal, technical issues, not ones that involve human, emotional concerns. Status attainment within the legal profession, therefore, contributes to a general withdrawal of lawyers from service to the greater public.[29] Even with a community of commitment, in the absence of outside social movements, efforts to increase representation for subordinate groups may be greatly restricted.

This book has argued that professional knowledge, ideology, and status all contribute to the withdrawal of law student interest in public interest practice. Producing greater numbers of public interest lawyers will require focusing on and changing fundamental aspects of professional training. It will in all likelihood mean that law schools must attempt to attract public-interest-oriented students, and to provide an educational and cultural experience that promotes alternatives to corporate practice. It also will require making law schools less insular learning environments.[30] Exposing law students to ideas and empirical findings from the social sciences, a pedagogy that was originally encouraged by legal realists several years ago, could help law students to better understand the relationship between law and society, as well as their role as legal practitioners.

The present contraction of employment opportunities in the corporate job market may actually provide the opportunity to institutionalize such changes. As a consequence of the recent economic recession, students may be forced to consider employment options in settings other than private law firms. Idealism among today's law students needs to be harnessed and cultivated within law school, particularly in the wake of the individualism and conservativism characterized by the emergence of the New Right. Doing this will require that law schools institute new courses and special volunteer requirements, in order to help facilitate greater commitment to alternative careers in law. However, it will also require that knowledge, status, and ideology be addressed in relation to the process of identity construction occurring in law school. Promoting greater public interest commitment may involve not only challenging the values of the legal profession, but those of the larger society as well. Such efforts, in the long run, would benefit not only America's unrepresented population, but would also allow individual lawyers to fulfill their idealistic goals and, by so doing, elevate the public image of the entire legal profession.

Methodological Appendix

A Natural History

I t was a cold, crisp December morning when I walked onto the Harvard Law School campus for my interview with one of the school's more colorful professors. As a graduate student in the mid-1980's with an interest in law and legal systems, I had become quite intrigued with the events taking place at the school. There was much being made in the local and national media of the intense debates taking place among students and faculty alike at Harvard Law regarding the role of law in modern society. With my curiosity piqued, I decided to venture "across the river" to investigate what the ruckus was all about. Although without an appointment, my host, a controversial professor at Harvard Law School for some fifteen years, graciously consented to speak with me in spite of the other appointments he had scheduled. We conversed about his views on law and legal education for a short time, after which he extended me an invitation to attend the course he was teaching for first-year law students.

The next day I arrived at Harvard Law feeling very much out of place.

Harvard Law School is a cultural icon in the American consciousness, and for someone from a working-class background studying, of all things, sociology in the 1980s, I felt a sense of anxiety overcome me as I ascended the concrete stairs of Langdell Hall to attend my first class at the law school. I entered the spacious lecture hall whose walls were adorned with portraits of eighteenth- and nineteenth-century English judges. After making my presence known to the professor, I took one of the empty seats in the back of the classroom, a seat I remember thinking that could have been occupied by any one of the Law School's famous graduates.

While I found the class interesting, though at times utterly incomprehensible, a significant event occurred, which lead to my further immersion into law student life at the school. Towards the end of the class the professor began discussing his approach to grading exams.[1] Since he had so many exams to grade and since he read each one very carefully in order to judge the exams's content, he informed students that he would not write comments. If anyone wished to discuss the exam grade, he told them, he would be more than happy to do so in his office.

Several students became noticeably uneasy and one student decided to confront the professor. After challenging the professor for shirking his professorial obligations, the student exclaimed that "I pay good money to come here and I expect some feedback on how I'm doing so just make the goddamn comments." Upon this, the class erupted with applause.

After class adjourned, I followed the students to the student center adjacent to Langdell Hall.[2] Upon entering one of the dining rooms, I noticed the student who confronted the professor sitting alone at a table. I approached him and commented on his bravery. After he discovered that I was not a member of the law school community, we proceeded to talk about his views on law and legal education. Realizing that I was interested in finding out more about law school life, he invited me to his classes the next day. So began my immersion into the daily life at Harvard Law School.

At first I was surprised by this student's almost immediate acceptance of me. Everything I had read on ethnography emphasized how the cultivation of relationships in the field takes considerable time and effort, particularly within elite institutions.[3] My initial hypothesis about the rapport I established with this informant was that it was due to our similar backgrounds, both being from the working class, and to the fact that we were both students who were interested in law. Within time, however, I came to an understanding of the role I was performing for most of the students with whom I talked; that of an uncritical counselor. In my interviews with students, I became aware of the conflicts they were experiencing, as well as the fact that they felt they had little opportunity to expose these conflicts to others. By my raising concerns about their experiences in non-threatening ways, and by using "deflection," they were able to talk about changes they had experienced, as well as their fears, without having to face possible reprisal.[4] Over the next six months, I regularly attended class with my initial informant and studied with him in the library. During this time, he introduced me to several other of his classmates as "a friend" who was interested in ongoings at Harvard Law. This fortuitous relationship helped establish my entry into the law school community.

During this initial fieldwork period, I did little more than observe and try to participate in the experiences of these students. In addition to attending classes with students, I accompanied some to their moot court,[5] visited with them in their apartments, and met with them socially on and off campus. During this time, I wrote and transcribed hundreds of pages of notes from my field observations as well as from informal interviews with students.

That summer I began to analyze the data I had collected and wrote a cursory article that later received an award from the Eastern Sociological Society and was published in the association's journal.[6] Although not firmly resolved about a focus, I decided to return to the Law School that next year to continue my investigations. At this stage in my fieldwork, I was primarily concerned with questions not unlike those that had been examined previously in regard to professional socialization. Everywhere I turned while at the Law School I saw resemblances to Becker's classic study of medical students, as well as to those developed by Merton and his associates in their earlier work on medical training.[7] However, as I continued my investigations I became increasingly dissatisfied with perspectives offered from past research. Functionalist analysis of professional socialization, as presented by Merton, offered no treatment of power and showed little interest in detailing the interpretive dimensions of life within medical school. On the other hand, interactionist perspectives on professional socialization, as seen in Becker's work, focused on these internal dimensions within school without saying much about their relationship to the structure and organization of professional work. As I continued my involvement at the Law School, it became increasingly clear to me that student orientations to law and legal practice develop through interpretive processes that are interrelated. The orientations that students develop about the law have implications for the orientations they formulate regarding legal practice. In addition, these orientations seem to have significant implications for the career choices made by law students.

This increased focus on the meaning systems and their relation to social structure led me toward hermeneutic analysis, that is, approaches in which meanings, understandings, and claims about the world are constructed in relation to some preexisting context.[8] Because I was interested in grasping the subjective dimensions of law student experience in ways that would make explicit their interpretive activities, and believing that the starting point of such an analysis lies in the analysis of dialogically established understandings, I began collecting life histories and student perceptions of the law and legal practice.

With the increasing specificity of various theoretical and methodological issues, I became significantly more focused in my data collection. While I continued fieldwork and observation, I proceeded to systematically conduct formal interviews with law students. At first, these interviews were conducted with those students with whom I had already developed rapport. Later, interviews were gathered from other students through "snowball" techniques. In order to get a fair representation of students for my interviews, I also selected student organizations to recruit interviewees. Some of the organizations I chose were the *Harvard Law Review*, the Harvard Women's Law Association, the Prison Legal Assistance Project, the Harvard Black-Americans Law Student Association, the Harvard Labor Law Association, and the *Journal of Law and Public Policy*. Each interview with students lasted approximately two hours and all were tape-recorded. Interviews resembled "guided conversations," allowing students to freely discuss the issues being raised.[9]

During the 1986 academic year, I conducted fifty-three interviews with students at Harvard Law. Although these interviews were proving a rich source of data to investigate the meaning systems of students, I grew increasingly concerned about the representativeness of my subjects. How could I be sure that the interpretations offered by the students I interviewed were not just isolated cases? Consequently, after I transcribed the recorded interviews, I constructed a questionnaire to be distributed to the entire body of students at Harvard Law. Taking the advice of Aaron Cicourel and constructing a questionnaire that sought to take account of the subject's understanding of the world rather than the researcher's, I developed a questionnaire that gathered information on student backgrounds, their motivations for attending law school, their perceptions regarding the personal changes that had occurred during law school, and their vision of future practice.[10]

After pre-testing the questionnaire with my original informants, I randomly distributed the questionnaire to half of the 1,540 students at the Law School in April of 1987. Of the 770 questionnaires distributed, 391 were returned, producing a response rate of 50 percent. This is an exceptionally high return rate considering that the questionnaire took about forty minutes to complete. Of those returning questionnaires, 61 percent were male, 85 percent were white, 70 percent reported having fathers who were professionals, 30 percent indicated having ivy league university degrees, and an additional 48 percent reported having attended "other highly prestigious" universities. The sample parameters appeared to be representative of the population; 64 percent of the students at the school were male and 84 percent were white.[11]

As suggested by Glaser and Strauss, I returned to the Law School the following year in order to confirm the patterns that were emerging in the data and pursue some leads from the questionnaires.[12] During this final phase of my data collection at Harvard, I participated in the school's orientation events for first-year students. I attended small group meetings with students, lectures on selected topics such as public interest practice, and the welcoming address given by the dean. I was able to participate in these events largely due to the fact that I had become acquainted with some students who were now in their third-year, and who had become student advisors. One role of these advisors was to participate in orientation exercises as well as conduct short courses on legal research for new students.

During this period, I collected an additional fifty interviews from students, many of whom I had interviewed a year or so earlier. These interviews closely resembled the ones conducted earlier, with the addition of a few questions developed after I had analyzed the questionnaire. Many of these interviews were selected from the questionnaires I had collected. These additional interviews brought the total number of interviews with Harvard Law students to 103 of which 32 percent were female.

Not only did I triangulate my methods—participant observation, interviews, and questionnaires—but I also added a comparative dimension to the research.[13] In the fall of 1987, while in the final stages of data collection at Harvard, I began investigations of a second Boston area law school. I selected this law school in order to increase the generalizability of my findings, as well as to examine the question of whether students in an "alternative" law school constructed identities and orientations that differed significantly from the ones identified at Harvard.[14] After receiving the consent of the dean, I started attending classes with first-year students.

Having acquired a familiarity with Harvard made it relatively easy for me to establish contacts with these students; everyone wished to know about Harvard Law School. For a period of the next six months, I regularly attended classes with students, participated in study groups both on campus and in their apartments, and accompanied them to organizational meetings and workshops.

In addition, I administered two hundred questionnaires to students in selected classes throughout the Law School.[15] A total of ninety-seven questionnaires were returned, producing a response rate of nearly 50 percent. Of those returning questionnaires, 44 percent were male.[16] Along with this data, forty

213

in-depth interviews were conducted and tape-recorded with law students from this school at various stages in the training. Of those interviewed, 53 percent were women and 85 percent were white.

The use of this multi-methodological approach, which combines participant observation, in-depth interviews, questionnaires, as well as public documents such as law school newspapers, placement statistics, and other non-reactive data sources, collectively outweighs the limitations associated with any singular method.[17] The interpretations and conclusions contained in this book are thus based on a wide assortment of data. While there are limitations to the methods employed in this study, I believe the utilization of a "plurality of methods" remains the most effective way of conducting social science research.

Notes

1 Power and Politics in Legal Education

1. See N. Abercrombie, S. Hill & B. Turner, *The Dominant Ideology Thesis* (London: George Allen & Unwin, 1980).

2. See C. Nelson and L. Grossburg, *Marxism and the Interpretation of Culture* (Urbana: University of Illinois Press, 1988).

3. M. Apple, "The Politics of Common Sense," in H. Giroux and P. McLaren, eds., *Critical Pedagogy, the State, and Cultural Struggle* (Albany: State University of New York Press, 1988), 36.

4. For a lucid discussion of these issues, see Paul Willis, "Cultural Production and Theories of Reproduction," in L. Barton and S. Walker, eds., *Race, Class and Education* (London: Croon Helm, 1983), 107–38. Also see J. Donald and S. Hall, *Politics and Ideology* (Philadelphia: Open University Press). For a particularly insightful discussion of this perspective, see Peter McLaren, "On Ideology and Education: Critical Pedagogy and the Politics of Empowerment," *Social Text* (fall 1988), 19/20.

5. For a recent discussion of the constitution of identities within educational institutions, see D. Holland and M. Eisenhart, *Educated in Romance* (Chicago: University of Chicago Press, 1990). Chapter 3 offers a succinct review of the theoretical and empirical work in this area.

6. See Linda Valli, *Becoming Clerical Workers* (Boston: Routledge, 1986) for an interesting ethnography on how high school women develop attitudes that correspond to their emerging work roles as secretaries.

7. G. Therborn, *The Power of Ideology and the Ideology of Power* (London: Verso, 1980).

215

8. Reginald Heber Smith, a Harvard Law School graduate, became head of the Boston Legal Aid Society in 1914.

9. Reginald H. Smith, *Justice and the Poor* (New York: Carnegie Foundation, 1919).

10. Quoted in P. Stern, *Lawyers on Trial* (New York: Times Books, 1980).

11. E. Bronner, "Harvard Plan Helps Law Graduates Enter Public Service," *Boston Globe* (24 May, 1987, 25.

12. These figures were reported in ABA president John Curtin's address to the American Bar Association house of delegates. A portion of this speech was published as "Themes for our Year Ahead: An Open, Independent Profession and an Open System of Justice," *American Bar Association Journal* (October 1990), 8.

13. Ibid.

14. See E. Kerlow, "Sign of the Times," *Legal Times,* February 1, 8, 1988.

15. This program was reinstated shortly after students protested its termination.

16. "Firm Growth Soars; Cutoff for Top 250 Hits 100 Lawyers," *National Law Journal* (Sept. 22, 1986), s–2.

17. R. Abel, *American Lawyers* (Berkeley: University of California Press, 1989). This is perhaps one of the most important and useful works on the American legal profession. It is not only lucid in its analysis but represents one of the best sources of statistics on the legal profession.

18. The actual meaning of the term "public interest law" is open to considerable debate. This is particularly the case with the rise of so-called "conservative" public interest law. In general, in this book it will be used in reference to types of legal practice that empower individuals or groups that have little access to legal representation. For this book, however, the actual meaning of public interest is less important than the ways that law students construct and reconstruct the meaning of this category of legal practice.

19. "Study Shows Average Starting Pay Jumps Nationwide for Class of 1986," *National Law Journal* (Nov. 9, 1987), 4.

20. "Firm Growth Soars; Cutoff for Top 250 Hits 100 Lawyers," *National Law Journal* (Sept. 22, 1986), s–2.

21. "Study Shows Average Starting Pay Jumps Nationwide for Class of 1986," *National Law Journal* (Nov. 9, 1987), 4.

22. "Employment of Recent Law School Graduates Report: The Class of 1986," National Association of Law Student Placement (Washington, D.C., 1987).

23. R. Abel, *American Lawyers* (Berkeley: University of California Press, 1989).

24. See B. Curran, "American Lawyers in the 1980's: A Profession in Transition," *Law and Society Review* 20 (1986), 19–52.

25. Abel, *American Lawyers.*

26. See ibid. Also see J. Heinz and E. Laumann, *Chicago Lawyers: The Social Structure of the Bar* (Chicago: American Bar Foundation, 1982).

27. See L. Freidman, "Lawyers in Cross-Cultural Perspective," In R. Abel and P. Lewis, eds., *Lawyers and Society: Comparative Theories* (Berkeley: University of California Press, 1989).

28. Magali Larson's classic book, *The Rise of Professionalism: A Sociological Analysis* (Berkeley: University of California, 1977) is one of the most important works on professions and capitalism. Also see Paul Starr, *The Social Transformation of American Medicine* (New York:

Basic Books, 1982). For a recent treatment of professions and capitalism see Derber et al., *Power in the Highest Degree* (New York: Oxford University Press, 1990).

29. Friedman, "Lawyers in Cross-Cultural Perspective."

30. See Ralph Nader's "Introduction" in *Verdicts on Lawyers* (New York: Cromwell Co., 1976).

31. In 1979, IBM had on its staff 243 full-time lawyers. This was about half the total number of lawyers in the Antitrust Division of the U.S. Department of Justice. In spite of this, IBM retained the services of a major Wall Street law firm who established two special branch offices solely for the IBM case. See Stern, *Lawyers on Trial*.

32. See Derber et al., *Power in the Highest Degree*. This was one of the findings these authors presented. They argue that while professions seem to be losing ideological control over their labor, they retain technical control. This control and the autonomy it brings was found to be important among the lawyers they studied.

33. See M. Powell, *From Patrician to Professional Elite: The Transformation of the New York City Bar Association* (New York: Russell Sage Foundation, 1988).

34. See Abel, *American Lawyers*.

35. For a review of this literature see J. Foster, "Legal Education and the Production of Lawyers to (Re)Produce Liberal Capitalism," *Legal Studies Forum* 9 (1985), 179–211; and "The Cooling Out of Law Students," *Law and Policy Quarterly* 3 (1983), 243–256. Also see, R. Pipkin, "Legal Education: The Consumer's Perspective," *American Bar Foundation Research Journal* 4 (1976), 1161; H. Erlanger and D. Klegnon, "Socialization Effects of Professional School: The Law School Experience and Student Orientations to Public Interest Concerns," *Law and Society Review* 13 (1978), 11–35; as well as D. Kennedy, *Legal Education and the Reproduction of Hierarchy: A Polemic Against the System* (Cambridge: AFAR Press, 1983). Most recently, Robert Stover has illustrated this point in *Making It and Breaking It: The Fate of Public Interest Commitment During Law School* (Urbana: University of Illinois Press, 1989).

36. Robert Stover, "From Myth to Myth: Eroding Preference for Public Interest Practice," paper presented at the annual meeting of the Law and Society Association, Boston, 1984, p. 31.

37. T. Schaffer and R. Redmount, *Lawyers, Law Students and People* (New York: McGraw Hill, 1977), p. 3.

38. Foster, "The Cooling Out of Law Students," 246.

39. Pipkin, "Legal Education: The Consumer's Perspective."

40. See J. Feinman and M. Feldman, "Pedagogy and Politics," *Georgetown Law Journal* 73 (1985), 875; and C. Byse, "Fifty Years of Legal Education," *Iowa Law Review* 71 (1985), 1063.

41. See A. Stone, "Legal Education on the Couch." *Harvard Law Review* 85 (1971), 392; and J. Taylor, "Law School Stress and the Deformation Professionele," *Journal of Legal Education* 27 (1975), 251.

42. See Feinman and Feldman, "Pedagogy and Politics." Also see R. Unger, *The Critical Legal Studies Movement* (Cambridge: Harvard University Press, 1986).

43. There are several exceptional ethnographies that examine how subordinate identities are constituted in primary and secondary school settings. See, particularly, Paul Willis, *Learning to Labor* (New York: Columbia University Press, 1977). In this critical ethnography, Willis

examines the processes which lead working-class youth to take working-class jobs. Also see Valli, *Becoming Clerical Workers* (New York: Routledge, 1986); R. Everhart, *Reading, Writing and Resistance* (New York: Routledge, 1983); and L. Weis, *Working Class Without Work* (New York: Routledge, 1990). For an exploration into gender subordination at the college level, see Holland and Eisenhart, *Educated in Romance* (Chicago: University of Chicago Press, 1990).

44. Perhaps the most significant work in the area of elite education is the collected work of Caroline Persell and Peter Cookson, particularly *Preparing for Power: America's Elite Boarding Schools* (New York: Basic Books, 1985). Their recent work demonstrates how elite schooling contributes to the production of class solidarity.

45. For a discussion of these issues, see C. Epstein, *Women in Law* (New York: Basic Books, 1981). Also see C. Menkel-Meadow, "Portia in a Different Voice: Speculations on a Women's Lawyering Process," *Berkeley Women's Law Journal* 1 (1985), 39. For a discussion of tokenism, see R. Kanter, *Men and Women of the Corporation* (New York: Basic Books, 1977). On tokenism within the legal profession, see R. Kanter, "Reflections on Women and the Legal Profession: A Sociological Perspective," *Harvard Women's Law Journal* 1, (1978), 1; and E. Spangler, M. Gordon, and R. Pipkin, "Token Women: An Empirical Test of Kanter's Hypothesis," *American Journal of Sociology* 84 (1978), 160–170.

46. See R. Abel, "Lawyers and the Power to Change." *Law and Society* 7 (1985), 1; and "Socializing the Legal Profession: Can Redistributing Lawyers' Services Achieve Social Justice?" *Law and Policy Quarterly* 5 (1978), 1. Also see Abel, *The Politics of Informal Justice* (New York: Academic Press, 1982).

47. Such an analysis is consistent with Abbott's important work on professional jurisdiction. For Abbott, a profession expands, contracts, or disappears altogether depending on its ability to gain and maintain control over the authority to provide professional services. See A. Abbott, *The System of Profession: An Essay on the Division of Expert Labor* (Chicago: University of Chicago Press, 1988).

48. J. Auerbach, "What Has the Teaching of Law to do With Justice?" *New York University Law Review* 53 (1978), 458.

49. See L. Hellman, "Considering the Future of Legal Education: Law Schools and Social Justice." *Journal of Legal Education* 29 (1978), 170.

50. See D. Bok, "The President's Report: 1981–1982," Harvard University, 1983.

51. For an interesting discussion of this, see R. Wasserstrom, "Legal Education and the Good Lawyer," *Journal of Legal Education* (1984), 155.

52. See Kennedy, *Legal Education and the Reproduction of Hierarchy.*

53. There are several sensitive accounts of law school life written by law students. Perhaps the most famous of these accounts has been written by Scott Turow. See S. Turow, *One L: An Insider Account of Life in the First Year at Harvard Law School* (New York: Penguin, 1977). Also see R. K. Wilkens, "The Person You're Suppose to Become: The Politics of the Law School Experience," *University of Toronto Faculty of Law Review* 45 (1987), 98. For accounts written about the experience of women, see J. Elkins, "Worlds of Silence: Women and Legal Education," *ASLA Forum* 8 (1984), 1. The most recent account of law school life by a law student is the compelling book by R. Kahlenberg, *Broken Contract: A Memoir of Harvard Law School,* New York: Hill and Wang, 1992. Kahlenberg's own experiences at Harvard Law School provide validation for many of the arguments contained within the present study.

54. For research on this see L. R. Reskin, "A Portrait of America's Law Students," *American Bar Association Journal* 71 (1985), 43. Also see R. Stevens, "Law Schools and Law Students," *Virginia Law Review* 59 (1973), 551; and D. Hedegard, "The Impact of Legal Education: An In-depth Examination of Career-Relevant Interests, Attitudes, and Personality Traits among First-Year Law Students," *American Bar Foundation Research Journal* (1979), 791. For recent work, see especially, Stover, *Making It and Breaking It.*

55. See the Methodological Appendix at the end of this book for further elaboration of the methods used.

56. See T. Parsons, *The Social System* (Glencoe: The Free Press, 1951); see also his "Professions," in D. Shils, ed., *International Encyclopedia of the Social Sciences,* vol. 12 (New York: Macmillian, 1968). For a Parsoninan-informed discussion of the professions, see W. Moore, *The Professions* (New York: Russell Sage, 1970).

57. I. Simpson, *From Student to Nurse: A Longitudinal Study of Socialization* (Cambridge: Cambridge University Press, 1979).

58. See R. Merton, "Some Preliminaries to a Sociology of Medical Education" and R. Fox, "Training for Uncertainty," both in R. Merton et al., *The Student Physician: Introductory Studies in the Sociology of Medical Education* (Cambridge: Harvard University Press, 1957).

59. H. Becker and B. Geer, "The Fate of Idealism in Medical School," *American Sociological Review* 23 (1958), 50–56; and H. Becker, et. al., *Boys in White* (Chicago: University of Chicago Press, 1961).

60. There is an extensive literature on this trend. See Becker and Geer, "The Fate of Idealism in Medical School"; J. Haas and W. Shaffir, "The Fate of Idealism Revisited," *Urban Life* 13 (1984), 63–81; G. Psathas, "The Fate of Idealism in Nursing School," *Journal of Health and Social Behavior* 9 (1968), 52–65; I. Simpson, "Patterns of Socialization into Professions," *Sociological Inquiry* 37 (1967), 47–54; R. Morris and B. Sherlock, "Decline of Ethics and the Rise of Cynicism in Dental School," *Journal of Health and School Behavior* 12 (1971), 290; D. Lortie, "Laymen to Lawmen: Law School, Careers and Professional Socialization," *Harvard Educational Review* 29 (1959), 352–369; and R. Harris, *The Police Academy: An Inside View* (New York: John Wiley, 1973).

61. See E. Freidson, *Professional Powers: A Study of the Institutionalization of Formal Knowledge* (Chicago: University of Chicago Press, 1986), and *Profession of Medicine: A Study of the Sociology of Applied Knowledge* (New York: Dodd, Mean and Company, 1970). Also see Larson, *The Rise of Professionalism.*

62. See Abbott, *The System of the Professions.*

63. Derber et al., *Power in the Highest Degree.*

64. See Larson, *The Rise of Professionalism,* and A. Abbott, "Professional Ethics," *American Journal of Sociology* 88 (1983), 855–885.

65. See H. Jamous and B. Peloille, *Professions and Professionalization* (London: Cambridge University Press, 1970). Also, P. Boreham, "Indetermination: Professional Knowledge, Organization and Control," *The Sociological Review* 31 (1983), 693–718; P. Atkinson, et al., "Medical Mystique," *Sociology of Work and Occupations* 4 (1977), 243–250; P. Atkinson, *The Clinical Experience: The Construction and Reconstruction of Medical Reality* (Farnborough: Grower, 1981); and J. Haas and W. Shaffir, "The Professionalization of Medical Students: Developing Competence and a Cloak of Competence," *Symbolic Interaction* 1 (1977), 71–88.

66. P. Atkinson, "The Reproduction of the Professional Community," in R. Dingwall and P. Lewis, eds., *The Sociology of the Professions: Lawyers, Doctors and Others* (New York: St. Martin's Press, 1983), 224–241.

67. My thanks to Michael Apple for suggesting this phrase.

68. R. Williams, *Marxism and Literature* (Oxford: Oxford University Press, 1977), 117–18.

69. See S. Bowles and H. Gintis, *Schooling in Capitalist America* (New York: Basic Books, 1976); P. Bourdieu, *Reproduction in Society, Culture and Education* (New York: Routledge, 1977); M. Apple, *Education and Power* (New York: Routledge, 1982); M. Apple, ed., *Cultural and Economic Reproduction in Education* (Boston: Routledge, 1982); and H. Giroux, "Theories of Reproduction and Resistance in the New Sociology of Education: A Critical Inquiry," *Harvard Educational Review* 53 (1983), 257–291. Also see David Liston's book, *Capitalist Schools* (New York: Routledge, 1988), for a comprehensive overview of this literature.

70. Bourdieu, *Reproduction in Society, Culture and Education.*

71. See P. Atkinson, *The Reproduction of the Professional Community.*

72. See R. Connell, D. Ashenden, S. Kessler and G. W. Dowsett, *Making the Difference* (Sidney: Allen & Unwin, 1982).

73. See Valli, *Becoming Clerical Workers;* and Holland and Eisenhart, *Educated in Romance.* Also see P. Wexler discussion of this in his "Symbolic Economy of Identity and Denial of Labor: Studies in High School Number 1," in L. Weis, ed., *Class, Race, and Gender in American Education* (Albany: State University of New York Press, 1988).

74. A Gramsci, *Selections from Prison Notebooks* (New York: International Publishers, 1971).

75. Williams, *Marxism and Literature,* 110.

76. See T. Gitlin, "Television's Screens: Hegemony in Transition," in M. Apple, ed., *Cultural and Economic Reproduction in Education* (London: Routledge, 1982); and *The Whole World is Watching: Mass Media in the Making and Unmaking of the New Left* (Berkeley: University of California Press, 1980).

77. P. Willis, *Learning to Labor: How Working Class Kids get Working Class Jobs,* New York: Columbia University Press, 1977.

78. See L. Valli, *Becoming Clerical Workers* on this point, where she writes that reproduction "is an adaptation or accommodation to the perceived structural limitations of their lives; it is a *choice* of the best alternative thought to be available" (emphasis added, see 190).

79. See A. Giddens, *Central Problems in Social Theory: Action, Structure and Contradiction in Social Analysis* (London: MacMillan, 1979).

2 American Legal Education and the Making of the Legal Profession

1. Magali Larson, *The Rise of Professionalism: A Sociological Analysis* (Berkeley: University of California Press, 1977).

2. A. Gouldner, *The Future of Intellectuals and the Rise of the New Class* (New York: Seabury Press, 1979).

3. See K. Llewellyn, *The Bramble Bush: On Law and Its Study* (New York: Oceana, 1930).

4. G. Lee, "The Lawyer's Position in Society," *The Green Bag* (1896), 246.

5. For a discussion of the law, lawyers and capitalism, see M. Tigar and M. Levy, *Law and the Rise of Capitalism* (New York: Monthly Review Press). See also, M. Weber's classic writings on this topic in *Economy and Society* ed. G. Roth and C. Wittich (Berkeley: University of California Press, 1978). For a discussion of Weber's analysis of law in relation to the rise of capitalism, see D. Trubeck, "Max Weber on Law and the Rise of Capitalism," *Wisconsin Law Review* 3 (1972), 720. Also see E. P. Thompson, *Whigs and Hunters: The Origin of the Black Act* (New York: Pantheon Books, 1975).

6. Most of those attending the Inns from the colonies resided in South Carolina and Virginia. See J. McKenna, *Tapping Reeve and the Litchfield Law School* (New York: Oceana, 1986). Between 1750 and 1776 a total of ninety-two colonialists attended the Inns, 60 percent of which were from either South Carolina or Virginia. See C. Warren, *A History of the American Bar* (Boston: Little, Brown and Company, 1913).

7. A. Fraser, "Legal Education and the Culture of Critical Discourse," unpublished manuscript, Harvard Law School, 1981.

8. McKenna, *Tapping Reeve.*

9. Ibid.

10. Ibid.

11. H. Eulau and J. Sprague, *Lawyers in Politics* (Indianapolis: Bobbs-Merrill, 1964).

12. P. Miller, *The Life of the Mind in America* (New York: Harcourt Brace Jovanovich, 1966).

13. For an interesting account of lawyers during the American Revolution, see Choust, *The Rise of the Legal Profession in America,* vol. 2 (Norman: University of Oklahoma Press, 1965). Also see R. Abel "Lawyers," in Leon Lipson and Stanton Wheeler, eds., *Law and the Social Sciences* (Russell Sage Foundation, 1986).

14. E. Brown, *Lawyers and the Promotion of Justice* (New York: Russell Sage, 1938).

15. Quoted in Brown, ibid.

16. Miller, *The Life of the Mind in America,* 111.

17. See Gouldner, *The Future of Intellectuals.*

18. D. Hay, "Property, Authority and the Criminal Law," in D. Hay, et al., eds., *Albion's Fatal Tree* (New York: Pantheon Books, 1973), 11–63.

19. See Gouldner, *The Future of Intellectuals.*

20. R. Stevens, *Law School: Legal Education in America from the 1850s to the 1980s* (Chapel Hill: University of North Carolina Press, 1983).

21. McKenna, *Tapping Reeve.*

22. Ibid.

23. Ibid.

24. For a review of the various law schools that emerged during this time, see Stevens, *Law School.*

25. R. Pound, "Work of the American Law School," *West Virginia Law Quarterly* (November 1923).

26. See McKenna, *Tapping Reeve.*

27. Stevens, *Law School.*

28. Ibid.

29. See Larson, *The Rise of Professionalism,* as well as M. Bloomfield, *American Lawyers in a Changing Society, 1776–1860* (Cambridge: Harvard University Press, 1976).

30. M. Horwitz, *The Transformation of American Law: 1780–1860* (Cambridge: Harvard University Press, 1977), 253–54.

31. Stevens, *Law School.*

32. Ibid., 8.

33. See Larson, *The Rise of Professionalism.*

34. See, J. Foster, *The Ideology of Apolitical Politics: The Elite Lawyers' Response to the Legitimation Crisis in American Capitalism* (Milkwood, N.Y.: Faculty Press, 1986). This is a particularly valuable book on elite lawyers in the 1800s.

35. Stevens, *Law School;* 11.

36. Bloomfield, *American Lawyers in a Changing Society.*

37. R. Lefcourt, *Democratic Influences on Legal Education from Colonial Times to the Civil War,* unpublished Ph.D. dissertation (Ann Arbor: University Microfilms, 1983).

38. Miller, *The Life of the Mind in America.*

39. Lefcourt, *Democratic Influences on Legal Education,* 181.

40. W. K. Hobson, *The American Legal Profession and the Organizational Society* (New York: Garland Press, 1986).

41. For a discussion of this, see R. Gordon, "Legal Thought and Legal Practice in the Age of American Enterprise: 1870–1920," in G. Geison, ed., *Professions and Professional Ideology in America* (Chapel Hill: University of North Carolina Press, 1986). Also see D. Kennedy, "Toward an Historical Understanding of Legal Consciousness: The Case of Classical Legal Thought in America, 1850–1940," in S. Spitzer, ed., *Research in Law, Deviance, and Social Control* (Greenwich, CT. JAI Press.) 3 (1980), 3–24.

42. M. Foucault, *The Archaeology of Knowledge and the Discourse on Language* (New York: Pantheon Book, 1972), 224–27.

43. J. W. Hurst, *Law and Markets in United States History* (Madison: University of Wisconsin Press, 1982).

44. R. Abel, "Torts," in D. Kairys, ed., *The Politics of Law: A Progressive Critique* (New York: Pantheon Books, 1982), 185–200.

45. W. Chambliss and R. Seidman, *Law, Order, and Power* (Massachusetts: Addison-Wesley Publishing Company, 1982).

46. R. Abel, "Lawyers." In Lipson and S. Wheeler, eds., *Law and the Social Sciences* (Russell Sage Foundation, 1986) 369–444.

47. M. Cain, "The General Practice Lawyer and the Client: Towards a Radical Conception," in R. Dingwell and P. Lewis, (eds.), *The Sociology of the Professions: Doctors, Lawyers and Others* (New York: St. Martin's Press, 1982), 106–130.

48. See J. Auerbach, *Unequal Justice: Lawyers and Social Change in Modern America* (London: Oxford University Press, 1976). This is perhaps the most engaging work on the history of lawyers.

49. See Stevens, *Law School;* W. Taft, "Legal Education and the University Law School," *Minnesota Law Review* 10 (1926); R. Chase, "The Birth of the Modern Law School," *American Journal of Legal History* 23 (1979), 329; E. Brown, *Lawyers and the Promotion of Justice* (New York: Russell Sage, 1938); and B. Manning, "American Legal Education: Evolution and Mutation—Three Models," Paper presented at the Western Assembly on Law and the Changing Society, June 12–15, 1969, San Diego, CA. For a critique of the narrowness of various histories of law school, see A. Konefsky and J. Schhlegel, "Mirror, Mirror on the Wall: Histories of American Law Schools," *Virginia Law Review* 95 (1982), 833.

50. J. Seligman, *The High Citadel: The Influence of Harvard Law School* (Boston: Houghton-Mifflin Co., 1978).

51. R. Pound, *The Lawyer From Antiquity to Modern Times: with Particular Reference to the Development of Bar Associations in the United States* (St. Paul, MI: West Publishing Co., 1953) 479.

52. For a similar critique of functionalist views of legal education, see D. Sugarman's, "Is the Reform of Legal Education Hopeless? or, Seeing the Hole Instead of the Doughnut," *Modern Law Review* 48 (1985), 728.

53. Auerbach makes this point in *Unequal Justice.*

54. See Chase, "The Birth of the Modern Law School," and Fraser, "Legal Education and the Culture of Critical Discourse."

55. Fraser, ibid., 12.

56. See D. Noble, *America by Design: Science, Technology, and the Rise of Corporate Capitalism* (New York: Oxford University Press, 1977), on how engineers contributed to the development of industrial capitalism. See B. Bledstein, *The Culture of Professionalism: The Middle Class and The Development of Higher Education in America* (New York: Norton, 1976), for an analysis of how the rise of the middle-class professional defended against the abuses of capitalism by conferring honor, dignity, and security to salaried employment. Also see R. LuBove, *The Professional Altruist: The Emergence of Social Work as a Career, 1880–1930* (New York: Antheum Press, 1980), on the rise of social work during industrial capitalism. For a discussion of the ideological disposition of professionals during this time see, C. W. Mills, "The Professional Ideology of Social Pathologists," *American Journal of Sociology* 49 (1943), 165–80.

57. Christopher Columbus Langdell is generally considered the founder of modern legal education. In 1870, Langdell was appointed dean of the Harvard Law School. While at Harvard, he initiated the "case method," which has come to be the established pedagogy within law school.

58. See Bledstein, *The Culture of Professionalism,* and Warren, *A History of the American Bar.*

59. Reform movements during this period were dominated by elite moral crusaders, who sought to protect children as well as rid American society of alcohol abuse. In most cases, these reformers were anything but ideologically disinterested. See A. Platt, *The Child Savers* (Chicago: University of Chicago Press, 1969), and J. Gusfield, *Symbolic Crusade: Status Politics and the American Temperance Movement* (Illinois: University of Illinois Press, 1964). For a more recent interpretation of the role of economic elites in alcohol reform, see J. Rumbarger, *Profits, Power and Prohibition: Alcohol Reform and the Industrialization of America, 1800–1930* (New York: SUNY Press, 1989).

60. Fraser, "Legal Education and the Culture of Critical Discourse."

61. Gordon, "Legal Thought and Legal Practice."

62. See Hobson, *The American Legal Profession*.

63. See H. Lasswell and M. McDougal, "Legal Education and Public Policy: Professional Training in the Public Interest," *Yale Law Journal* 52 (1942), 2.

64. Talcott Parsons was one of the first to assert that professionals such as lawyers were distinct from business interests because of their dedication to public service and altruism. Many have criticized this presentation of professional life, seeing altruism merely as a way of gaining legitimacy.

65. For a critique of the unequal distribution of lawyers, see Lefcourt, *Democratic Influences on the Legal Education;* and Stern, *Lawyers on Trial*.

66. H. Hadley, "Legal Education, Considered in Relation to Professional Standards and Ideals," *Minnesota Law Review* 7 (1922), 122.

67. W. Johnson, *Schooled Lawyers: A Study in the Clash of Professional Cultures* (New York: New York University Press, 1978), 118.

68. See Brown, *Lawyers and the Promotion of Justice*.

69. See J. Katz, *Poor People's Lawyer in Transition* (New Brunswick: Rutgers University Press, 1984), for a history of the legal aid movement in the U.S.

70. These figures are taken from Brown, *Lawyers and the Promotion of Justice*. See also Abel, *American Lawyers*.

71. For an insightful history of the conflict between Harvard Law School and Suffolk Law School in Boston, see T. Koenig and M. Rustad, "The Challenge to Hierarchy in Legal Education: Suffolk and the Night School Movement," in S. Spitzer and R. Simon, eds., *Research in Law, Deviance, and Social Control* 7 (Greenwich, CT: JAI Press, 1985) 189. R. Abel also examines this in *American Lawyers*.

72. J. Tinnelly, *Part-Time Legal Education: A Study of the Problems of Evening Schools* (New York: Foundation Press, 1975), 63.

73. I. Smith, "The Evolution of the Ambulance Chaser," *The Green Bag* (1920), 203–4.

74. For a discussion of the underlying foundations in legal realism, see M. Tushnet, "Critical Legal Studies: An Introduction to its Origins and Underpinnings," *Harvard Law Review* (1986). Also see A. Hunt, *The Sociological Movement in Law* (New York: Academic Press, 1985); E. Schur, *Law and Society* (Englewood Cliffs: Prentice-Hall, 1964); W. Twinning, *Karl Llewellyn and the Realist Movement* (London: Weidenfeld & Nicolson, 1973); and D. Livingston, "Round and Round the Bramble Bush: From Legal Realism to Critical Legal Scholarship" *Harvard Law Review* 95 (1982), 1669.

3 Contradictions and Disjunctures: Motives, Values and Career Preferences among Law Students

1. D. Kennedy, "The Structure of Blackstone's Commentaries," *Buffalo Law Review* 28 (1979), 205.

2. R. Stevens, "Law Schools and Law Students," *Virginia Law Review* 59 (1973), 551.

3. D. Hedegard, "The Impact of Legal Education: An In-depth Examination of Career-Relevant Interests, Attitudes, and Personality Traits among First-Year Law Students," *American Bar Foundation Research Journal* (1979), 791.

4. F. K. Zemans and V. Rosenblum, *The Making of a Public Profession* (Chicago: American Bar Foundation, 1981).

5. A. N. Katz and M. P. Denbeaux, "Trust, Cynicism and Machiavellianism among First Year Law Students," *Journal of Urban Law* 53 (1976), 397.

6. B. Ehrenreich, *Fear of Falling: The Inner Life of the Middle Class* (New York: Harper and Row, 1989).

7. L. R. Reskin, "A Portrait of America's Law Students," *American Bar Association Journal* 71 (1985), 43.

8. S. Turow, *One L: An Inside Account of Life in the First Year at Harvard Law School* (New York: Penguin Books, 1977).

9. See A. Stone, "Legal Education on the Couch," *Harvard Law Review* 85 (1971), 392; P. Carrington and J. Conley "The Alienation of Law Students." *Michigan Law Review* 75 (1977), 887, and A. Benjamin et al., "The Role of Legal Education in Producing Psychological Distress Among Law Students and Lawyers," *American Bar Foundation Research Journal* (1986), 225.

10. See J. Elkins, "Worlds of Silence: Women and Legal Education," *ASLA Forum* 8 (1984), 1, and "On the Significance of Women in Legal Education," *ASLA Forum* 7 (1983), 290. Also see C. Weiss and L. Melling, "The Legal Education of Twenty Women," *Stanford Law Review* 40 (1988), 98. I will review this literature in greater detail in chapter 6.

11. "The Special Sadness of Liberal Law Students," *Reptile* 2 (1987), 3. Harvard Law School.

12. Halpern, "On the Politics and Pathology of Legal Education," *Journal of Legal Education* 32 (1979), 383.

13. "Three Receive HFIPIL Fellowships," *Harvard Law Record*, 27 April 1984.

14. "Students to Study Children's Representation," *LA Daily Journal*, 21 March 1988.

15. "Harvard Law School Alumni Fund New Program," *Massachusetts Lawyers Weekly*, 14 March 1988.

16. Harvard Law School, *Reptile* 2 (1987), 1.

17. Reduced to its most elementary definition, this is a jurisprudential philosophy that places ultimate importance on the economic rationality of human behavior. See R. Posner, "The Economic Approach to Law," *Texas Law Review* 53 (1975), 757.

18. T. Schaffer and R. Redmount, *Lawyers, Law Students, and People* (New York: McGraw Hill, 1977).

19. It should be noted, however, that a higher proportion of third-year students evaluated tax law more favorably than did first-year students. Significantly fewer third-year students found tax law unfulfilling than did first-year students, 56 percent and 77 percent, respectively. This finding is consistent with previous studies on legal education.

20. For example, see H. Becker, et al., *Boys in White* (Chicago: University of Chicago Press, 1961), and I. Simpson, *From Student to Nurse: A Longitudinal Study of Socialization* (Cambridge: Cambridge University Press, 1977).

21. See table 3.2 for the figures on political ideology. With regard to student attitudes toward

business, significantly more third-year students indicated a hostility toward business than did first- and second-year students.

Table 3.4   Attitude toward Business by Year

	Anti-business	Same	Pro-business
First	19.5%	61.7%	18.8%
Second	27.0	36.0	37.0
Third	32.5	44.2	23.3

X2 = 22.37; df = 4; P < .000

22. D. Bok, "The President's Report: 1981–1982" (Harvard University, 1983), and E. Griswold, *Legal Times,* 30 October 1989.

23. See C. Goodrich, *Anarchy and Elegance: A Journalist's Confessions of the First Year at Yale Law School* (New York: Basic Books, 1991).

24. J. Curtin, "Themes for our year Ahead." *American Bar Association Journal,* Oct. 1990, 8.

25. Harvard's loan forgiveness policy is designed to encourage students to take lower paying legal positions in public interest law upon graduation. If the student earns an income that is less than twenty-nine thousand dollars, the school will forgive the student's loan for each year he/she remains under the wage cap set by the administration. Several other law schools have loan forgiveness programs as well. Some of these include Yale, Stanford, and Michigan.

4   Discovering the Law: The Emergence of Legal Consciousness

1. Correspondence theories of schooling posit that specific dispositions and habits of thought required by a capitalist economy are inculcated in students. The forms of consciousness fostered during schooling, for instance, are seen as legitimizing the social division of labor between mental and manual workers that characterizes advanced capitalist society. The arguments posed by supporters of correspondence theory maintain that knowledge and consciousness are unequally distributed in schools. Working-class students, for instance, are taught to be punctual and respectful of authority, while their more privileged counterparts are taught to think critically and solve problems. This differential development of consciousness within school is seen as corresponding to the systemic needs of a capitalist economy. See S. Bowles and H. Gintis, *Schooling in Capitalist America* (London: Routledge, 1976), and R. Sharp, *Knowledge, Ideology and the Politics of Schooling: Towards a Marxist Analysis of Education* (London: Routledge, 1980) for further review.

2. See H. Giroux, "Theories of Reproduction and Resistance in the New Sociology of Education: A Critical Inquiry," *Harvard Educational Review.* 53 (1983), 257–91, and P. McLaren, "On Ideology and Education: Critical Pedagogy and the Politics of Empowerment," *Social Texts* 19/20 (fall 1988).

3. Learning to "think like a lawyer" is said to be one of the most direct changes that occur during law school. See M. Lowy and C. Haney, "The Creation of Legal Dependency: Law School in a Nutshell," *The People's Law Review* (1980), 36–41; and H. Erlanger and D. Klegnon, "Socialization Effects of Professional School: The Law School Experience and

Student Orientations to Public Interest Concerns," *Law and Society Review* 13 (1978), 11–35; and T. Schaffer and R. Redmount, *Lawyers, Law Students, and People* (New York: McGraw Hill, 1977). The most recent exploration of this cognitive ability by Goodrich presents an engaging account of how legal pedagogy develops this skill. See C. Goodrich, *Anarchy and Elegance: A Journalist's Confessions of the First Year at Yale Law School* (New York: Basic Books, 1991). In all these accounts, however, there is little attention given to how law students develop and interpret legal consciousness.

4. K. Mannheim, *Ideology and Utopia* (New York: Harvest Books, 1936).

5. E. Griswold, "Educating the Lawyer for New Responsibilities," speech given on the occasion of the occupation of the new building of the Dalhousie University Law School, Halifax, Nova Scotia, 1952.

6. See Goodrich, *Anarchy and Elegance*.

7. Most of the cases in law school, particularly during the first year, are appellate cases. This means that the case was heard in a lower court but was appealed. The students generally read the appealed case and the decision rendered by the appellate court. Many of these cases are Supreme Court cases, the highest appellate court in the land.

8. Such groups are informally designed not only to facilitate the learning of legal skills, but also as an economizing mechanism. In many instances, students divide the work in their classes among the members of the group. Subsequently, a student is responsible for a certain section of a course. Students exchange notes and outlines of their sections as a way of preparing for exams.

9. K. Llewellyn, *The Bramble Bush: On Law and Its Study* (New York: Oceana, 1930), 35.

10. Ibid, 141.

11. E. Goffman, *Asylums: Essays on the Social Situation of Mental Patients and Other Inmates* (Garden City, N.J.: Doubleday, 1961).

12. P. Bonsignore, "Law Schools Caught in a Paradigmatic Squeeze," *ALSA Forum* 2, 1977, 65–74.

13. See J. Haas and W. Shaffir, "The Fate of Idealism Revisited" *Urban Life* 13 (1984), 63–81, for a discussion of this in relation to medical school.

14. E. Gofman, *Frame Analysis* (New York: Harper and Row, 1974), 21.

15. See P. Bourdieu, *Distinction: A Social Critique of the Judgment of Taste* (Cambridge: Harvard University Press, 1984), and P. Bourdieu and J. C. Passeron, *Reproduction in Education, Society and Culture* (London: Routledge, 1990). Bourdieu's notion of "habitus" refers to the distinctive modes of perception, thinking, appreciation, and action associated with a given group. The habitus is typically part of the taken-for-granted part of social life.

16. See Becker et al., *Boys in White* (Chicago: University of Chicago Press, 1961); Haas and Shaffir, "The Fate of Idealism Revisited"; M. J. Huntington, "The Development of a Professional Self-Image," in R. Merton et al., *The Student Physician* (Cambridge: Harvard University Press, 1957); and D. Light, *Becoming Psychiatrists: The Professional Transformation of Self* (New York: W. W. Norton, 1980).

17. See Becker et al., *Boys in White*.

18. See R. Unger, *Social Theory: Its Situation and Its Task* (Cambridge: Harvard University Press, 1987), for a discussion of "false necessities."

19. L. Eron and R. Redmount, "The Effect of Legal Education on Attitudes," *Journal of Legal Education* 9 (1957), 431.

20. For related views on legal reasoning, see P. Williams, *The Alchemy of Race and Rights* (Cambridge: Harvard University Press, 1991).

21. For an overview of the resistance literature, see P. Willis, *Learning to Labor* (New York: Columbia University Press, 1977); H. Giroux, *Theory and Resistance in Education* (South Hadley: Bergin and Garvey, 1983); S. Aronowitz and H. Giroux, *Education Under Seige: The Conservative, Liberal and Radical Debate Over Schooling* (South Hadley: Bergin and Garvey, 1985); R. Everhart, *Reading, Writing and Resistance* (Boston: Routledge, 1983); and M. Apple, *Education and Power* (Boston: Routledge, 1982).

22. Mannheim, *Ideology and Utopia,* 88.

23. See Stover, *Making It and Breaking It: The Fate of Public Interest Commitment During Law School* (Urbana: University of Illinois Press, 1989), particularly his final chapter on retaining commitment to public interest law. A recent review essay on Stover's book devotes a good deal of attention on ways to retain student idealism in law school. See D. Raack, "Law School and the Erosion of Student Idealism," *Journal of Legal Education* 41 (1991), 121.

24. See P. Starr, *The Social Transformation of American Medicine* (New York: Basic Books, 1982), and A. Abbott, *The System of Professions* (Chicago: University of Chicago Press, 1988).

5 The Moral Transformation of Law Students: Constructing Symbolic Boundaries in Law School

1. C. Sumner, *Reading Ideology* (London: Academic Press, 1979).

2. C. MacKinnon, *Towards a Feminist Theory of the State* (Cambridge: Harvard University Press, 1989); S. Estrich, *Real Rape* (Cambridge: Harvard University Press, 1987); and K. Bumiller, "Fallen Angels: The Representation of Violence against Women in Legal Culture," in M. Fineman and N. Thomadsen, eds., *At The Boundaries of Law: Feminism and Legal Theory* (New York: Routledge, 1991), 95–111.

3. See K. Bumiller, *The Civil Rights Society* (Johns Hopkins Press, 1989). Also see D. Bell, *And We Are Not Saved: The Elusive Quest for Racial Justice* (New York: Basic Books, 1987).

4. Terdimann, "Editor's Translation: Pierre Bourdieu and the Force of Law," *Hastings Law Review* 38 (1987), 805.

5. See M. Shapiro, *The Politics of Representation* (Madison: University of Wisconsin Press, 1987).

6. G. Peller, "The Metaphysics of American Law," *California Law Review,* 73 (1985), 1151.

7. S. Burton, "Reaffirming Legal Reasoning: The Challenge from the Left," *Journal of Legal Education* 36 (1986), 358.

8. For a discussion of the symbolic power within law, see P. Bourdieu, "The Force of Law," *Hastings Law Review* 38, (1987), 805.

9. Wexler makes this point in "Symbolic Economy of Identity and Denial of Labor: Studies in High School Number 1," in L. Weiss, ed., *Class, Race, and Gender in American Education* (Albany: State University of New York Press, 1988).

10. This is a major debate within the legal education literature. There is a substantial body of statistical literature that suggests that the basic moral values of law students do not change in law school. See Shaffer and Redmount, *Lawyers, Law Students, and People* (New York: McGraw Hill, 1977); D. Lortie, "Laymen to Lawmen," *Harvard Educational Review* 29 (1959), 352; W. Thielens, "Some Comparisons of Entrants to Medical and Law School," in R. Merton et al., *The Student Physician* (Cambridge: Harvard University Press, 1957); J. Carlin, *Lawyers on their Own* (New Brunswick: Rutgers University Press, 1962); A. Schwartz, "The Paper Chase Myth: Law Students of the 1970s," *Sociological Perspectives* 28 (1985), 87–100; A. Schwartz, "Law, Lawyers and Law School: Perspectives From the First-Year Class," *Journal of Legal Education* 30 (1980), 437; and H. Erlanger and D. Klegnon, "Socialization Effects of Professional School." *Law and Society Review* 13 (1978) 11. From this literature, many have concluded that law schools are less monolithic than commonly assumed. However, most of these studies seek to identify distinct changes in values and political ideologies. The moral transformation that I am suggesting is much more subtle, and relates to the ways that law students come to understand the law and the world around them. Such changes tend to be difficult to quantify.

11. See M. Lamont, "The Nature of Virtue: Symbolic Boundaries in the French & American Upper-Middle Classes" (unpublished manuscript, Princeton University, 1990).

12. See P. Bourdieu, *Distinction: A Social Critique of the Judgment of Taste* (Cambridge: Harvard University Press, 1984).

13. For a review of this position, see E. Freidson, *Professional Powers: A Study of the Institutionalization of Formal Knowledge* (Chicago: University of Chicago Press, 1986); C. Derber et al., *Power in the Highest Degree* (New York: Oxford University Press, 1990); and A. Gouldner, *The Future of Intellectuals and the Rise of the New Class* (New York: Seabury Press, 1979).

14. See M. Larson, *The Rise of Professionalism* (Berkeley: University of California Press, 1977); R. Collins, *The Credential Society* (New York: Academic Press, 1979); and R. Abel, *American Lawyers* (Berkeley: University of California Press, 1989).

15. The view that professions represent "communities" was developed by T. Parsons. See T. Parsons, *The Social System* (Glencoe: The Free Press, 1951). See also, W. Moore, *The Professions* (New York: Russell Sage Foundation, 1970). The community view of professions has been subject to great criticism.

16. See M. Lowy and C. Haney, "The Creation of Legal Dependency: Law School in a Nutshell," *The People's Law Review* (1980), 36–41.

17. See C. Goodrich, *Anarchy and Elegance: A Journalist's Confessions of the First Year at Yale Law School* (New York: Basic Books, 1991).

18. This was a phrase D. Lortie used in "Laymen to Lawmen," 1958.

19. M. Lowy and C. Haney argue this same point in "The Creation of Legal Dependency."

20. G. W. Domhoff, *Who Rules America Now?* (Englewood Cliffs, N.J.: Prentice-Hall, 1983), 128.

21. See K. Erikson, *Wayward Puritans: A Study in the Sociology of Deviance* (New York: John Wiley and Sons, 1964), for a discussion of the functions of "boundary maintenance."

22. K. Worden, "Overshooting the Target: A Feminist Deconstruction of Legal Education," *American University Law Review* 34 (1985), 1141.

23. See E. Goffman, *Asylums* (Garden City, NJ: Doubleday, Anchor Books, 1961).

24. See Becker et al., *Boys in White* (Chicago: University of Chicago Press, 1961).

25. See H. Becker and B. Geer, "The Fate of Idealism in Medical School," *American Sociological Review* 23 (1958), 50–56.

26. Becker et al., *Boys in White*, 425.

27. D. Kennedy, "How Law Schools Fail: A Polemic," *Yale Journal of Law and Social Action* 1 (1970), 1. This same point has recently been made by former Harvard Law dean, Erwin Griswold. See *Legal Times*, October 1990.

28. This conflict will be examined in greater detail in chapter 9.

29. See D. Kennedy, *Legal Education and the Reproduction of Hierarchy: A Polemic Against the System* (Cambridge: AFAR Press, 1983); and J. Foster, "Legal Education and the Production of Lawyers to (Re)Produce Liberal Capitalism," *Legal Studies Forum* 9 (1985), 179–211. Each argue that law school depoliticizes students without necessarily examining the processes law students go through.

30. See R. Stover, *Making It and Breaking It: The Fate of Public Interest Commitment During Law School* (Urbana: University of Illinois Press, 1989).

31. Ibid.

32. See P. Atkinson, "The Reproduction of the Professional Community" in R. Dingwall and P. Lewis, eds., *The Sociology of the Professions: Lawyers, Doctors and Others* (New York: St. Martin's Press, 1983).

33. See C. Derber et al., *Power in the Highest Degree* (New York: Oxford University Press, 1990), for a discussion of this.

34. B. Ehrenreich, *Fear of Falling: The Inner Life of the Middle Class* (New York: Harper and Row, 1989).

6 *The Contradictions of Gender: Competing Voices among Women at Harvard Law School*

1. On knowing and thinking, see M. Belenky, et al., *Women's Way of Knowing* (New York: Basic Books, 1986); and A. Hochschild, *The Managed Heart: The Commercialization of Human Feeling* (Berkeley: University of California Press, 1983). On morality and voice, see C. Gilligan, *In A Different Voice: Psychological Theory and Women's Development* (Cambridge: Harvard University Press, 1982). On personality orientations, see M. Johnson, *Strong Mothers Weak Wives: The Search For Gender Equality* (Berkeley: University of California Press, 1988); S. Gill, et al., "Measuring Gender Differences: The Expressive Dimension and Critique of Androgyny Scales," *Sex Roles* 17 (1988), 7, 375–400; and N. Chodorow, "What is the Relation Between Psychoanalytic Feminism and the Psychoanalytic Psychology of Women?" in D. Rhode, ed., *Theoretical Perspectives on Sexual Difference* (New Haven: Yale University Press, 1990), and *The Reproduction of Mothering: Psychoanalysis and the Sociology of Gender* (Berkeley: University of California Press, 1978).

2. See Johnson, *Strong Mothers, Weak Wives,* for an in-depth discussion of this issue. Johnson maintains that while women are characterized by greater degrees of expressiveness, they are no different from men in terms of instrumentality.

3. See J. Elkins, "Worlds of Silence: Women and Legal Education," *ASLA Forum* 8 (1984),

1; C. Weiss and L. Melling, "The Legal Education of Twenty Women," *Stanford Law Review* 40 (1988), 98; and P. Carrington and J. Conley, "Alienation of Law Students," *Michigan Law Review* 75 (1977), 877.

4. J. Tabor, "Gender, Legal Education, and the Legal Profession: An Empirical Study of Stanford Law Students and Graduates," 40 *Stanford Law Review* 40 (1988), 1209.

5. J. Abrahamson and B. Franklin, *Where Are They Now: The Story of the Women of Harvard Law 1974* (New York: Doubleday, 1986); and C. Epstein, *Women in Law* (New York: Basic Books, 1981).

6. R. Stevens, "Law Schools and Law Students," *Virginia Law Review* 59 (1973), 551.

7. J. White, "Women in the Law," *Michigan Law Review* 65 (1967), 1051; and Tabor, "Gender, Legal Education, and the Legal Profession."

8. G. Benjamin, et al., "The Role of Legal Education in Producing Psychological Distress Among Law Students and Lawyers," *American Bar Foundation Research Journal* (1986) 225; R. Pipkin, "Legal Education: The Consumers Perspective," *American Bar Foundation Research Journal* 4 (1976), 1161.

9. Tabor, "Gender, Legal Education, and the Legal Profession."

10. S. Homer and L. Schwartz, "Admitted but Not Accepted: Outsiders Take an Inside Look at Law School," *Berkeley Women's Law Journal* (1990).

11. K. Worden, "Overshooting the Target: A Feminist Deconstruction of Legal Education," *American University Law Review* 34 (1985), 1141, 1151.

12. Ibid.

13. C. F. Epstein, *Deceptive Distinctions: Sex, Gender, and The Social Order* (New Haven: Yale University Press, 1988), 11–12.

14. See D. Rhode, ed., *Theoretical Perspectives on Sexual Difference* (New Haven: Yale University Press, 1990); K. Gerson, *Hard Choices: How Women Decide about Work, Career, and Motherhood* (Berkeley: University of California Press, 1985); and S. Freeman, *Managing Lives: Corporate Women and Social Change* (Amherst: University of Massachusetts Press, 1990).

15. For a review of this literature, see M. Johnson, *Strong Mothers Weak Wives.* Also see Gill, et al., "Measuring Gender Differences"; and T. Parsons and E. Shils, *Toward A General Theory of Action* (Cambridge: Harvard University Press, 1952).

16. See chapter 6 for explanation.

17. See D. Holland and M. Eisenhart, *Educated in Romance* (Chicago: University of Chicago Press, 1991), for a discussion of identity construction among women.

18. R. Klatch, "Conflict and Coalition among Women of the New Right," *Signs* 13 (1988), 671–94.

19. See Freeman, *Managing Lives,* for a discussion of how women corporate executives feel about their opportunities and managed their careers so as to be successful.

20. R. Klatch, *Women of the New Right* (Philadelphia: Temple University Press, 1987).

21. Weis makes this point in her book on working-class students. She argues that working-class women have less an opportunity to rely on the free market. See L. Weis, *Working Class without Work: High School Students in a De-Industrializing Economy* (New York: Routledge, 1990).

◆ *Making Elite Lawyers* ◆

22. N. Black, *Social Feminism* (Ithaca: Cornell University Press, 1989).

23. R. Kanter, "Reflections on Women and the Legal Profession: A Sociological Perspective," *Harvard Women's Law Journal* 1 (1978).

24. See Homer and Schwartz, "Admitted but Not Accepted," and C. Menkel-Meadow, "Portia in a Different Voice: Speculations on a Women's Lawyering Process," *Berkeley Women's Law Journal* 1 (1985), 39.

25. Epstein, *Deceptive Distinctions*.

26. The "social justice" category refers to students who reported attending law school for the reasons of social change, social justice, or to help others.

27. The "other" category refers to those who reported attending law school for reasons other than in the social justice category, such as career and academic interest.

28. See Black, *Social Feminism*.

29. Freeman, *Managing Lives*.

30. See S. Hardesty and N. Jacobs, *Success and Betrayal: The Crisis of Women in Corporate America* (New York: Franklin Watts, 1986), for the position that women who are successful in the corporate world are denying their expressive side.

31. See Weis, *Working Class without Work,* for this point.

32. Black, *Social Feminism*.

7 Making It by Faking It: Working-class Students at Harvard Law

1. See P. Willis, *Learning to Labor* (New York: Columbia University Press, 1977) for a discussion of this.

2. R. Zweigenhaft and G. W. Domhoff, *Blacks in the White Establishment: A Study of Race and Class in America* (New Haven: Yale University Press, 1991).

3. See E. Smigel, *The Wall Street Lawyer: Professional Organization Man?* (New York: The Free Press, 1969); J. Heinz and E. Laumann, *Chicago Lawyers: The Social Structure of the Bar* (Chicago: American Bar Foundation, 1982); M. Useem and J. Karabel, "Paths to Corporate Management," *American Sociological Review* 51 (1986), 184–200.

4. See P. Bourdieu and C. Passeron, *Reproduction in Education, Society, and Culture* (London: Routledge 1990). For an elaboration of how elite schools instill cultural capital, see the works of P. Cookson and C. Persell, *Preparing for Power: America's Elite Boarding Schools* (New York: Basic Books, 1985); "The Reproduction of Social Elites," *Comparative Education Review* 29 (1985), 283–98; "Chartering and Bartering: Elite Education and Social Reproduction," *Social Problems* 33 (1985) 114–128.

5. E. Goffman, *Stigma: Notes on the Management of Spoiled Identity* (Englewood Cliffs: Prentice-Hall, 1963).

6. See E. Schur, *Labeling Women Deviant: Gender, Stigma, and Social Control* (New York: Random House, 1984).

7. See E. Pfuhl, *The Deviance Process* (Belmont, CA: Wadsworth, 1984), for further discussion of these concepts.

8. See Goffman, *Stigma*, 5.

9. Ibid, 145.

10. Goffman uses the concept of asymmetrical relations to describe deference rules regarding status disparity, see *Interaction Ritual: Essays on Face to Face Behavior* (New York: Pantheon, 1967). These status differences are inherent within unequal interactions, such as those between doctor and patient in mental institutions (see Goffman, *Asylums* (Garden City, NJ: Doubleday, 1961). However, while Goffman saw asymmetrical encounters as frequently strained, he did not see this as the result of social structure; see Goffman, "The Interaction Order," *American Sociological Review* 48 (1983), 1–17. Interactional practices and social structure are seen as "loosely-coupled." Goffman's emphasis on local determinism suggests that interaction is situationally defined and not predetermined by external factors such as race, age, gender, or class. Consequently, asymmetrical social class encounters inhibit equal interactions in some cases, while facilitating this interaction in others.

11. R. Sennett and J. Cobb, *The Hidden Injuries of Class* (New York: Random House, 1973).

12. Ibid, 33–34.

13. See A. Cohen, *Delinquent Boys: The Culture of the Gang* (New York: The Free Press, 1955); and Willis, *Learning to Labor.*

14. In the case of Willis' "lads," I do not wish to suggest that they willingly accepted their subordinate position within society. In fact, as Willis demonstrates, members of the working class who penetrate the structure of social class relations are anything but passive. They often feel superior to their middle class counterparts. This social construction of meaningfulness is what leads the "lads" to choose working-class jobs. However, such behavior is consistent with Goffman's notion of "flaunting," in which individuals who experience devaluation assert their superiority. The celebration of the informal status system among the working-class youth Willis studied seems, at least in part, related to their attempts to resist a class-imposed devalued identity, by glorifying the traits associated with the working class.

15. Measurement of class background was accomplished by asking students to subjectively identify with a particular social class. This identification was then compared with their father's occupation and education. Among those identifying with the working class, 83 percent indicated their father's occupation as being either in the service, craft, or technical sectors of the labor market. The remaining 17 percent identified themselves as working class, but failed to report their father's occupation. Nearly 80 percent reported that the highest level of education attained by their father was high school or less. The percentage distribution of class background is as follows: upper class (2.8), upper-middle (44.6), middle (30.9), lower-middle (8.0), working (13.1), and lower (.5).

16. See V. Steinitz and E. Solomon, *Starting Out: Class and Community in the Lives of Working Class Youth* (Philadelphia: Temple University Press, 1986).

17. Ibid.

18. See B. Bernstein, *Class Codes and Control, Vol. 4: Towards a Theory of Educational Transmission* (London: Routledge, 1990). Bernstein's work on language codes associated with class position is useful in this regard. Bernstein maintains that working-class students develop a "restricted" language code, thereby limiting their ability to compete in the middle-class world where "elaborated" codes are used.

19. See Sennett and Cobb, *The Hidden Injuries of Class.*

20. For a discussion of these issues see, E. Schur, *The Politics of Deviance* (Englewood Cliffs,

N.J.: Prentice-Hall, 1980), and *Labeling Deviant Behavior* (New York: Harper and Row, 1971).

21. See D. Baltzell, *Philadelphia Gentlemen* (New York: The Free Press, 1958).

22. See K. Newman, *Falling From Grace: The Experience of Downward Mobility in the American Middle Class* (New York: The Free Press, 1988). This is a brilliant piece of scholarship that examines the experience of unemployment among the middle class.

23. Similar findings are reported by Zweigenhaft and Domhoff, *Blacks in the White Establishment* (1991) in which they describe the experiences of Black students enrolled in elite prep schools.

24. G. Stone, "Appearance and the Self," in G. Stone and H. Farberman, eds., *Social Psychology through Symbolic Interaction* (New York: John Wiley, 1970).

25. For a discussion of how appearance excludes, see M. Lamont and A. Lareau, "Cultural Capital: Allusions, Gaps, and Glissandos in Recent Theoretical Development," *Sociological Theory* 6 (1988), 153–68; and R. Jackell, *Moral Mazes: The World of the Corporate Manager* (New York: Oxford University Press, 1988).

26. R. Kanter, *Men and Women of the Corporation* (New York: Basic Books, 1977).

27. Jackell, *Moral Mazes.*

28. See R. Abel, *American Lawyers* (Berkeley: University of California Press, 1989).

29. A recent study of hiring policies among large firms found that "personal characteristics" ranked second among the criteria for selecting new lawyers. See P. Buller and C. Beck-Dudly, "Performance, Policies and Personnel," *American Bar Association Journal,* 76 (1990), 94.

30. See Sennett and Cobb, *The Hidden Injuries of Class.* The authors feel that members of the working class lack a sense of dignity and attempt to pass as competent when they believe they're actually incompetent.

31. Goffman, *Stigma,* 107.

32. See Sennett and Cobb, *The Hidden Injuries of Class* for their discussion of ambivalence members of the working class experience through upward mobility. For a contrasting analysis of upward mobility among the working class, see Steinitz and Solomon, *Starting Out.*

33. See J. Ryan and C. Sackrey, *Strangers in Paradise: Academics from the Working Class* (Boston: South End Press, 1984).

34. See Goffman, *Stigma.*

35. See R. Connell, et al., *Making the Difference* (Australia: Allen and Unwin, 1982).

36. Steinitz and Solomon, *Starting Out,* 3.

37. See J. Katz, *Poor People's Lawyer in Transition.* (New Brunswick: Rutgers University Press, 1984).

38. Steinitz and Solomon, *Starting Out.*

39. See Zweigenhaft and Domhoff, *Blacks in the White Establishment.*

8 Learning Collective Eminence: The Social Production of Elite Lawyers

1. I wish to thank Tom Koenig for his collaboration on this chapter. The term "collective eminence" was developed together. We have published portions of this chapter in *Critical Criminologist, Research on Politics and Society,* and *Sociological Quarterly.* Tom is as much a part of this chapter as I am.

2. J. Kilmer, "Where Do You Fall in the Legal Caste System?" *American Bar Association Journal* (Fall 1976), 18–26.

3. C. Munneke, "History of National Association for Law Placement," paper presented at the 11th annual conference for the National Association of Law Placement, St. Petersburg, Fl. May 9–12, 1982.

4. For discussion of the bifurcation within the bar, see W. S. Van Alstyne, J. Julin, and L. Barnett, *The Goals and Mission of Law Schools* (New York: Peter Lang, 1990); M. Rustad and T. Koenig, "An Empirical Study of A Prestige Image in Transition: Suffolk Law Graduates in Large New England Law Firms," *The Advocate* (1991); J. Heinz and E. Laumann, *Chicago Lawyers: The Social Structure of the Bar* (Chicago: American Bar Foundation, 1982); R. Abel, *American Lawyers* (Berkeley: University of California Press, 1989); and F. K. Zemans and V. Rosenblum, *The Making of a Public Profession* (Chicago: American Bar Foundation, 1981).

5. Most of the recent research on schooling examines how educational institutions contribute to subordinate identities. For example, see L. Valli, *Becoming Clerical Workers* (Boston: Routledge, 1986); P. Willis, *Learning to Labor* (New York: Columbia University Press, 1977); and P. McLaren, *Schooling as a Ritual Performance* (London: Routledge, 1986).

6. See C. Cappell and R. Pipkin, "The Inside Tracks: Status Distinctions in Allocation to Elite Law Schools," in P. Kingston and L. Lewis, eds., *The High Status Track: Studies of Elite Schools and Stratification* (New York: State University of New York Press, 1990).

7. J. Meyer, "Education as an Institution." *American Journal of Sociology* 83 (1977), 55–77.

8. P. Cookson and C. Persell, *Preparing for Power* (New York: Basic Books, 1985).

9. Van Alstyne, Julin, and Barnett, *The Goals and Mission of Law Schools.*

10. Kilmer, "Where Do You Fall in the Legal Caste System?"

11. See Rustad and Koenig, "An Empirical Study of A Prestige Image in Transition"; and T. Blake, "Alienation: The Hidden Agenda of American Law Schools," unpublished manuscript, University of Denver, 1990.

12. The finding that Harvard Law School is not as competitive a place as depicted in the popular literature should not be considered unusual. Audrey Schwartz found a similar lack of competitiveness in the elite law schools she studied. See Schwartz, "The Paper Chase Myth: Law Students of the 1970s," *Sociological Perspectives* 28 (1985), 87.

13. Cookson and Persell, *Preparing for Power.*

14. On the collective values of elites, see G. W. Domhoff, *Who Rules America Now?* (Englewood Cliffs, N.J.: Prentice-Hall, 1983); Cookson and Persell, *Preparing for Power;* and D. Baltzell, *Philadelphia Gentlemen* (New York: The Free Press, 1958). Cookson and Persell are especially insightful in documenting the importance of a collective identity in prep school.

15. S. Keller, *Beyond the Ruling Class: Strategic Elites in Modern Society* (New York: Random House, 1964), 220.

16. On fostering a collective identity, see Cookson and Persell, *Preparing for Power;* M. Useem and J. Karabel, "Paths to Corporate Management", *American Sociological Review,* 51 (1986), 184–200; C. W. Mills, *The Power Elite* (New York: Oxford University Press, 1958); R. Collins, *The Credential Society* (New York: Academic Press, 1979); and Baltzell, *Philadelphia Gentlemen.* On inhibiting a collective working-class identity, see P. Wexler, "Movement, Class, and Education," in L. Barton and S. Walker, eds., *Race, Class, and Education* (London: Croon Helm, 1983).

17. "O-groups" refer to the orientation group meetings for One L's at Harvard Law.

18. For example, at the University of Denver School of Law, the dean gives students a taste of how difficult law school will be by subjecting selected neophytes to an intimidating round of legal questions and warns that many will fail to graduate. See T. Blake, "Alienation: The Hidden Agenda of American Law Schools" (unpublished manuscript, University of Denver, 1990).

19. The "no hassle pass" option is available in most classes. A student who feels unprepared to answer questions simply informs the professor before class. The professor will then not call on that student if he/she does not wish to respond to a professor's queries.

20. See chapter 6 for details.

21. See M. Granovetter, *Getting a Job: A Study of Contacts and Careers* (Cambridge: Harvard University Press, 1973); "The Strength of Weak Ties," *American Journal of Sociology* 78 (1973), 1460; and M. Granovetter and C. Tilly, "Inequality and Labor Processes," in N. Smelser, ed., *Handbook of Sociology* (Newbury Park: Sage, 1988).

22. For a rich description of these fly-outs, see R. Kahlenberg, *Broken Contract: A Memoir of Harvard Law School,* New York: Hill and Wang, 1992.

23. See Cookson and Persell, *Preparing for Power.* These authors draw much of their analysis from P. Bourdieu, *Reproduction in Education, Culture, and Society* (London: Routledge, 1977).

24. P. Buller and C. Beck-Dudly, "Performance, Policies and Personnel," *American Bar Association Journal* 76 (1990), 94.

25. See Abel, *American Lawyers.*

26. Cookson and Persell make a similar point about students from the working class. In their study of prep schools, they found that although working-class students lacked appropriate social skills, they found they could adapt by receiving assistance from their more elite peers. See chapter 7 for further details.

27. E. Bronner, "Harvard Plan Helps Law Graduates Enter Public Service," *Boston Globe* 24 May 1987, 25.

28. D. Kaplan, "Out of 11,000, 243 Went into Public Interest," *The National Law Journal,* 8 August 1988, 1, 46.

9 The Dilemma of Job Selection: Ideological Work among Harvard Law Students

1. See M. Apple, *Education and Power* (Boston: Routledge, 1982), for a discussion of this irony.

2. See P. Cookson and C. Persell, *Preparing for Power* (New York: Basic Books, 1985).

3. In the psychological literature, see L. Festinger, *A Theory of Cognitive Dissonance* (London: Row Peterson, 1957). The theory of cognitive dissonance, as outlined by Festinger, depicts individuals as seeking to maintain consistency in their thoughts. From this perspective, individuals avoid thoughts that result in disharmony. On ideological dilemmas, see M. Billig et al., *Ideological Dilemmas: A Social Psychology of Everyday Thinking* (Newbury Park: Sage, 1988). These authors diverge from "balance" theories by arguing that ideological themes run through "common sense," and that individuals make sense of the dilemmas they experience by giving reasonable justification for the seeming inconsistency. Also see C. Reinarman, *American States of Mind* (New Haven: Yale University Press, 1987), for further exploration of ideological dilemmas.

4. Billig et al., *Ideological Dilemmas,* 17.

5. M. Edelman, *Political Language* (New York: Academic Books, 1977); and J. Nilson, "Reconsidering Ideological Lines: Beliefs about Poverty in America," *Sociological Quarterly* 22 (1981), 531.

6. G. Myrdal, *An American Dilemma* (New York: Harper and Row, 1944); J. Potter and M. Wetherall, "Accomplishing Attitudes: Fact and Evaluation in Racist Discourse," *Text* 18 (1988), 51.

7. Reinarman, *American States of Mind.*

8. See J. Potter and M. Wetherall, *Discourse and Social Psychology* (London: Sage, 1987).

9. See Billig et al., *Ideological Dilemmas.*

10. See M. Oppenheimer, *White Collar Politics* (New York: Monthly Review Press, 1985).

11. See R. Jackell, *Moral Mazes* (New York: Oxford University Press, 1988).

12. See R. Merton, *Sociological Ambivalence and Other Essays* (New York: The Free Press, 1976).

13. A. Abbott, "Professional Ethics" *American Journal of Sociology* 88 (1983), 5.

14. See Jackell, *Moral Mazes.*

15. See J. Schevitz, *The Weaponsmakers: Personal and Professional Crisis During the Vietnam War* (Cambridge: Schenkman, 1979).

16. C. Derber, *Professionals as Workers: Mental Labor in Advanced Capitalism* (Boston: G. K. Hall, 1982).

17. See M. Burawoy, *Manufacturing Consent* (Chicago: University of Chicago Press, 1979).

18. B. Berger, *The Survival of the Counterculture* (Berkeley: University of California Press, 1981).

19. Ibid., 22–24.

20. E. Rochford, *Hare Krishna in America* (New Brunswick: Rutgers University Press, 1986).

21. K. Knorr-Cetina and A. Cicourel, *Advances in Social Theory and Method* (New York: Routledge, 1981).

22. For research that applies this perspective, see M. Apple, "The Politics of Common Sense," in H. Giroux and P. McLaren, eds., *Critical Pedagogy, the State, and Cultural Struggle* (Albany: State University of New York Press, 1989); P. McLaren, "On Ideology and Education: Critical Pedagogy and the Politics of Empowerment," *Social Texts* 19/20 (Fall 1988); P. McLaren, *Schooling as a Ritual Performance* (London: Routledge, 1986); and P. Willis, *Learning to Labor* (New York: Columbia University Press, 1977).

23. See P. Anderson, *In The Tracks of Historical Materialism* (London: Verso Press, 1983); G. Therborn, *The Power of Ideology and the Ideology of Power* (London: Verso Press, 1980); and R. Williams, *Marxism and Literature* (Oxford: Oxford University Press, 1977).

24. See M. Apple, *Teachers and Texts: A Political Economy of Gender and Class* (New York: Routledge, 1986), and *Education and Power* (Boston: Routledge, 1982). Also see L. Valli, *Becoming Clerical Workers* (Boston: Routledge, 1986).

25. See Cookson and Persell, *Preparing for Power.*

26. P. Willis, *Learning to Labor;* L. Weis, *Working Class without Work;* and J. MacLeod, *Ain't No Making It* (Boulder: Westview, 1986).

27. See R. Connell, et al., *Making the Difference* (Australia: Allen and Unwin, 1982); D. Holland and M. Eisenhart, *Educated in Romance* (Chicago: University of Chicago Press, 1990).

28. S. Fordham and J. Ogbu, "Black Students' School Success: Coping with the Burden of Acting White," *Urban Review* 18 (1986), 18.

29. This was a term I had heard used on several occasions to describe students who join large law firms. Although this is a disparaging term, I felt comfortable asking this question since I had established considerable rapport with this student.

30. See Apple, *Education and Power.*

31. On "accounts," see H. Garfinkel, *Studies in Ethnomethodology* (Englewood Cliffs: Prentice-Hall, 1967); and R. Scott and S. Lyman, "Accounts," *American Sociological Review* 33 (1968), 46. According to Scott and Lyman, accounts typically involve discourse that is offered to justify or otherwise excuse an activity so as to reduce responsibility. Such accounts are used to try to ease a situation by convincing other people and oneself of the reasonableness of an activity.

32. See C. W. Mills, "Situated Actions and Vocabularies of Motive," *American Sociological Review* 5 (1940), for a discussion of vocabulary of motives.

33. This name is in reference to the law firm of Cravath, Moore and Swaine in New York City. Within the professional hierarchy, this firm is considered as one of the most prestigious law firms in the country.

34. D. Chambers, "Educational Debts and the Worsening of Small Firm, Government, and Legal Services Lawyers." *Journal of Legal Education* (1990), 709.

35. See Rochford, *Hare Krisna in America,* and P. Berger and T. Luckmann, *The Social Construction of Reality* (New York: Doubleday, 1966).

36. See C. Derber, *Professionals as Workers: Mental Labor in Advanced Capitalism* (Boston: G. K. Hall, 1982).

37. R. Stover, *Making It and Breaking It: The Fate of Public Interest Commitment During Law School* (Urbana: University of Illinois Press, 1989), 84.

38. See R. Zweigenhaft and G. W. Domhoff, *Blacks in the White Establishment: A Study of Race and Class in America* (New Haven: Yale University Press, 1990), for a similar discussion on this point.

39. Fulbright and Jaworski is a Houston based law firm. A group of radical law students picketed this firm because of its alleged involvement in union-busting. The term "prolicide" was used to define the practice of killing the proletariat.

40. See R. Nelson, *Partners Without Power: The Social Transformation of the Large Law Firm*

(Berkeley: University of California Press, 1988); and E. Spangler, *Lawyers for Hire: Salaried Professionals at Work* (New Haven: Yale University Press, 1986).

41. G. Sykes and D. Matza, "Techniques of Neutralization: A Theory of Delinquency," *American Sociological Review,* 22 (1957), 664–70.

42. See H. Trice and P. Roman, "Delabeling, Relabeling, and Alcoholics Anonymous," *Social Problems* 17 (1970), and J. Gusfield, "Moral Passage: The Symbolic Process in Public Designations of Deviance," *Social Problems* 15 (1967). While these articles are primarily about the disavowal of deviant activities such as heavy drinking, they illustrate the importance of being repentent. This is particularly true within self-help programs like Alcoholics Anonymous.

43. For discussions of resistance in schooling, see H. Giroux, "Theories of Reproduction and Resistance in the New Sociology of Education: A Critical Inquiry," *Harvard Educational Review* 53 (1983), 257–91; H. Giroux and P. McLaren, *Critical Pedagogy, the State, and Cultural Struggle* (New York: State University of New York Press, 1989); and S. Aronowitz and H. Giroux, *Education Under Siege: The Conservative, Liberal and Radical Debate Over Schooling* (South Hadley: Bergin and Garvey, 1986).

44. Apple, *Education and Power,* 25.

45. See Abel, *American Lawyers.*

46. E. J. Pollock, "Big Law Firms Learn That They, Too, Are a Cyclical Business," *Wall Street Journal,* 5 August 1991, A 1, 14.

47. C. Derber et al., *Power in the Highest Degree* (New York: Oxford University Press, 1990).

48. See I. Szelenyi and B. Martin, "The Legal Profession and the Rise and Fall of the New Class," in R. Abel and P. Lewis, *Lawyers in Society: Comparative Theories* (Berkeley: University of California, 1989).

49. S. Benson, "Why I Quit Practicing Law," *Newsweek,* November 4, 1991.

10   The Public Interest Law School: An Alternative Challenge or the Illusion of Difference?

1. S. Aronowitz and H. Giroux, *Education Under Seige: The Conservative, Liberal and Radical Debate Over Schooling* (South Hadley: Bergin and Garvey, 1985), 108.

2. E. Marston, *Origins and Development of Northeastern University, 1898–1960* (Boston: Northeastern University Press, 1961).

3. See T. Koenig and M. Rustad, "The Challenge to Hierarchy in Legal Education: Suffolk and the Night School Movement," in S. Spitzer and R. Simon, eds., *Research in Law, Deviance, and Social Control* (Greenwich, CT: JAI, Press 1985); and R. Stevens, *Law School: Legal Education in America from the 1850s to the 1980s* (Chapel Hill: University of North Carolina Press, 1983).

4. Stevens, Ibid.

5. Marston, *Origins and Development of Northeastern University.*

6. Ibid.

7. Ibid.

8. See M. Rustad, "Turning Carthorses into Trotters: Suffolk Evening Law School as a Counter-Hegemonic Movement in Legal Education," *The Advocate* 17 (1986), 18; and Stevens, *Law School: Legal Education in America*.

9. Marston, *Origins and Development of Northeastern University*.

10. A. Frederick, *Northeastern University: An Emerging Giant: 1959–1975* (Boston: Northeastern University Press, 1982).

11. Quoted in Frederick, *Northeastern University*, 214.

12. Ibid.

13. Ibid., 215.

14. Program, Northeastern University School of Law, 7.

15. S. Adler, "Northeastern Through Crimson-Colored Glasses," *The American Lawyer*, 26 August 1982.

16. See Z. Bankowski and G. Mungham, "A Political Economy of Legal Education," *New Universities Quarterly* 32 (1978), 448, for an interesting economic analysis of the rise of "alternative" schools.

17. "Co-op" is the term used for cooperative education at Northeastern University.

18. The oral argument is this school's equivalent to Moot Court. The exercise consists of giving teams of first-year students a legal problem which they must do research on for several months. They then present their argument in a mediation type of setting. This exercise is intended to teach legal skills, but in a non-adversarial way.

19. See R. Stover, *Making It and Breaking It: The Fate of Public Interest Commitment During Law School* (Urbana: University of Illinois Press, 1989).

11 Legal Education and Professional Powers: Reflections on Theory and Practice

1. See L. Valli, *Becoming Clerical Workers* (New York: Routledge, 1986); P. Wexler, "Symbolic Economy of Identity and Denial of Labor: Studies in High School Number 1," in L. Weis, ed., *Class, Race, and Gender in American Education* (Albany: State University of New York Press, 1988); and P. Willis, *Learning to Labor* (New York: Columbia University Press, 1977).

2. See K. Marx, *The Eighteenth Brumaire of Louis Bonaparte* (New York: International Publishers, 1969).

3. M. Larson, *The Rise of Professionalism: A Sociological Analysis* (Berkeley: University of California Press, 1977).

4. See chapter 1 of Eliot Freidson's work, *Professional Powers: A Study of the Institutionalization of Formal Knowledge* (Chicago: University of Chicago Press, 1986) for a review of arguments related to the power/knowledge relationship.

5. See C. Derber et al., *Power in the Highest Degree* (New York: Oxford University Press, 1990).

6. See T. Johnson, *Professions and Power* (London: MacMillian, 1970); and P. Boreham,

"Indetermination: Professional Knowledge, Organization and Control," *Sociological Review* 31 (1983), 693.

7. See M. Apple, *Teachers and Texts: A Political Economy of Gender and Class* (New York: Routledge, 1986).

8. See N. Chomsky, *Necessary Illusions: Thought Control in Democratic Societies* (Boston: South End Press, 1989); T. Gitlin, "Television's Screens: Hegemony in Transition," In M. Apple, ed., *Cultural and Economic Reproduction in Education* (London: Routledge, 1982); and Gitlin, *The Whole World is Watching: Mass Media in the Making and Unmaking of the New Left* (Berkeley: University of California Press, 1980).

9. H. Braverman, *Labor and Monopoly Capital* (New York: Monthly Review Press, 1976); D. Noble, *America by Design: Science, Technology and the Rise of Corporate Capitalism* (New York: Oxford University Press, 1977).

10. See K. Bumiller, *The Civil Rights Society* (Johns Hopkins Press, 1989); K. Klare, "The Law-School Curriculum in the 1980s: What's Left?" *Journal of Legal Education* 32 (1982), 336.

11. See M. Foucault, *Madness and Civilization: A History of Insanity in the Age of Reason* (New York: Mentor Book, 1945); B. Ehrenreich and D. English, *Complaints and Disorders: The Sexual Politics of Sickness* (New York: The Feminist Press, 1973).

12. J. Auerbach, "What Has the Teaching of Law to do With Justice?" *New York University Law Review* 53 (1978), 42.

13. R. Collins, *The Credential Society* (New York: Academic Press, 1979).

14. See P. Cookson and C. Persell, *Preparing for Power* (New York: Basic Books, 1985); and, M. Useem and J. Karabel, "Paths to Corporate Management," *American Sociological Review* 51 (1986), 184–200.

15. For extensive critiques of reproduction theory, see D. Liston, *Capitalist Schools* (New York: Routledge, 1988); P. Wexler, *Social Analysis of Education: After the New Sociology* (Boston: Routledge, 1987); and Valli, *Becoming Clerical Workers*.

16. J. Meyer, "Education as an Institution," *American Journal of Sociology* 83 (1977), 55–77.

17. See J. Heinz and E. Laumann, *Chicago Lawyers: The Social Structure of the Bar* (Chicago: American Bar Foundation, 1982); and, F. K. Zemans and V. Rosenblum, *The Making of a Public Profession* (Chicago: American Bar Foundation, 1981).

18. See M. Granovetter, *Getting a Job: A Study of Contacts and Careers* (Cambridge: Harvard University Press, 1974). Also, for a discussion of the importance of networks in locating professional jobs in law, see R. Granfield and T. Koenig, "Pathways Into Elite Law Firms: Professional Stratification and Social Networks," in G. Moore and A. Whitt, eds., *Research on Politics and Society* (Greenwich, CT: JAI Press, 1992).

19. See Granfield and Koenig, "Pathways Into Elite Law Firms."

20. See G. Ritzer and D. Walczak, *Working: Conflict and Change,* 3rd edition (Englewood-Cliffs: Prentice-Hall, 1986).

21. G. Geison, "Introduction," in G. Geison, ed., *Professions and Professional Ideology in America* (Chapel Hill: University of North Carolina Press, 1983), 7.

22. See G. Miller, "Work as Reality Maintaining Activity: Interactional Aspects of Occupational and Professional Work," in H. LoPata, *Current Research on Occupations and Professions* (Greenwich, CT: JAI Press, 1990).

23. See I. Kaufman, "Idealism vs. Reality," *The National Law Journal,* 22 October 1990.

24. Ibid.

25. See Harvard Law School Council, "A Program in the Public Interest For Harvard Law School," 1990.

26. It is important to point out, however, that the volunteer argument is certainly limited in that only a small percentage of the nation's attorneys provide pro bono legal services on any regular basis. This would suggest that the spirit of volunteerism among lawyers is limited at best.

27. Quoted in P. Rubin, "Harvard Law Grads Chose the Private Life," *Harvard Crimson*, 9 February 1990.

28. See J. Costello, "Training Lawyers for the Powerless: What Law School Should do to Develop Public Interest Lawyers," *Nova Law Journal* 10 (1986), 431, and, C. Halpern, "A New Direction in Legal Education: The CUNY Law School at Queens College," *Nova Law Review* 10 (1986), 549. See also, R. Stover's recommendations in, *Making It and Breaking It: The Fate of Public Interest Commitment During Law School* (Urbana: University of Illinois Press, 1989). Also, A. Sarat, "Lawyers and Clients: Putting Professional Service on the Agenda of Legal Education," *Journal of Legal Education* 41 (1991), 43. See also H. Erlanger, "Social Reform organizations and the Subsequent Careers of Participants: A Follow-Up Study of Early Participants in the OEO Legal Services Program," *American Sociological Review*, 42 (1977), 233–48. Erlanger concludes that identification with the interests of underrepresented clients lead to accepting jobs in public interest law.

29. See A. Abbott, "Status and Status Strain in the Professions," *American Journal of Sociology* 86 (1981), 819, for a similar point.

30. Cynthia Fuchs Epstein makes a similar point. See Epstein, "Reworking the Latent Agenda of Legal Education," *Nova Law Review* 10 (1986), 449.

Methodological Appendix: A Natural History

1. This class had only about two weeks remaining in the semester. After the course ended students would leave for the Christmas break and then return to take their first-year exams.

2. The student center, Harkness Commons, is known as "the Hark" to Harvard Law students.

3. See J. E. Hoffman, "Problems of Access in the Study of Social Elites and Boards of Directors," in W. Shaffir, R. Stebbins and A. Turowetz, eds., *Fieldwork Experience: Qualitative Approaches to Social Research* (New York: St. Martin's Press, 1980). Although I had no personal ties to anyone at Harvard Law, I found that I was able to collect data. Hoffman speaks of the importance of using personal ties when studying elites. R. Jackell, in his book *Moral Mazes: The World of the Corporate Manager* (New York: Oxford University Press, 1988), also describes the problems he had in studying corporate managers. Only after making the right contact and using the right phrasing to express his research interest was he able to gain access to the data he sought. In most interviews with the law students at Harvard, I told them that I was interested in following up on Scott Turow's observations in *One L,* a book that most Harvard Law students are very familiar with.

4. See Hoffman, "Problems of Access."

5. This is a first-year requirement in which students select a case, research it, and conduct an oral argument that is evaluated by a team of three judges.

6. See R. Granfield, "Legal Education as Corporate Ideology: Students Adjustment to the Law School Experience," *Sociological Forum* 1 (1986), 514–523.

7. See Becker et al., *Boys in White* (Chicago: University of Chicago Press, 1961); and R. Merton et al., *The Student Physician,* (Cambridge: Harvard University Press, 1957).

8. See Josef Bleicher, *The Hermeneutic Imagination* (New York: Routledge, 1982), for a detailed and enlightening discussion of hermeneutics in relation to methodological positivism.

9. See J. Lofland and L. Lofland, *Analyzing Social Settings: A Guide to Qualitative Observation and Analysis* (California: Wadsworth Press, 1984).

10. See A. Cicourel, *Method and Measurement in Sociology* (New York: The Free Press, 1964).

11. As reported in a personal communication with one school administrator.

12. See B. G. Glaser and A. Strauss, *The Discovery of Grounded Theory: Strategies for Qualitative Research* (Chicago: Aldine, 1967).

13. See N. Denzin, *The Research Act* (Englewood Cliffs, NJ: Prentice-Hall, 1989), and N. Fielding and S. Fielding, *Linking Data* (Newbury Park: Sage, 1982) on methodological triangulation.

14. The description of the "alternative" nature of this school is discussed in chapter 10.

15. These questionnaires were identical to those administered at Harvard with the exception of minor adjustments to account for the specific features of this school.

16. This higher percentage of women is not an anomaly. This law school is known as a "feminist" law school in that it has always ranked far above the national average in admitting women.

17. See E. Webb et al., *Unobtrusive Measures: Non-Reactive Research in the Social Sciences* (Chicago: Rand McNally, 1966), for a discussion of non-reactive measures.

Index

Abbott, A., 218–219, 228, 237, 242
Abel, R., 216, 216–218, 221–222, 224, 229, 234, 236, 239
Abercrombie, N., 215
accommodation: affinity and, 156–157; autonomy and, 161–162; effectiveness and, 153–156; good firms and, 157–160; loan debt and, 151–153; professional development and, 160–161; resistance and, 164–165; strategies of, 149–151; working class and, 119, 154
accounts, 17, 149, 163–164, 238
alienation, 11, 40–41, 66, 189
allocation theory, 201–202
Althusser, L., 2, 16
altruism: among women, 102; law and, 37; student motivation and, 38–40, 42, 175–177
American Bar Association, 30, 38, 49, 136, 204
American Social Science Association, 29
Amnesty International, 69
Anderson, P., 238
Apple, M., 3, 164, 215, 220, 228, 236–239, 241
apprenticeship, 21–22
Aronowitz, S., 168, 228, 249
Atkinson, P., 14, 219–220, 230
Auerbach, J., 10–11, 200, 218, 222, 241

Babbitt, B., 127
backbenching, 131
Baltzell, D., 234, 236
Bankowski, Z., 240
Benjamin, A., 225, 231
Becker, H., 13, 61, 84, 211, 219, 225, 227, 230, 243
Benson, S., 239
Berger, B., 144–145, 237
Bernstein, B., 233
bifurcated bar, 123
Billig, M., 237
Black, N., 101, 231
Blackmun, H., 127
Bledstein, B., 223

Bleicher, J., 243
Bloomfield, M., 222
Bok, D., 11, 218, 226
Bonsignore, P., 56, 227
Boreham, P., 219, 240
Bork, R., 9
Bourdieu, P., 15, 60, 74, 220, 227–229, 232, 236
bourgeosie, 19, 28
Bowers v. Hardwick, 76–77
Bowles, S., 51, 220, 226
Brandeis, L., 170, 206
Braverman, H., 241
Brennan, W., 127
Bronner, E., 216
Brown, E., 221, 223, 224
Bumiller, K., 228, 241
Burawoy, M., 144, 237
Byse, C., 217

Cain, M., 222
Carter, J., 4
Carrington, P., 225, 231
case method, 29, 74, 185
Chambers, D., 238
Chambliss, W., 222
charter, 124, 202
Chase, R., 223
Chodorow, N., 230
Chomsky, N., 241
Chroust, A., 221
Clark, R., 43
Cicourel, A., 212, 237, 243
Cobb, J., 111, 113, 233–234
Code Critical, 140
cognitive dissonance, 144, 237
Cohen, A., 111, 233
collective eminence: classroom and, 129–133; recruitment and, 133–138; results of, 141–142; threats to, 138–140
Collins, R., 201, 229, 236, 241
Connell, R., 220, 234, 238
Cookson, P., 124, 218, 232, 235–238, 241
corporate tool, 140, 146–150
correspondence, critique of, 51–52, 226, 241

Costello, J., 242
Counter-Hegemonic Front, 69, 138–139
Cravath, Swaine, and Moore, 25, 149, 238
critical legal studies, 9, 35, 45, 79, 169
critical theory, 2
cultural capital, 15, 19, 23, 27, 37, 64, 113, 136–137, 202
culture of critical discourse, 23
Curran, B., 216
Curtin, J., 216, 226
cynicism: in law school, 8, 61–65, 192–193; resistance of, 65–71

Declaration of Independence, 22
deflection, 211; Also see, Methods
Denbeaux, M., 37, 225
Denzin, N., 243
Derber C., 13, 153, 167, 200, 217, 219, 229, 230, 237, 240
detached concern, 13
de Tocqueville, A., 24, 32
Dodge, R., 170
Domhoff, G. W., 81, 109, 122, 229, 232, 234–235, 238–239
Dukakis, M., 127
du Pont, P., 127

Eastern Sociological Society, 211
Edelman, M., 237
education, and inequality, 15; critical pedagogy and, 168–169; sociology of, 14–18, 201; subordinate identities and, 17, 123, 217, 235
Ehrenreich, B., 93, 226, 230, 241
Eisenhart, D., 215, 220, 231, 238
elaborated speech codes, 113, 233
Eliot, C., 29–30
elites: collective identity and, 124–125; moral crusades and, 30, 223; scientific authority and, 31
Elkins, J., 218, 225
Epstein, C. F., 95, 218, 231–232, 242
Erikson, K., 229
Erlanger, H., 217, 226, 229, 242
Eron, L., 228
ethnography, See methods
Eulau, H., 221
evaluative thought, 68
Everhart, R., 218

false necessities, 62
Feinman, J., 217

feminism: equity, 101, 107; reactions to, 79, 81, 98–99; social, 101, 107–108
Festinger, L., 237
Fielding, N., 243
fly-outs, 117, 133–136
Fordham, S., 238
Foster, J., 8, 217, 222, 230
Foucault, M., 27, 222, 241
Fox, R., 209
Fraser, A., 221, 223–224
Freeman, S., 231
Freidman, L., 216–217
Friedson, E., 13, 219, 229, 240
functionalism, 12

gamesmanship, 61–65, 193–194; See also, legal consciousness
Garfinkel, H., 238
Geer, B., 219, 230
Geison, G., 241
Gerson, K., 231
Giddens, A., 220
Gilligan, C., 230
Gintis, H., 51, 220, 226
Giroux, H., 168, 220, 226, 228, 237, 239
Gitlin, T., 220, 241
Goffman, E., 56, 60, 83, 110–111, 118, 122, 146, 227, 229, 232–234
Goodrich, C., 53, 226–227, 229
Gordon, R., 222, 224
Gouldner, A., 20, 23, 220–221, 229
Glaser, B., 213, 243
Gramsci, A., 16, 220
Granfield, R., 241, 243
Granovetter, M., 236, 241
Griswold, E., 52, 227, 230
Grossburg, L., 215
Gusfield, J., 223

Haas, J., 219, 227
habitas, 15, 60, 227
Hadley, H., 31, 224
Harvard Law Review, 138
Harvard Law School: and the modern law school movement, 28–31; Boston YMCA and, 170; competitiveness at, 125–133; crisis at, 9–10; loan forgiveness and, 50, 141, 151–153, 204–205, 226; orientation week at, 127–128; public interest law at, 5, 48–49, 141, 147, 205–206, 216;

women at, 94–108; working class students at, 109–122
Hay, D., 23, 221
Hedegard, D., 37, 219, 225
hegemony, 14, 16, 79, 99
Heinz, J., 216, 232, 235, 241
Hellman, L., 218
hermeneutics, 211
hidden curriculum, 198
Hill, S., 215
Hobson, K., 222, 224
Hoffman, J. E., 242
Holland, D., 215, 220, 231, 238
Homer, S., 231–232
Horwitz, M., 222
Hunt, A., 224
Hurst, J. W., 222

IBM, 7, 217
identity: ambivalence, 118; collective, 123–125; professional, 73; stigma and, 110–122
ideological cooptation, 153
ideological dilemmas, 144, 237
ideological work: 143–167, 204; Harvard Law students and, 146–166; fragility of, 167
ideology: approaches to, 2–4; as lived experience, 145–146; education and, 14–18, 145–146
Inns of Court, 21–22, 24, 221

Jackell, R., 117, 234, 237, 242
Jacksonian democracy, 25–26
Jamous, H., 219
Johnson, M., 230
Johnson, T., 240
Johnson, W., 32, 224

Kahlenberg, R., 218, 236
Kanter, R., 101, 117, 217, 231, 234
Katz, A., 37, 225
Katz, J., 224, 234
Kaufman, I., 204, 241
Keller, S., 124, 236
Kennedy, D., 37, 54, 86, 217–218, 222, 224, 230
Kilmer, J., 235
Klare, K., 241
Klatch, R., 100, 231
Knorr-Cetina, K., 237

Knowles, A., 171
Koenig, T., 224, 234, 239, 241
Konesfky, A., 223

Lamont, M., 73–74, 229, 234
Langdell, C., 29–30, 32–33, 170, 223
Langdellian formalism, 29, 32–33, 35
Larson, M., 13, 19–20, 199, 216, 219–220, 222, 229, 241
Laumann, E., 216, 232, 235, 241
law: and economics, 9, 43, 225; and power, 72–73; as ideology, 2–3; as symbolic boundaries, 73–93; 72–73; as tool for social change, 69–70, 201; capitalism and, 30–31; indeterminacy in, 68–69; individualism in, 37; transformation of, 25
law school: idealism in, 8, 84; levelling of requirements in, 25; part-time, 32–35; See also, legal education
lawyers: American Revolution and, 22; capitalism and, 6, 24–32; hostility toward, 20–25
Lee, G., 221
Lefcourt, D., 26, 222, 224
legal aid, 4, 6, 48
legal consciousness: argumentation as, 58–61; as justification, 54–56; drawing connections and, 56–58
legal education: conservatizing effects of, 85; crises in, 32–35; criticism of, 49–50; early American developments in, 23–28; elite foundations and, 20–23; legitimation and, 29–32
legal positivism, 30–31
legal profession: contradictions within, 7–8; entrance into, 24–26; expansion of, 6; legitimation in, 29–32; market control and, 22; satisfaction in, 204; See also, lawyers
legal realism, 35
legal services, 6–7, 37, 146, 173; maldistribution of, 4–7, 36
Levy, M., 221
Light, D., 227
Liston, D., 220, 241
Litchfield, law school at, 23–24; See also, Reeve
Livingston, D., 224
Llewellyn, K., 55, 221, 227
Lofland, J., 243
Lortie, D., 219, 229
Lowy, M., 226, 229

LuBove, R., 223
Lyman, S., 238

MacKinnon, C., 228
Mannheim, K., 52, 68, 227–228
Manning, B., 223
Marcuse, H., 2
Marston, E., 239–240
Marx, K., 51, 198–199, 240
master status, 118
Matza, D., 162, 239
McLaren, P., 215, 226, 235, 237, 239
McKenna, J., 221
Menkel-Meadow, C., 218
Merton, R., 211, 219, 237, 243
methods: comparative, 213; fieldwork and, 11, 211–212; interviews and, 11, 210–212; questionnaires and, 11, 212–214; plurality of, 214; triangulation of, 213–214
Meyer, J., 124, 202, 235, 241
Miller, G., 241
Miller, P., 26, 221–222
Mills, C. W., 223, 236, 238
Moore, W., 219, 229
moral career, 83
Myrdal, G., 237

Nader, R., 6, 49, 217
National Law Journal, 204
Nelson, C., 215
Nelson, R., 238
Newman, K., 234
Nilson, J., 237
no hassle pass, 131, 236
Noble, D., 223, 241
non-reactive measures, See methods
normative values, 69
Northeastern University School of Law: career choices at, 187–88; closing of, 171; cooperative education at, 173; curriculum at, 170, 172–174; fate of idealism at, 183–185; history of, 169–74; "jammin for justice at," 205; motives for attending, 174–178

One L, 125, 127, 242
Oppenheimer, M., 237

Parsons, T., 219, 224, 229, 231
Peller, G., 73, 228
Peloille, B., 219
Persell, C., 124, 218, 232, 235–237, 241
Pipkin, R., 8, 217–218, 231, 235

Platt, A., 223
Pollock, E. J., 239
Posner, R., 225
Potter, J., 237
Poulantzas, N., 2
Pound, R., 28, 221, 223
Powell, M., 217
power: ideology as, 203–204; knowledge as, 200–201; status as, 201–203
practical consciousness, 145
pragmatism, 81, 84, 87, 90–91
prep schools, 109, 124, 201, 122
pro bono, 43–44, 88, 92, 134, 184, 203–206
professions: cultural authority and, 200; knowledge and, 15–16, 200–201; new class and, 199; socialization in 13–14; theories of, 12–14
professional autonomy, 7, 217
promissory estoppal, 53
Psathas, G., 219
public interest law: declining rates of, 4–5; redefinition of, 84–92; salaries and, 6; studies on, 7–8, 37
Puritans, 20–21

Reagan, R., 9, 38
recruitment, see collective eminence
Reeve, T., 23
Reinarman, C., 237
religion, 68
repentant role, 163, 239
reproduction: as lived experience, 3; choice in, 17; cultural, 15; inequality and, 15–18; resistance and, 164–165; social, 17
res ipso loquitur, 53
res judicata, 53
Reskin, L. R., 219
restricted speech codes, 19, 233
Ritzer, G., 241
Rochford, E., 237–238
Rosenblum, V., 37, 225, 235, 241
Rumbarger, J., 223
Rustad, M., 224, 234, 239–240

Scalia, A., 127–128
Schevitz, J., 144, 237
Schlegal, J., 223
Schwartz, A., 229, 235
Scott, R., 238
Seidman, R., 222
Seligman, J., 223
selling-out, 147–149, 204

Sennett, R., 111, 113, 233–234
Shakespeare, W., 22
Shaffer, T., 217, 225, 227, 229
Shaffir, W., 219, 227
Shapiro, M., 228
Sharp, R., 226
Shaw, G. B., 19
Simpson, I., 219, 225
slippery slope, 58
Smigel, E., 232
Smith, I., 224
Smith, R. H., 4, 216
social class, as experienced, 121–122; asymmetrical relations, 111, 233
social networks, 135, 166, 202–203, 241
socialization, into medical school, 12–13, 61, 91, 211
Solomon, E., 112, 121, 233–234
Spangler, E., 218, 239
Sprague, J., 221
Starr, P., 216, 228
Steinitz, V., 112, 121, 233–234
Stern, P., 216, 224
Stevens, R., 23, 25, 37, 219, 221–224, 231, 239–240
stigma: concealment of, 115–116; flaunting and, 233; management of, 110–111; research on, 110; social class and, 110–111, 122
Stone, A., 217, 225
Stone, G., 116, 234
Stover, R., 7–8, 217, 219, 228, 230, 238, 240, 242
Strauss, A., 213, 243
structuralism, 2, 16, 145
Suffolk, University Law School, 170, 178, 202
Sugarman, D., 223
Sumner, C., 228
Sykes, G., 162, 239
symbolic boundaries: and students, 78–81; and faculty, 75–78; professional identity as, 73–74; the self and, 81–92
symbolic interactionism, 13
symbolic violence, 15

Tabor, J., 231
Taft, W., 223
Taylor, J., 217
taylorization, 24
techniques of neutralization, 162

Tigar, M., 221
Tinnelly, J., 224
Therborn, G., 215, 238
The Paper Chase, 40, 124–125, 127, 130, 133
thinking like a lawyer, 52, 59, 70, 98, 181, 226; See also, legal consciousness
Thompson, E. P., 221
tokenism, 9, 218
total institution, 56
Trubeck, D., 221
turkey bingo, 81, 132
Turow, S., 218, 225, 242
Tushnet, M., 224
Twinning, W., 224

undesired differentness, 110
Unger, R., 217, 227
Useem, M., 232, 241

Valli, L., 215, 218, 220, 235, 238, 240–241
Van Alstyne, W. S., 235
Vietnam, 144
vocabulary of motives, 149

Warren, C., 221, 223
Wasserstrom, R., 218
Webb, E., 243
Weber, M., 199, 221
Weis, L., 218, 231
Weiss, C., 231
Wetherall, M., 237
Wexler, P., 220, 228, 236, 240–241
Wilkins, R. K., 218
Williams, P., 228
Williams, R., 14, 220, 238
Willis, P., 17, 111, 215, 217, 220, 227, 232–233, 235, 237, 240
women: and difference, 94–95; free market and, 100; in law school 9, 79, 94–95, 101; legal reasoning and, 98
Worden, K., 95, 229, 231
working class: culture, 17; idealism and, 112; identity management and, 115–118; in elite institutions, 109–110; stigma and, 110–113; stress and, 113–114
wounded narcissism, 130

Young Men's Christian Association, 169–171

Zemans, F. K., 37, 225, 235, 241
Zweigenhaft, R., 109, 122, 232, 234, 238